ANIMAL HISTORY

BY THE SAME EDITORS

Animal Ethics for Veterinarians
The Ethical Case against Animal Experiments
The Palgrave Handbook of Practical Animal Ethics
The Routledge Handbook of Religion and Animal Ethics
Ethical Vegetarianism and Veganism
An Ethical Critique of Fur Factory Farming
Animal Ethics and Animal Law
Animal Theologians
The Ethics of Fur: Religious, Cultural, and Legal Perspectives

ANIMAL HISTORY

History as if Animals Mattered

Edited by ANDREW LINZEY and CLAIR LINZEY

RESOURCE *Publications* · Eugene, Oregon

ANIMAL HISTORY
History as if Animals Mattered

Copyright © 2025 Wipf and Stock Publishers. All rights reserved. Except for brief quotations in critical publications or reviews, no part of this book may be reproduced in any manner without prior written permission from the publisher. Write: Permissions, Wipf and Stock Publishers, 199 W. 8th Ave., Suite 3, Eugene, OR 97401.

Resource Publications
An Imprint of Wipf and Stock Publishers
199 W. 8th Ave., Suite 3
Eugene, OR 97401

www.wipfandstock.com

PAPERBACK ISBN: 979-8-3852-4866-7
HARDCOVER ISBN: 979-8-3852-4867-4
EBOOK ISBN: 979-8-3852-4868-1

VERSION NUMBER 051925

Chapters reproduced with permission from the University of Illinois Press.

Contents

Introduction: The Meaning of Animal History | vii
    —*Andrew Linzey and Clair Linzey*

PART I: CONCEIVING ANIMAL HISTORY

1. Do "Animals" Have Histor(ies)? Can/Should Humans Know Them?: A Heuristic Reframing of Animal-Human Relationships | 3
    —*Jacob Brandler*

2. Animal Biographies: Beyond Archetypal Figures | 13
    —*Violette Pouillard*

PART II: INTELLECTUAL FIGURES

3. "Higher" and "Lower" Political Animals: A Critical Analysis of Aristotle's Account of the Political Animal | 23
    —*Cheryl E. Abbate*

4. Augustine of Hippo on Nonhuman Animals | 36
    —*Christina Hoenig*

5. "Mad Madge": The Contribution of Margaret Cavendish to Animal Ethics | 49
    —*Lauren Bestwick*

6. Frances Power Cobbe and the Philosophy of Antivivisection | 59
    —*Alison Stone*

PART III: HISTORICAL CONTROVERSIES: MEAT EATING

7. Biblical Veganism: An Examination of 1 Timothy 4:1–8 | 71
    —*Marcello Newall*

8. On Imitating the Regimen of Immortality or Facing the Diet of Mortal Reality: A Brief History of Abstinence from Flesh-Eating in Christianity | 96
    —*Carl Tobias Frayne*

9. Morality and Meat in the Middle Ages and Beyond | 121
    —*Christene d'Anca*

10. The Anarchist Diet: Vegetarianism and Individualist Anarchism in Early Twentieth-Century France | 140
 —*Carl Tobias Frayne*

PART IV: HISTORICAL CONTROVERSIES: VIVISECTION

11. Vivisection, Virtue Ethics, and the Law in 19th-Century Britain | 157
 —*A. W. H. Bates*

12. "The New Superstition, the New Tyranny": The Ethics and Contexts of John Cowper Powys's Antivivisection | 172
 —*Felix Taylor*

13. Boycotted Hospital: The National Anti-Vivisection Hospital, London, 1903–1935 | 179
 —*A. W. H. Bates*

14. Animal Research, Safeguards, and Lessons from the Long History of Judicial Torture | 190
 —*Adam Clulow and Jan Lauwereyns*

About the Editors and Contributors | 203

Introduction: The Meaning of Animal History

ANDREW LINZEY AND CLAIR LINZEY

I

History has been famously described by a student in the film *The History Boys* as "just one [expletive deleted] thing after another." The "thing" or "things" in question are of course events, circumstances, or politics that relate almost entirely to human beings. That is how history is written, as we commonly understand it. The idea that animals also have a history jolts our common understanding and invites incredulity.

Animals are not purposive agents, it will be protested. History involves decisions made by rational agents, it will be protested further. But neither of these objections quite captures the nature and scope of what may be meant by the term animal history. In the first place, humans do not exist in a vacuum. We exist in a myriad of relations, many of them with animals. Millions of people keep (for better or worse) millions of companion animals. The lives of these animals and their human carers are intertwined. And, at a more basic level, humans largely exist by using, exploiting, and eating animals. Properly conceived, animals cannot be written out of the human narrative. For good or ill, our lives are in almost daily contact with other sentient creatures.

Second, it is by no means clear that animals (at least sentient ones) are not purposive, by which we mean capable of making decisions as to what course of action to follow. When our cat chooses not to eat the food we make available and meows for another more palatable kind, we are pretty sure that a choice is being made. It may be driven by pleasure, or instinct, or other influences (as are most human decisions) but we can be quite sure that a choice is being made. Moreover, the old idea that animals cannot think (at least in their own terms); that they are simply machines without any sense of self has been slowly but surely eroded by empirical research (see for example Bekoff, 1998, pp. 17–26; and Low, 2012). We now know more about the complexity of animal awareness than we ever did (see Griffin, 1990; and Rollin, 1990). It is that which has fuelled a fundamental change in moral attitudes towards them. An animal does not just have a biology, but also a biography.

Introduction: The Meaning of Animal History

Third, many, if not most, human actions are not driven by, or are the result of, deliberate choices. Humans, like most other sentient beings, are creatures of habit, or routine, which means that only a few of our actions are dictated by rational assessment of the options we may take. As Bertrand Russell reportedly quipped: "Most English people would rather die than think, and most of them actually do." To disregard animals simply because we believe we are the only thinking beings capable of making deliberate choices is not only inaccurate, but also myopic. It is myopic in the correct sense of the word, namely short-sighted.

And here we reach the rub. It is short-sighted to think that the business of living is simply a human affair. Many other creatures are also living, breathing, and feeling – and doing their business also. Humans are not the only beings in the world. The world is populated with millions, if not billions, of other species whose business of living makes possible (in almost all cases) our living.

II

How, then, have we managed to conceive of history (at least as an academic subject) without also concerning ourselves with the lives of animals to whom we relate or who live alongside us as fellow sojourners? The answer it seems is the dogma of anthropocentricity (perhaps better described as humanocentricity) that has permeated almost all academic disciplines. Apart from, arguably, the natural sciences and literature, the latter of which has been perhaps the most perceptive and sensitive to our relations with animals (see Regan and Linzey, 2010; and Scholtmeijer, 1993) other disciplines, such as theology, philosophy, ethics, anthropology, geography, law - to name just a few – have been overwhelming concerned with human beings to the detriment of other beings in the world. Only recently, with the advent of ecology and environmentalism, have human eyes begun to see more far-sightedly.

The best analogies are women's history, black history, and LGBTQ+ history. In the past, women's history was largely written by men, black history by whites, and LGBTQ+ history by heterosexuals. These narratives more than often have silenced the voices of the people they wrote about. As Winston Churchill apparently remarked, "History is written by the victors." Now, however, the voices that were previously silenced or overlooked have begun to find their rightful place, not only in common discourse, but also in academia. Now, students can study and investigate the forces that have side-lined the voices of the oppressed. This process has helped us enlarge our understanding of the world and its human inhabitants. It also serves as a warning of how easily humans can succumb to prejudice, bigotry, and discrimination. Now, previously unheard voices can be heard, and we do well to listen.

But, it may be protested, animals cannot speak for themselves, they cannot write their own history and, therefore, they cannot be part of anything like similar developments that have liberated side-lined human beings. But, while it is true that animals cannot obviously speak (in a language that we can easily understand), it does not follow that their presence, their feelings, and their interests cannot be represented by human beings. Yes, it may take some use of our imaginative capacity, but arguably no less perhaps than it took for white, heterosexual men to understand women's, black, and LGBTQ+ identities.

Another objection, however, is that attempts at "representation" have unfortunate connotations. In the past, oppressors have often claimed to "represent" others, to speak for them, while actually eclipsing their actual needs or identity. An example is given by Noam Chomsky. He narrates how he came across a gravestone inscription, placed by the National Parks "as a testimonial." It read: "Here lies an Indian woman, a Wampanoag, whose family and tribe gave of themselves of their land that this great nation might be born and grow." As Chomsky rightly comments: "she and her family didn't 'give of themselves and their land.' Rather they were murdered by our forefathers and driven out of their land" (Chomsky, 1992, p. 14). The question, then, has to be faced: is animal history a new form colonialism in which the voiceless are subject to further speciesist human control by the taking over of their voices? "We know what's best for you" has historically been the slogan of many oppressors.

But is it true that *all* representation is prejudicial to those represented? Not necessarily. In the US, for example, some courts have appointed guardians who represent the interests of children in legal cases, and a similar development is now being advanced in relation to animals (Rubin, 2018). There is also another, major consideration. While some, even many, representation of animals may well have been prejudicial, animals exactly like children need representation in order to be heard at all. If genuinely benign and compassionate human beings do not advance their interests, animals will remain voiceless and almost entirely defenceless. What is true in the law courts is equally, if not especially, true when it comes to positing narratives that influence how we treat animals and what moral status, if any, they are granted. History, in this sense, is the intellectual framework in which humans live and from which animals so often suffer and die. The stories we tell shape our understanding of who we are and who animals are.

III

So what is history if animals matter? Well, first of all, it is to *see* them. Seeing is much more than just looking. John Ruskin, the famous artist and advocate for animals wrote that "Hundreds of people can talk for one who can think, but thousands can think for one who can see. To see clearly is poetry, prophecy, and religion – all in one" (Ruskin quoted in Kemp, 1990). It is only by properly seeing that we can know and understand. And, most importantly, extend our imaginative sympathy and gain some sense of the joys and travails they are experiencing. As Henry Beston put it in eloquent prose:

> We patronize them [animals] for their incompleteness, for their tragic fate of having taken form so far below ourselves. And therein we err, and greatly err. For the animal shall not be measured by man. In a world older and more complete than ours they moved finished and complete, gifted with extensions of the sense we have lost or never stained, living by voices we shall never hear.

They are "other nations," as he poignantly concludes:

> We need another and wiser and perhaps more mystical concept of animals . . . They are not brethren; they are not underlings; they are other nations, caught with ourselves in the net and life of time, fellow prisoners of the splendour and travail of the earth. (Beston, 1928, p. 25)

Second, and relatedly, we are going through little less than a revolution in *how* we see animals. As we have frequently written: we are moving through a new paradigm shift away from the idea that sentient animals are things, tools, machines, commodities, resources here for us to the realisation that animals have their own intrinsic value, dignity, and rights (see Linzey and Linzey, 2018a, pp. 34–43). This awareness has emerged slowly, but as the intellectual work over the last 50 years has shown, seeing has led to a fundamental intellectual change and thus to some significant shifts of behavior, not least of all dietary changes (see for example Linzey and Linzey, 2018b). Animal history is one way in which we can look again beyond humanocentric myopia.

Third, animal history challenges our animal-blindness or indifference. It demands that we take account of the point of view of other creatures. Summed up in a line often attributed to Max Weber: "All knowledge comes from a point of view." In seeing that animals matter, we posit that their lives, their suffering, their joys, their perceptions (both of themselves and ourselves) are taken in to account. What matters then is that animals matter: They should not be written out of our story or our story told without them. Humans do not live in a vacuum, we are not encapsulated beings who live alone, atomistic individuals without relations to each other or fellow creatures. Once this is grasped, a whole new perspective on history can emerge. Instead of restricting our vision, it can enlarge it, and with it empower our moral vision. Future generations will be amazed that our history could be written without any account of the non-human creatures that live alongside us. The *animal's* point of view has yet to be fully represented.

IV

This book is a primer for those who want to know what animal history is and how it can be done or, rather, how it is being done. It should especially appeal to history and animal studies students, as well as animal protectionists, who are increasingly interested in their own intellectual history and in understanding the controversies

Introduction: The Meaning of Animal History

the animal movement engendered. The book brings together a range of pioneering articles that all deserve careful study.

Part One focuses on how we conceive of animal history. Jacob Brandler ("Do 'Animals' Have Histor(ies)? Can/Should Humans Know Them?: A Heuristic Reframing of Animal-Human Relationships") confronts the neglect of animals as historical subjects in Western history, and how it illustrates human frailty and partiality. He even provides an example of how history could be reframed by taking seriously the lives of animals in Oxford that live alongside us. Violette Pouillard ("Animal Biographies: Beyond Archetypal Figures") reviews two important studies that focus our attention on how "animal celebrities," i.e. famous animals (notably in zoos) have their own biographies that we often overlook. She concludes that: "Due to their experimental nature, animal biographies are also historiographical laboratories paving the way for further questioning and avenues of research."

Part Two examines four key intellectual figures – two ancient and two more modern – who have historically influenced our understanding of animals. Both Aristotle and Augustine of Hippo are critical here in propounding negative views of animals that have had long lasting historical significance. Cheryl E. Abbate ("'Higher' and 'Lower' Political Animals: A Critical Analysis of Aristotle's Account of the Political Animal") introduces us to Aristotle in his apparent rejection of the view that animals cannot be "political" like their human counterparts. While Aristotle's instrumentalist view of animals is well known, it seems that what we now know of animals' cognitive ethology means that his position should be revised, and so should our attitudes as well. Christina Hoenig ("Augustine of Hippo on Nonhuman Animals") also confronts the instrumentalist view of animals found in Augustine, but indicates the complexity of his approach to animals within the Christian (actually Aristotelian in origin) concept of a hierarchical view of creation. Given animals' closeness to humans within that hierarchy should perhaps have necessitated a more sensitive treatment of them, but, alas, Augustine only reinforces the long-standing idea that animals exist to serve human beings.

Two other, more modern voices are also examined. Lauren Bestwick ("'Mad Madge': The Contribution of Margaret Cavendish to Animal Ethics") shows how in 17th-century England, a radical pro-animal and pro-feminist aristocrat took on both the instrumentalist ideas of Aristotle and Augustine of Hippo, and also the emerging philosophy of Cartesianism. Central to her work is the conviction that animals are also rational and because humans could not grasp this (to her) obvious fact so that "the Ignorance of Men concerning other Creatures is the cause of despising other Creatures, imagining themselves as petty Gods in Nature."

Alison Stone ("Frances Power Cobbe and the Philosophy of Anti-Vivisection") examines the thought of a leading Victorian anti-vivisectionist. Focusing on Cobbe's 1875 article, "The Moral Aspects of Vivisection," she emphasizes the philosophical considerations that led her to systematically refute the defenses for vivisection. Cobbe argues that "As the main work of civilization has been the vindication of the rights of the weak" whereas vivisection is "is a retrograde step in the progress of our race, a backwater in the onwards flowing stream of justice and mercy."

One of the ways in which we may conceive of animals in history is by looking at human relations to animals through time. Some of those relationships have crystalized around controversies about animal use. This is the subject of the last two parts. Part Three addresses how meat eating has been construed through time as a divisive issue. Marcello Newall's chapter ("Biblical Veganism: An Examination of 1 Timothy 4:1–8") considers the use of 1 Timothy to criticize the practice of abstaining from meat. Taking a closer look at the historical theological context, Newall argues a vegan diet upholds Paul's original intention which is to celebrate the glory of God and his creation. Carl T. Frayne's ("On Imitating the Regimen of Immortality or Facing the Diet of Mortal Reality: A Brief History of Abstinence from Flesh-Eating in Christianity") chapter provides an historical overview of abstinence from meat in the Christian tradition. He argues that "abstinence from animal flesh is no trivial matter … it has been a subject of much controversy and friction from the dawn of Christian history and remains in question to this day."

Continuing the discussion of meat-eating in Christianity, Christene d'Anca ("Morality and Meat in the Middle Ages and Beyond") focuses on the concern about Cathars and meat-eating in the Middle Ages. Abstinence from meat was one of the ways people could be identified as Cathars and thus followers of practices deemed heretical. Her historical analysis is used to frame an exploration of the ways in which meat is used to form a "social covenant" which those who abstained from meat were seen as breaking. In the last chapter of this part, Frayne ("The Anarchist Diet: Vegetarianism and Individualist Anarchism in Early Twentieth-Century France") considers how vegetarianism became a core value of individualist anarchism in early 20th-century France. Vegetarianism was here conceived as a transformative act, of individual revolution, as opposed to awaiting the transformation of society.

In terms of historical controversy regarding animals, few areas have been so contentious as the use of animals in experiments. Vivisection is thus the focus of Part Four. A. W. H. Bates's chapter ("Vivisection, Virtue Ethics, and the Law in 19th-Century Britain") provides a historical study of the early 19th-century opposition to vivisection, particularly focused on the moral character of the vivisector. The pro-experimentation scientists argued for the scientific necessity of animal experiments, while opponents to vivisection portrayed the scientists as callous and indifferent to suffering. Bates digs deep into the historical writings of the period to explore the debate. Felix Taylor's chapter ("'The New Superstition, the New Tyranny': The Ethics and Contexts of John Cowper Powys's Antivivisection") examines the anti-vivisectionist writing of novelist and philosopher John Cowper Powys. Taylor uses Powys's fiction and newspaper articles to detail how he pre-figured the modern animal rights movement in his objection to experimentation.

Introduction: The Meaning of Animal History

In an example of the historical study of buildings and animals, Bates ("Boycotted Hospital: The National Anti-Vivisection Hospital, London, 1903–1935") details the history of London's only anti-vivisection hospital. Bates explores the opposition from the state and monarchy to the hospital's stance on vivisection, and the struggles it faced as a result. In our final chapter, Adam Clulow and Jan Lauwereyns ("Animal Research, Safeguards, and Lessons from the Long History of Judicial Torture") compare the history of reforming judicial torture with the use of the 3R's as an attempt to reform animal experimentation. Using historical comparison, they argue that "In the case of judicial torture, attempts to refine the system from within produced limited results, and effective change only took place when individual legal systems succeeded in enforcing clear absolutes." They argue there are lessons to be learned here about how to reform the institutionalization of animal experimentation.

V

We would like to conclude by focusing on the issue of language. Language is the means through which we think the world – and also represent it to others as well as ourselves.

As we say in most of our books, we have, as editors, have tried to pay special attention to the question of ethical language. So much of our historic language denigrates animals as "beasts," "brutes," "subhumans," or "dumb brutes" or deploys negative metaphors about animals, such as "snake in the grass," "cunning as a fox," "greedy as a pig," and "stupid cow." With these terms we libel animals, and not only animals, of course. Therefore, we have found it essential to pioneer an ethical or at least more objective terminology. We have used "he" or "she" instead of "it" for individual animals. We have used "free-living," "free-roaming," or simply "free" instead of "wild" because wildness has negative connotations. We have also used the term "farmed animals" rather than "livestock" or "farm animals." Where substitution has proved problematic, we have simply placed the objectionable words in quotation marks. Needless to say, exceptions to ethical language have been made in the quotation of texts, particularly historical writings.

This work is a project of the Oxford Centre for Animal Ethics, which aims to pioneer ethical perspectives on animals through academic research, teaching and publication. The articles originally appeared in the *Journal of Animal Ethics*, which we co-edit in partnership with the University of Illinois Press. Our special thanks to Stephanie Ernst for her expert copy-editing. We also wish to thank the wonderful team at Wipf and Stock especially James Stock, Matthew Wimer, George Callihan, and Ian Creeger.

We hope that this book will be a contribution to the re-writing of history with other animals included.

REFERENCES

Bekoff, M. (Ed.) (1998). *Encylopedia of animal rights and animal welfare*. Westport, CT: Greenwood Press.

Beston, H. (1928). *The outermost house: A year of life on the Great Beach of Cape Cod*. Harmondsworth: Penguin.

Chomsky, N. (1992). *Chronicles of dissent: Interviews with David Barsamian*. Stirling, Scotland: AK Press.

Griffin, D. R. (2001). *Animal minds: Beyond cognition to consciousness*. Chicago, IL: University of Chicago Press.

Kemp, W. (1990). *The desire of my eyes: The life and work of John Ruskin*. New York, NY: Farrar, Straus, and Giroux.

Linzey, A., and Linzey, C. (Eds). (2018a). *The ethical case against animal experiments*. Urbana, IL: University of Illinois Press.

Linzey, A., and Linzey, C. (Eds). (2018b). *Ethical vegetarianism and veganism*. London: Routledge.

Low, P. (2012). *The Cambridge declaration on consciousness*. Jaak Panksepp, Diana Reiss, David Edelman, Bruno Van Swinderen, Philip Low, and Christof Koch, (Eds.). Francis Crick Memorial Conference on Consciousness in Human and Non-Human Animals, Churchill College, University of Cambridge, England. July 7, 2012. Retrieved from: http://fcmconference.org/img/CambridgeDeclarationOnConsciousness.pdf.

Regan, T., and Linzey, A. (Eds.) (2010). *Other nations: Animals in modern literature*. Waco, TX: Baylor University Press.

Rollin, Bernard E. (1990). *The unheeded cry: Animal consciousness, animal pain and science*. Oxford: Oxford University Press.

Rubin, J. (2018). Desmond's law: A novel approach to animal advocacy. *Animal Law Review*, 24: 243–275.

Scholtmeijer, M. (1993). *Animal victims in modern fiction*. Toronto: University of Toronto Press.

PART I

Conceiving Animal History

Do "Animals" Have Histor(ies)? Can/Should Humans Know Them? A Heuristic Reframing of Animal-Human Relationships

JACOB BRANDLER
University of Oxford

Abstract: The Western history discipline has recently experienced a growing appreciation of animals as subjects of historical concern, part of what has been described as the "animal turn" in the humanities. While briefly examining some historiographical points related to this burgeoning trend, this article looks to the question of whether animals have history itself as a device to reframe the relationship humans have with both animals and history. Through this process, this article highlights how respecting the unknown possibility and the possibility of the unknown history from the animal perspective recasts the inquiry into "history" as a parochial human endeavor, entangled in the limits of human knowledge, perception, and frailty. It is this same human frailty that explains why humans must understand animal history if only from a human perspective—because humans have fundamentally depended on animals for their survival and development in their own history. Taking these points together, this article asserts that appreciating the existence (and weakness) of the human lens gives new meaning and a sense of humility to the inquiry into animal history, such as how animal history may be better understood in the plural ("histories"), how humans might be freed from universal history and human exceptionalism, and how this humility encourages more ethical treatment of animals.

Key Words: "animal turn," history, animal history, animal mind, human exceptionalism, humility, reflection

Looking at the past and present, it is of such certainty that most humans who have ever lived encountered animals in some capacity during their daily lives, often as part of satisfying their basic needs, that such a statement hardly requires citation. Similarly, one can say without fear of serious controversy that all those humans are seen, at least now in contemporary times, as subjects of history.[1] But interactions are not one sided, and one can ask what of those animals who lived intimately in and out of human society and what of the perhaps greater number of animals who lived their lives content without human interference—do they belong to history as well? Not too long ago, such a question would have been met with general incredulity, and even of the past few decades, a proposal to embark on greater historical research into animal lives would have been seen as radically avant-garde. But today, while still far from fully mainstream,[2] animal history is a blossoming area of research, part of the "animal turn" occurring within and outside the Western history discipline (Ritvo, 2007).

But while history, as a field of research, has moved in some step forward in noticing animals, the question of whether animals have history still remains a vibrant matter for contemplation in and of itself. Inspired as an ontological exercise, this article proposes to look to the process of answering this question, rather than simply to the answer itself, as a way of expanding knowledge. While this article ultimately presents an answer in a nuanced affirmative—a yes within an "I don't know, maybe"—it does so in a way that reframes the position of humans in relation to these histories. This intention, in turn, explains the "quirks" of the question as transformed into what appears in the article's title: The quotation marks around animals exposes the supposed separation between humans and animals (if humans have history, of course, at least one animal history must exist since humans are animals!); the parenthesized plural challenges the conglomeration of diverse nonhumans into one group; and the slash between can and should invokes human weakness, the difference between what humans can and ought to do. Thus, by employing this question as a heuristic, this exercise in addressing the existence of animal history will illuminate these elements while illustrating how the reframing of the relationship humans have with animals and the inquiry of history gives new meaning to that relationship. This includes, among other things, how this reframed relationship frees humans from the constraints of universal history and human exceptionalism and fosters a view more favorable to the ethical treatment of animals.

But first, why should anyone even ask this question about animals and histories at all? For one, recent historiographical developments in the West have made this question particularly relevant. More specifically, the field of history has witnessed a renaissance due in large part to what has been traditionally treated as objective history being revaluated as a parochial view. A central element of this development has been an expanded appreciation by the mainstream of overlooked minority perspectives, minority in terms of institutional power, not numbers, as illustrated with women's and non-White histories.[3] As such, there is a temptation to ask how animals, particularly given their status as an exploited class, might similarly possess an overlooked history that could likewise vitalize historical analysis.[4] This provides a related animal ethics reason to consider this question: Looking to animals as subjects of history rather than merely as objects of natural science can infuse a new appreciation of their inherent dignity—such denial of history having been previously used to deny human groups of the very same.[5] But even outside these manifestations in historiography and considerations of animals, the question of whether animals have histories remains fruitful ontologically for its utility in probing the meaning of history itself.

REFLECTION IN HISTORY

Now, this article does not intend to answer the age-old question of "what is history?" But even a brief discussion can take notice that there seems to be something different between "the past," memories, and history. The past, if one may be pardoned for straying too close to a reductionist account, is something that materially happens in space and time—an objective existence, if such a concept is reliable. Given that humans are temporal beings, which in turn serves as a reminder of their communion with other animals, the past is something that can no longer be experienced in the present. In other words, this current second ("now") is gone, things happened, but all that humans have of it are memories—and here, one might be moved by Mrs. Goforth's rumination in Tennessee Williams's (1964) *The Milk Train Doesn't Stop Here Anymore*: "Has it ever struck you . . . that life is all memory except for the one present moment that goes by you so quick you hardly catch it going?" (p. 38). Memories may be false, two individuals might recall the same event very differently, but that does not make them unreal or without significant meaning.

When it comes to having a past and memories, humans have, at least recently in Western thought, accepted that some animals do possess both.[6] But history appears to be different, involving a sense of reflection. On this, people can debate its purpose: Is reflection meant to ascertain an accurate picture of the past or to view the past for the utility of the present? Perhaps these are second-order considerations: Reflection may be more primordially involved in history as a need for a sense or consciousness of the past to begin with. And to the extent that history is reflective, it of course matters who is doing the reflecting and how this invites subjectivity, perhaps inseparably, into history. But whatever the case, reflection is there as a crucial ingredient for history, leading some, even proponents of animal studies, to question the possibility of animal history without humans. In other words, there is this idea that history demands, if one is agnostic to angels and aliens, a human observer, and a world without humans would be one without history. For example, Erica Fudge (2002) asserts that a true "history of animals . . . is impossible" because, among other things, animals fail to either document or periodize their past; instead, what is described as animal history is more accurately "the history of human attitudes toward animals" (pp. 5–6). Similarly, David Gary Shaw (2013) sees history as a progression of the social group reflecting on the past, expanding the "we" of who counts, and that until now, history was not about animals, "it couldn't have been" (p. 1). Thus, Shaw (2013) points to historical reasons—the materialism of Darwinian thought and shifting intellectual epistemes and struggles that pushed Europeans and Americans to the nature of suffering—that changed the ideas of humans to allow animals to become subjects of historical concern in the West (p. 2).

Putting these historiographical doubts to the side, accepting that reflection has a crucial role in doing history, what can be made of animals; do they have any reflective abilities? Despite some physical and metaphysical presumptions, there are indications that some animals react to the past in a way that might be reflective. In a popular example, researchers at the University of Washington wore cavemen masks when capturing crows; later, when they donned these same masks in public outside, they were harassed by crows, and not just by those who were previously captured. Moreover, the crows did not attack those researchers wearing similar but different masks—a Dick Cheney mask instead of a caveman (Nijhuis, 2008). To say these crows on the University of Washington campus had a history with researchers wearing cavemen masks is quite apt, both in the vernacular of the phrase and the meaning of it. Of course, it may be the case that humans do not think enough like crows (or any other animal) to design experiments that will reveal their reflective capacities. But these tests and others like them, while not definitive, do open the door wider to considerations of the possibility that animals possess overlooked capabilities that are constitutive to history, much more than the Cartesian version of animals as unthinking automata.[7]

RECONSIDERING HISTORY FROM THE ANIMAL PERSPECTIVE

So maybe animals have some sort of reflective ability. Or maybe not. But humans are not some divine arbitrators of reality, and should animals reflect in a way to germinate their own history, this would exist whether or not humans recognized it. And this is rather a good thing if one appreciates the flawed track record of human empathy—if truth depended upon human recognition, much would be lost. So perhaps, in another world where humans could enter an anthill, the home of one of nature's most social creatures, they might find ant historians doing their histories. But the fact that humans cannot shrink nor communicate with ants in this world does not mean that ants do not have histories. It is accounting for this unknown possibility (and the possibility of this unknown) that is key, serving more than an epistemological point about human knowledge; the fact humans may never know animal history from animal perspectives is a metaphysical reminder of human weakness. Crucially, this hanging question mark on whether animals can do histories offers an opportunity for humbling humans, one that can unlock for them a greater perspective of the world for which they are desirous to know.

Perhaps this dynamic and its opportunity can be better illuminated with a parable from history. There is a story that the Bishop of Polignac, upon seeing a chimpanzee at the Jardin du Roi in Paris, declared, "Speak and I shall baptize thee" (Corbey, 2005, p. 54). As Raymond Corbey (2005) speculates, such an invitation was most likely proffered ironically, to deny the chimpanzee communion with humans at a time when captivatingly never-before-seen humanlike creatures were testing the metaphysical boundary between human and animal in 18th-century Europe (pp. 54–55). Regardless of this invitation's sincerity, or whether this encounter even occurred, it epitomizes the false choice humans give to other animals, including the question of history. What if the chimpanzee can speak but does not wish to be baptized? Or what if this chimpanzee wishes to be baptized, but cannot speak as the bishop understands? Stepping back, is this a tale of the chimpanzee not speaking or that of the bishop not hearing? And why should the ability to speak and be heard by human ears, and the ceremony of baptism, be the door to freedom from the cage of the zoo? These considerations and others that show the falsity of the choice will likely be missed if the bishop approaches the chimpanzee with a sense of arrogance, even with the purest of intentions. However, if the bishop considers his own incapacity to understand the chimpanzee and how this may contribute to this interaction, one housed in uncertainty, he may be humbled. In turn, not only will this humility give him a clearer reflection of this interaction, but with it, an opportunity to better understand himself, his endeavors, and the world around him, one that is also inhabited by the chimpanzee.

The same applies to history. When Fudge (2002) explains in the context of why animal histories are impossible—because of a lack of documentation—that a dog's bark "cannot be understood," she misses an opportunity to stress the difference between human knowledge of the world (accessibility) and how the world may actually exist (possibility; p. 5). The fact that humans do not hear the historical meaning of the bark does not mean that it is not necessarily there. Likewise, while Fudge (2002) intimates the limits of human knowledge when discussing how animals do not periodize their past, "as far as [humans] know," her conclusion that they "clearly" do not leaves an objective impression (p. 6). Even if this is the only perspective available to humans, such that they have to move forward without history from the animal's perspective, reframing the approach as one of human lack of knowledge changes the nature of the reflection—the issue becomes not whether animals have histories but whether humans have or will ever have access to them. Reconsidering the interaction between human and animal histories in this way, like with the bishop in meeting the chimpanzee, gives new opportunities to humans to appreciate their place in the world and their relationship with animals. For example, if Shaw (2013) is correct that history is of a "we" social group that has only recently expanded to include animals, recognizing this frame of the unknown recasts history as either less universal (more parochial or tautologically human) or that the "we" social group that has made history its project may not be the only "we" group out there (there are some—perhaps inaccessible—"we" groups outside what is human; p. 1). In other words, the history that humans do may be neither universal nor exceptional. This would leave the possibility of animals having their own histories as well as recasting the place of human history as something to the side, rather than above, the place of animals.

REAPPRECIATING HISTORY FROM THE HUMAN PERSPECTIVE

Thus, one answer to the question "do animals have histories?" is an enigmatic maybe, but one that is a crucial reminder of human partiality and inability that reframes the relationship between humans and animals via the latter's possible history. But whether humans can know or not know animal history from animal perspectives, they need to recognize and understand animal history from a human perspective, a point that Fudge (2002) and Shaw (2013) rightly emphasize. This is so because animals have played a vital part in the foundation of human history. And not simply as passive objects, but as agents of influence. Take the colonization of North America as one case example. Virginia Anderson (2004), in *Creatures of Empire*, describes how the uncontrolled behavior of European domesticated animals forced interactions between settlers and indigenous peoples, a process that was integral to the history of colonization. Likewise, Andrea Smalley (2017) illustrates, in *Wild By Nature*, how "wild" American animals arrested (and in many ways reshaped) plans by colonizers to master the country, provided means for indigenous peoples to resist, and, in the process, became legal actors as authorities sought to "contain and preserve the wildness" (p. 3). Whether domesticated or free-living, animals have significantly shaped the development of America, and if one wants to have a full understanding of American history, one must have an understanding of animals, even if only through the feeble attempt to understand animals from the outside. This, of course, is in addition to the fundamental role animal exploitation had in building America, from the beaver "pelt" trade that was foundational to America's early growth, economically and spatially, to the sinew of bovine that cleared the land, fed the population, pulled the wagon trains, and gave cowboys their fame, to name a few examples of just a small subset of animals.[8] In a word, human history, assuming American history is not exceptionally unrepresentative, cannot be fully written without due consideration of animals.

But, even from the human perspective, what is the history of animals? The animal examples above were chosen deliberately, with one being domesticated and one being free-living, because it evinces how animals, often thrown together, are eclectic. This is important to highlight as not all animals, itself a human categorization, are the same and their relationships to humans (and vice versa) can be very different. This includes *how* they contributed to human history. As such, if history is about an accurate reflection of the past, their different roles must be highlighted, and casting them in the same lot does a disservice to this mission. Similarly, if history is also about the utility of present, it also matters that animals are not all lumped together in one artificially constructed category. Consider the fact that in *Zoopolis*, Sue Donaldson and Will Kymlicka (2013) make a potent argument that domesticated animals should enjoy citizenship rights as members of human societies while free-living animals should be seen as their own sovereign communities with protected rights of self-determination. Whether one is convinced by these arguments or not,[9] *Zoopolis* raises a key point: Various animals stand in different relationships with humans and, consequently, may have unique justifications and attendant rights in their diverse standings. In both cases, the past is alive in the present through history, and in this it is helpful to see animals as not just possessing a history, but histories (in the plural).

This division between domesticated and free-living animals is just one example of how the socially constructed category of animals can be broken down, and there are many different ways—indeed, *Zoopolis* also discusses liminal animals (Donaldson & Kymlicka, 2013, pp. 210–251). But one thing that these taxonomies are likely to have in common is that they are elementally human creations. This alone does not make them bad nor anthropocentric. Instead, as the anteater has its long tongue, the mallard has its buoyancy, or the orb-weaving spider has its web, these taxonomies can be seen as part of the human condition utilized for survival. And, indeed, some scholarship has suggested that these sorts of taxonomies may be a product of cognitive disposition in *Homo sapiens* to understand their world (Smith, 2015, pp. 47–51). If so, to deny this biological function to humans among all animals would be a retreat back into human exceptionalism. But in employing this tool, humans must not succumb to the hazard of instrumentalizing animals, a common critique of animal histories performed by humans (Specht, 2016). At the end of the day, humans are not taxonomizing animals from the center of the universe, but rather as a means of surviving as a small part of it. Reframing the inquiry into animal history as one of what humans know and do not know aids in this realization and serves to free humans in their reflection of animal history by giving greater appreciation to their human lens. In turn, acknowledging that humans are examining history for themselves from a position of their own partiality, one that respects their ignorance of the animal perspective, they are released from the weight of universal history and the taint of human exceptionalism. Among other things, this allows humans to escape from "the Scylla of anthropomorphism and the Charybdis of anthropocentrism" of animal history (Pearson & Weismantel, 2012, p. 17). By seeing those "isms" for what they are, human tools that bend light to give a clearer picture to weak eyes, humans can better process their own understanding of the world while still regarding the possibility and the search for different ways of seeing animals as they exist independent of the human perspective.

THE PRACTICE OF ANIMAL HISTORY, REFRAMED

Considering all this, what might animal histories look like? In a place like Oxford, England—whose very etymology traces to animals crossing a ford—the perspective of those eponymous oxen on their history to the town and university may be out of the grasp of humans. However, humans need to strive to understand local ox history given their integral role played in Oxford's development, which may itself lead to considerations of what might be owed to them in the present as part of that history. But this would just be one animal history of Oxford, and there are many interactions between different animals. In fact, even the lowly pigeon, denizen of Oxford streets, dodger of human traffic, has a significant history. Take one example from the human perspective: A careful onlooker might notice, among the august architecture that populates the "the city of dreaming spires," the infestation of metal spikes jutting out of many structures. These are meant to prevent pigeons from roosting, yet a closer inspection reveals many instances of pigeons circumventing these attempts, leading one to wonder how future architects might craft their designs to incorporate this consideration as a result. Thus, even pigeons have left their mark and have a worthwhile history to study; Oxford history has human history, ox history, and pigeon history, all intermingling, each informing the other. And viewed in this way, human history appears more like another type of animal history than as something separate and above. In turn, taking a step back away from human exceptionalism—which is not the same as disregarding the individuality of humanity—with this humbled view encourages humans to perceive better treatment for animals; if they consider how pigeons are part of Oxford's history, both in known and unknown ways, they might be more considerate of pigeons in the present—if they want to protect the architecture of Oxford, they could do so in a more respectful manner, to raise just one consideration, than demeaning spikes.

Though a groundbreaking work in animal history, Anderson (2004) has an interesting line in *Creatures of Empire*, writing that "livestock" was "the one set of characters incapable of making [a] plan" that ironically "proved fully capable of upsetting the plans of all of the people around them" (p. 7). What this article wishes to emphasize is how such a passage, while drawing needed attention to animals as historical actors, too quickly writes off animals, making a paradigmatic assumption that equates human proof to objective existence. Here, Anderson assumes that a lack of human evidence of animal plan-making is conclusive and, thus, animals do not make plans. In reality, "animals still allude [humans]" (Pearson & Weismantel, 2012, p. 17) and reframing the approach as a teleological matter from what exists toward what humans know of existence—here, from the incapability of animals to make plans to perhaps the incapability of humans to know if and how animals make plans—would highlight the weakness of the human perspective rather than that of the animal. It would be wise for humans to take notice of such a moment of self-awareness as it is this very weakness that has contributed to humans needing to know animals because, as Anderson's passage appreciates, animals have been an integral part of human history. And this includes the historical reliance humans, vulnerable creatures that they are, have had on their cohabitants of earth, whatever else can be said of animals independent of humans. Thus, other animals may have their own histories, but humans need to know animal histories in their quest to know themselves, and being aware that it is from an "all-too-human" perspective, rather than some objective historical view, aids in this journey.

CONCLUSION

In the end, this article ultimately answers the question of whether animals have histories with a "maybe" *and* a "yes." On the one hand, humans may not know, and may never know, history from the animal perspective, though this lack of knowledge does not mean it does not exist. Acknowledging this uncertainty and this possibility of the animal perspective reframes the inquiry into what humans know rather than what definitively exists, not only giving a more honest reflection, but one that illuminatingly draws attention to human partiality and frailty. It is this same frailty that demands, on the other hand, that humans know animal history from a human perspective; humans have depended on animals for their survival and, accordingly, animals played an integral role in human history, often with their own agency. Putting together this possibility of the animal perspective and the need for animal history because of the human perspective sheds new light on the human reflection of animal history. By giving greater appreciation to the humanness of the lens by which they view the world, humans are humbled into considering how they are among, rather than separate from, animals, giving a new view of the tools they employ in considering the world and informing them of how animals more appropriately have histories (in the plural), of which humans just might be one. This humility may also make them more considerate of their treatment of animals, an ethical consequence of this reframing. All this uncovered in the process of stepping back to consider the question of animal history itself, even as the field of history in the West has progressed in some step, albeit long overdue, of viewing animals as subjects of historical concern.

Notes

1. For an interesting perspective considering a "history from below" with animals, see Hribal, 2007.

2. As an illustration of the lack of acceptance of animals within the history discipline, consider Amir Zelinger's (2019) assessment of the positive reaction to the hoax article in the journal *Totalitarisumus un Demokratie* about German shepherds in East-West German relations: "In what might be seen as a rebuttal of the hoaxers' claim that Human-Animal Studies have become mainstream, [the] scheme [of ridiculing animal history] garnered widespread approval within and outside academia" with many working "to ensure that reputable historical research would not be contaminated by the German Shepherd and other creatures of its kind" (pp. 360–362).

3. For a discussion of how women's liberation has impacted historical analysis, including as an example of this expanded appreciation, see Alexander and Davin, 1976.

4. Harriet Ritvo (2004) describes this as the "democratizing tendency within historical studies" (p. 205). See also Brantz, 2012, pp. 2–6

5. For instance, in the United States, Frederick Douglass (1854/1950) critiqued how White anthropologists sought to deny Black history and civilization as a defense for slavery. Approximately a century later, James Baldwin (1963/1998) expounded on how Black history was denied and what consequence it had for identity. Both these examples are also interesting in how they engage with the conceptions of animals—Douglass establishing human subjectivity through animal alterity and Baldwin discussing how Black slaves were treated as animals and how humans are social animals.

6. For example, see de Waal, 2019.

7. For a discussion of the Cartesian conception of animals and an assessment of René Descartes's particular treatment of animals, see Miller, 2013.

8. There is a growing literature about the fundamental role animal exploitation had in the development of America. For a few examples, see Cronon, 1991 (particularly Chapter 5, "Annihilating Space: Meat"); Dolin, 2010; Flores, 2008; Greene, 2008; and Specht, 2019.

9. For critiques of *Zoopolis*, see Hinchcliffe, 2015 and Ladwig, 2015. See Donaldson and Kymlicka (2015) for their rejoinder. For a critique of how *Zoopolis*'s portrait is incomplete, see von Essen and Allen, 2016.

References

Alexander, S., & Davin, A. (1976). Feminist history. *History Workshop: A Journal of Socialist Historians*, 1, 4–6.

Anderson, D. V. (2004). *Creatures of empire: How domestic animals transformed early America*. Oxford, England: Oxford University Press.

Baldwin, J. (1998). A talk to teachers. In T. Morrison (Ed.), *James Baldwin: Collected essays* (pp. 678–686). New York, NY: Library of America. (Original work published 1963)

Brantz, D. (2012). Introduction. In D. Brantz (Ed.), *Beastly natures: Animals, humans, and the study of history* (pp. 1–13). Charlottesville: University of Virginia Press.

Corbey, R. (2005). *The metaphysics of apes: Negotiating the animal-human boundary*. Cambridge, England: Cambridge University Press.

Cronon, W. (1991). *Nature's metropolis: Chicago and the great west*. New York, NY: W. W. Norton.

de Waal, F. (2019, June 2). The surprising complexity of animal memories. *The Atlantic*. Retrieved from: https://www.theatlantic.com/science/archive/2019/06/surprising-complexity-animal-memories/589420/

Dolin, E. J. (2010). *Fur, fortune, and empire: The epic history of the fur trade in America*. New York, NY: W. W. Norton.

Donaldson, S., & Kymlicka, W. (2013). *Zoopolis: A political theory of animal rights*. Oxford, England: Oxford University Press.

Donaldson, S. & Kymlicka W. (2015). Interspecies politics: Reply to Hinchcliffe and Ladwig. *Journal of Political Philosophy, 23*(3), 321–344.

Douglass, F. (1950). The claims of the negro ethnologically considered. In P. S. Foner (Ed.), *The life and writings of Frederick Douglass* (Vol. 2, pp. 289–309). New York, NY: International Publishers. (Original work published 1854)

Flores, D. (2008). Bring home all the pretty horses: The horse trade and early American West, 1775–1825. *Montana: The Magazine of Western History, 58*(2), 3–21, 94–96.

Fudge, E. (2002). Left-handed blow: Writing the history of animals. In N. Rothfels (Ed.), *Representing animals* (pp. 3–18). Bloomington: Indiana University Press.

Greene, A. N. (2008). *Horses at work: Harnessing power in industrial America*. Cambridge, MA: Harvard University Press.

Hinchcliffe, C. (2015). Animals and the limits of citizenship: *Zoopolis* and the concept of citizenship. *Journal of Political Philosophy, 23*(3), 302–320.

Hribal, J. C. (2007). Animals, agency and class: Writing the history of animals from below. *Human Ecology Review, 14*(1), 101–112.

Ladwig, B. (2015). Animal rights—politicised, but not humanised: An interest-based critique of citizenship for domesticated animals. *Historical Social Research/Historische Sozialforschung, 40*(4), 32–46.

Miller, M. R. (2013). Descartes on animals revisited. *Journal of Philosophical Research, 38*, 89–114.

Nijhuis, M. (2008, August 26). Friend or foe? Crows never forget a face, it seems: Science desk. *The New York Times*. Retrieved from: https://www.nytimes.com/2008/08/26/science/26crow.html

Pearson, S. J., & Weismantel, M. (2012). Does "the animal" exist? Toward a theory of social life with animals. In D. Brantz (Ed.), *Beastly natures: Animals, humans, and the study of history* (pp. 17–37). Charlottesville: University of Virginia Press.

Ritvo, H. (2004). Animal planet. *Environmental History, 9*(2), 204–220.

Ritvo, H. (2007). On the animal turn. *Daedalus, 136*(4), 118–122.

Shaw, D. G. (2013), A way with animals. *History and Theory, 52*(4), 1–12.

Smalley, A. L. (2017). *Wild by nature: North American animals confront colonization*. Baltimore, MD: Johns Hopkins University Press.

Smith, J. E. H. (2015). *Nature, human nature, and human difference: Race in early modern philosophy*. Princeton, NJ: Princeton University Press.

Specht, J. (2016). Animal history after its triumph: Unexpected animals, evolutionary approaches, and the animal lens. *History Compass, 14*(7), 326–336.

Specht, J. (2019). *Read meat republic: A hoof-to-table history of how beef changed America*. Princeton, NJ: Princeton University Press.

von Essen, E., & Allen, M. P. (2016). A rabble in the zoopolis? Considering responsibilities for wildlife hybrids. *Journal of Social Philosophy, 47*(2), 171–187.

Williams, T. (1964). *The milk train doesn't stop here anymore*. London, England: Secker & Warburg.

Zelinger, A. (2019). Race and animal-breeding: A hybridized historiography. *History and Theory, 58*(3), 360–384.

Animal Biographies: Beyond Archetypal Figures

VIOLETTE POUILLARD
French National Centre for Scientific Research

Obaysch. A Hippopotamus in Victorian London. By John Simons. (Sydney, Australia: Sydney University Press, 2019. 226 + xx pp. with color illustrations. Paperback. A$14.99. ISBN 978–1–74332–586–5.).

Biographies animales: Des vies retrouvées. By Éric Baratay. (Paris, France: Seuil, 2017. 304 pp. Paperback. €22.00. ISBN: 978–2–02–118295–8.) (English translation by Georgia University Press, *Animal Biographies: Toward a History of Individuals.*)

Abstract: The biographies of animal celebrities published by the historians John Simons and Eric Baratay aim to place animals in and of themselves at the center of academic narratives. Both excavate the lived experiences concealed behind official discourses and collective representations, notably by relying on cross-fertilization with ethological research. They unveil the ways in which information was reshaped in order to portray animal celebrities as benevolent members of human-animal communities, and thereby shed light on the mechanics of animal commodification. The close examination of a few individual animal trajectories enlightens the condition of many historical animals living under human tutelage in the 19th and early 20th century and highlights long-term historical evolutions, such as the succession of animal cultures and generations largely determined by human actions.

Key Words: historical animals, animal celebrities, zoos, Obaysch, bullfighting, animals used in entertainment, companion dogs, animal commodification, animal agency

The two books referred to in this review article, which appear among several recently published animal biographies and works on animal biographies (see, for a recent overview, Krebber & Roscher, 2018), intend "to put the animals at the centre of their own narratives" (Simons, 2019, p. 9) in reaction to the fact that animal history has largely been built up for the purpose of illuminating human history. Admittedly, placing animals at the center of historical narration is a difficult exercise, and it is therefore necessary, as underlined by Éric Baratay (2017), to accept that any animal biography is "amendable or replaceable" (p. 30). However, both John Simons and Baratay argue that we should not use these difficulties as a pretext for not looking at animals.

Simons devotes a book to the life of Obaysch, a hippopotamus born on the island of Obaysch, on the Nile, more than 2,200 kilometers from Cairo, in 1848 or 1849. He was subsequently imported to the London Zoo in 1850 to inaugurate a policy of animal starification, where he spent 28 years in his pen, dying in 1878. Obaysch appears in this work as a focal point upon which a broad range of human interests converged: the scientific and recreational thirst for zoological "specimens," the institutional and managerial requirements of the London Zoo, Egyptian diplomatic and political strategies, and material and cultural imperial greed: The young Obaysch arrived at the zoo with his keeper, Hamet Safi Cannana, who was dressed in Oriental clothing, and snake charmers, and all were transformed into Orientalist icons. The story of Obaysch therefore reveals new perspectives on the politics and policies of both Victorian England and the Zoological Society of London, which runs the London Zoo. But Obaysch is not, for John Simons, a pretext. He is a historical actor in his own right, "a real living being who had thoughts and feelings," which "deserve acknowledgment" and make him a subject of "our moral concern" (Simons, 2019, p. xii). This interest in Obaysch makes it possible, as is most often the case with biographies and microhistories, to transcend the singularity of the individual, the place, and the time and to recount the common condition through the singular experience (see, for example, Ginzburg, 2013)—in this case to reflect on the common ground of relationships between humans and animals held in captivity.

Simons first reconstructs the life and experiences of Obaysch in context and his interactions with keepers and visitors, who were at first enormously eager and curious—Obaysch was probably the first hippopotamus exhibited alive in Europe since Roman times—but then rapidly tired of a nocturnal animal who spent most of his day sleeping. The second chapter focuses on the meanings attributed to Obaysch, and on the ways they influenced material relationships with him. It demonstrates how the displaying of a hippopotamus—a species considered so dangerous that it was perceived as an obstacle to colonial expansion in Africa—in the heart of London, and the subsequent redefinition of this hippopotamus as an element of English culture, was part of a colonial undertaking that aimed to domesticate/civilize the "savage." Chapter 3 extends the scope of the work to captive hippos who succeeded Obaysch in Europe and the United States from 1850 to 1900. This widening of the scope sheds additional light on Obaysch's life as well as sketches a broader context, which turned out to be "a bloody narrative" (p. 202) of the hippos' captive condition.

Throughout the book, a clear disparity gradually appears between the hippopotamus's life, marked by coercion and routine, and representations of Obaysch, "constructed and manipulated" by his keepers, the zoo administrators, and the news media (Simons, 2019, p. xiii), who drew a picture of "a gentle giant fully acclimatised to the genteel rhythms of English life, but with a loveably grumpy side" (Simons, 2019, p. 90). This reshaping of the public image of animals, denying them their lived experiences and identity (Simons, 2019, p. 83), proves to be one of the main components of the development of the "animal entertainment" industry, allowing the legitimization of captive institutions as places of harmonious human-animal relationships (see Nance, 2013). Animal biographies, by putting the light back on the animals in and of themselves, help to deconstruct these collective strategies that form part of the mechanics of animal commodification.

In *Biographies animales*, Baratay (2017) retraces the biographies of 11 famous animals over a period spanning from the 1820s to the 1950s, mainly by examining certain chapters of their lives and placing them within the fuller perspective of their whole lives (p. 81). In the first part, which demonstrates the methodology of animal biographies, Baratay highlights the possibility of reconstructing animal trajectories through two case studies. The first is the journey of the first giraffe presented in Europe for centuries, destined for the Jardin des Plantes menagerie in Paris, in 1827. The second is the life of the horse Warrior during its mobilization in the British army in the course of the First World War. The second part deals with more concise episodes, lasting from a few days to only a few minutes: the donkey Modestine's journey under the guidance of the writer Robert Louis Stevenson in the Cévennes in 1878 and the bullfighting in which Islero was forced to participate, during which he killed the famous *torero* Manolete. This section further develops the reconstruction of animal experiences through the development of a "sensitive ecology" (Baratay, 2020, p. 60), or the study of animal feelings in their context, which the reader is invited to experience in the moment alongside the animals, and the role of these feelings in interactions with humans.

Baratay intends to demonstrate through these narratives both the idiosyncrasy of each animal's life journey as well as their insertion in a meta-animal history, comprised of a succession of different epochs. Part 3 thus explores the era of the "civilization" of chimpanzees in the West (ca. 1850-ca. 1950), characterized by their integration into (some) human activities, through the lives of the chimpanzee Consul at the Belle Vue Zoological Gardens in Manchester in 1893–1894 and of the chimpanzee Meshie in New York in the early 1930s, in the home of the naturalist Henry Cushier Raven. In Part 4, the lives of dogs demonstrate that specific epochs are formed by a succession of animal generations. Baratay considers the life trajectories of the stray dogs Bummer and Lazarus, who became mascots in San Francisco from 1861 to 1863, and the lives of three writers' dogs—Pritchard, with Alexandre Dumas (1846–1850); Bauschan, with Thomas Mann (1915–1920); and Douchka, with Colette Audry (1954–1960). These accounts testify to the increasing integration of dogs into human social relationships and the family circle. However, in such relationships, animal epochs and generations appear to be largely determined by human actions.

ANIMAL METHODOLOGIES

Highlighting animal experiences requires the development of specific methodologies. Both Simons and Baratay rely mainly on official and published sources, a large part of which were intended for a wide audience. Archival and internal sources, when they exist (such as the minutes of meetings of the London Zoo) would have provided the reader with more certifiable facts. However, both authors cross the sources with less standardized documents and carry out a considerable amount of work in deconstructing official narratives, reading between the lines and against the grain.

This work is further supplemented by cross-fertilization with research in the life sciences, mainly ethology, biology, and cognitive psychology, in order to better understand the historical documents and shed light on some of their shortcomings. Simons makes use of general information on the life of free-living hippopotamuses, which enables him to contrast the free life with the deprivations of captive life. However, according to Simons (2019), reconstituting the animals' experiences presents certain limits: "We cannot reconstruct their feelings or perceptions" (p. 9). Baratay, for his part, tries to reconstruct the animals' mental universes, their feelings, sensations, and behaviors, which cannot be easily distinguished from their corporeal universe, their perceptions, faculties, and needs. The research work then consists in "translating and transposing into the human world, with human words" the animals' lived experiences in order to reach the animal flesh of anthropozoological relationships (Baratay, 2012, p. 70). Reading such animal biographies constitutes an original, and sometimes arduous, experience, which requires the reader to undertake a shift in focus, away from their own human-centered perspective, notably by means of typographical variations that distinguish the animal and human points of view. The experience is at its best when the text, not unlike experimental literature, achieves its goal in placing the reader alongside the animal. This is particularly true for the journey of the donkey Modestine in the Cévennes by suffering under Stevenson's blows, for Islero's bullfighting ordeals, or for the trajectories of the companion dogs.

BIOGRAPHY HIGHLIGHTS

Beyond their methodological specificities, Simons's and Baratay's works share a de-anthropocentric perspective that helps us "to get away from the evidence and beliefs of our situated perspective" (Baratay, 2017, p. 123). The biographies offer often striking contrasts to the collective images surrounding famous animals, regularly portrayed as debonair characters and embodiments of the bond between humans and animals. By virtue of their exceptionality, these animals probably received much better care and treatment than their anonymous counterparts—with the notable exception of the donkey Modestine and the bull Islero, who became famous after being used. However, as exceptional as they were, the weight of human violence permeates their biographies. Obaysch's life is "a story of misery and pain" (Simons, 2019, p. 9), while the other zoo animals (the giraffe and the chimpanzee Consul) endured grueling trapping and transport, followed by the daily routine of captive life, interrupted by physical ailments. The chimpanzee Meshie, who seems to have been more integrated into Raven's home, spent most of her time chained or locked up in a cage in the basement before being sold to a zoo. The horse Warrior was enlisted in the war where he experienced cold, exhaustion, boredom, and stress associated with fighting. Dogs involved in loose relationships with humans (Bummer, Lazarus, Pritchard) were nonetheless victims of human violence (poisoning, beatings, mutilation). Dogs subsequently more included in the family circle had their life "organised according to the availability of humans" (Baratay, 2017, p. 215), a situation that involved, for Bauschan, long periods of solitary confinement in the cold of the yard. Douchka's situation, despite being promoted to a real "family member" (Baratay, 2017,

p. 239) involved "an often solitary confinement" (Baratay, 2017, p. 256) that she found increasingly difficult to cope with, to the point of needing to be calmed down by means of an antipsychotic used for captive big cats (Baratay, 2017, p. 259).

Violence toward the individual animals described in these biographies are embodiments of structural violence. One can decipher the lives of many animals used in zoos, menageries, circuses, entertainment, and film, scripted for the crowds, yet coerced behind the scenes, through the trajectories of Obaysch, Consul, or Meschie; the severe training imposed on utilitarian animals through the lives of Modestine, Warrior, or Pritchard; the extremes of violence endured by fighting bulls through Islero's trajectory, invalidating "the widespread idea that modern bullfighting has reduced violence or that it represents a fair fight" (Baratay, 2017, p. 104); and, in the case of companion animals, the dullness and uncertainties of lives more or less fortunately tied to those of their human "masters."

Despite the many cultural specificities, Simons's study emphasizes the ubiquity of the violent common ground permeating human relationships with animals. Obaysch's trajectory indeed testifies to both the imperial appetite for exoticized animals and the role of the Egyptian ruling elites and hunters in the extraction of free-living animals. The history of animals has much to contribute to imperial and colonial environmental historiography, by shedding light on transcultural modes of exploitation: "underlying all the process of colonisation, decolonisation and postcolonisation is a more fundamental process of speciesism" (Simons, 2019, p. 13).

All this does not mean that virtuous dynamics between humans and animals do not exist. Official sources value collaboration both as a tool to conceal the constraints imposed upon the animals and as a result of a sincere desire to exist in a community with them. However, the desire for animal company itself determines a large part of the constraints. The limits of such a companionship leads to the confinement or chaining of free-living animals for training or for the purposes of discipline. Collaboration with animals does not take place outside of asymmetrical power relationships, but within them. Thus, the chimpanzee Consul developed a close relationship with his keeper John Webb, but under his guard or in his cage. Similarly, the dogs Bauschan and Douchka experienced moments of great complicity with their "master," but only within the latitude conceded by the spatial and disciplinary framework that governed their existence.

Human-animal dynamics also encompass chain reactions that follow the pattern of animal reactions to imposed coercion; human perceptions of these reactions and, through them, of the failings inflicted upon the animals; and subsequent human disapproval and protest. The latter could eventually pave the way for potential adaptations and improvements in the conditions of the animals. Animal biographies bear witness to several occurrences of public protests. The *Knight's Cyclopedia of London* (1851) noted "that porridge was no diet for a hippo, and that a large free-ranging animal needed more than a small pool to swim in" (cited in Simons, 2019, p. 59). Stevenson met inhabitants of the Cévennes outraged by the treatment he inflicted on Modestine (Baratay, 2017, p. 102). However, the strength of human protest as a product of animal agency was regularly countered by animal keepers and users, who worked on staging animals and reframing information about their treatment. This process appeared at work in the entertainment industry as well as in most official accounts and film and literary works. For example, Stevenson translated the violent episodes to which he subjected the donkey Modestine into a sanitized account tinged with sentimentality, so as not to offend the readership (Baratay, 2017, p. 103).

Accordingly, the stage animal often proved to be a fragile construction, always likely to be challenged by the animals themselves (including by their own mortality, as was the case with Consul). Obaysch, for example, rapidly became a "furious" animal—"the Obaysch the Zoological Society didn't want people to see" (Simons, 2019, p. 82)—but also, "like most [zoo] animals," an animal "radically different and distant," (Simons, 2019, p. 85) in short, "a disappointment in the flesh" (Simons, 2019, p. 113). It thus transpired that there was little more to say about him—nor about the giraffe nor any other mascots—than a dull routine punctuated by rare incidents or anecdotes. Animals used in entertainment were thus doomed to gradually fade away behind the archetypal figure imposed upon them, which was itself increasingly disembodied (Baratay, 2017, pp. 55–56). Biographies can give animals back their full agency by excavating these concealed existences.

Other animals did transgress the expectations surrounding them to such an extent that they could barely be contained to the semantic categories associated to taming. From the female hippopotamus Adhela, who arrived at the London Zoo a few years after Obaysch, to the bull Islero, who killed his matador, they were portrayed as intrinsically dangerous beings and "vicious monster[s]" (Baratay, 2017, p. 104). Such depictions, which avoided acknowledging the human role in the production of animal violence, were, as Baratay (2017) points out, "double negation[s]": of what animals were and of what they were subjected to (p. 121).

Lastly, the re-creation of animals can take one final form that is more deeply rooted within the animal bodies: a remodeling inscribed in the gene itself. Collective animal biographies can help to highlight social as well as biological animal generations (Baratay, 2017, p. 176): the generations of zoo captives, increasingly docile, a product of both purposeful selection and the mortality of those who could not adapt to captivity, the generations of companion dogs, increasingly standardized, as the most appreciated were carefully selected through controlled reproduction, and the generations of bullfighting bulls, less and less dangerous. However, Islero—a bull "belonging to the transformed type, less dangerous" (Baratay, 2017, p. 106)—reminds us of how some individuals have exposed the deceptive nature of this genetic reshaping.

BIOGRAPHICAL PATHS

Due to their experimental nature, animal biographies are also historiographical laboratories paving the way for further questioning and avenues of research. Baratay and Simons have studied famous animals, while making it a point to evoke through their trajectories the mirrored lives of the anonymous animal masses swept away by history. However, in contrast with research into human biographies, historians have not yet produced biographies of unknown animals (see, for example, Corbin, 2001). Internal sources produced for management purposes, by making it possible to reconstruct living conditions, offer more direct access to the average animal condition. In such narratives, the part dedicated to human-animal interactions and dynamics will probably be further reduced. It will thus be necessary to reflect on ways of providing adequate space for the description of the broken relationships, apathy, or boredom that impregnated coerced animal lives in order to avoid reproducing in our historical narratives the marginalization or negation of such experiences. The history of bodies could serve as an auxiliary by replacing the animal experiences within the confines of underdeveloped (Obaysch), suffering and malnourished (Bauschan, Warrior), sick (the giraffe in the Paris menagerie, Consul), damaged (Modestine, Pritchard), mutilated (Islero), or drugged (Douchka) bodies. Further interdisciplinary cross-pollination could also be imagined by relying on preserved archaeozoological remains. Finally, interdisciplinary crossings themselves invite some reflexive questioning. Academic works on animals do not take place outside the history of anthropozoological relationships, but within them, which assigns them de facto ethical implications. In the multidisciplinary dialogue conducted with ethologists, zoo technicians, or veterinarians, how can human and social scientists distance themselves from epistemological practices that are intrinsically coercive toward animals? By addressing such issues, history can take a leading role in the critical dialogue between animal studies and the natural sciences thanks to its disciplinary propensity to inscribe power asymmetries in a long-term perspective. Thus history can highlight the cultural prominence of such asymmetries, as well as their contingent character, as demonstrated in particular by ethologists practicing animal research "as a social science and cultural activity itself" (Chrulew, 2018, p. 24).

References

Baratay, É. (2012). *Le point de vue animal: Une autre version de l'histoire*. Paris, France: Seuil.

Baratay, É. (2017). *Biographies animales : Des vies retrouvées*. Paris, France: Seuil, 2017.

Baratay, É. (2020). Penser les individus: Retour sur *Biographies animales*. In A. Choné, I. Iribarren, M. Pelé, C. Repussard, & C. Sueur (Eds.), *Les études animales sont-elles bonnes à penser?* (pp. 55–79). Paris, France: L'Harmattan.

Chrulew, M. (2018). Living, biting monitors, a morose howler and other infamous animals: Animal biographies in ethology and zoo biology. In A. Krebber & M. Roscher (Eds.), *Animal biography. Re-framing animal lives* (pp. 19–40). Basingstoke, England: Palgrave Macmillan.

Corbin, A. (2001). *The life of an unknown: The rediscovered world of a clog maker in nineteenth-century France*. New York, NY: Columbia University Press.

Ginzburg, C. (2013). *The cheese and the worms: The cosmos of a sixteenth-century miller*. Baltimore, MD: Johns Hopkins University Press. (Original work published 1980)

Krebber, A., & Roscher, M. (Eds.). (2018). *Animal biography. Re-framing animal lives*. Basingstoke, England: Palgrave Macmillan.

Nance, S. (2013). *Entertaining elephants: Animal agency and the business of the American circus*. Baltimore, MD: Johns Hopkins University Press.

Simon, J. (2019) *Obaysch. A hippopotamus in Victorian London*. Sydney, Australia: Sydney University Press.

PART II

Intellectual Figures

"Higher" and "Lower" Political Animals: A Critical Analysis of Aristotle's Account of the Political Animal

CHERYL E. ABBATE
University of Colorado, Boulder

While Aristotle's proposition that "Man is by nature a political animal" is often assumed to entail that, according to Aristotle, nonhuman animals are not political, some Aristotelian scholars suggest that Aristotle is only committed to the claim that man is more of a political animal than any other nonhuman animal. I argue that even this thesis is problematic, as contemporary research in cognitive ethology reveals that many social nonhuman mammals have demonstrated that they are, in fact, political in the Aristotelian sense, as they possess a sense of both general and special justice. Keeping this in mind, I conclude that some nonhuman animal communities very well might be identified as highly political communities, leading us to question whether it is really the case that humans are more political than socially complex, group-living nonhuman animals.

KEY WORDS: Aristotle, justice, cognitive ethology, animal minds, animal morality

"Man is by nature a political animal" (Aristotle, 1998, 1253a1). This is perhaps one of Aristotle's most famous sayings, which is motivated by his claim that "every man, by nature, has an impulse toward a partnership with others" (Aristotle, 1998, 1253a29). According to Aristotle, humans have an impulse toward a partnership with others because humans cannot flourish on their own—happiness for humans requires that they form partnerships with others. While Aristotle discusses various types of human partnerships, such as the household and village, one important partnership that enables humans to achieve the highest good, and to which humans are drawn naturally, is the city or the *polis*: a political partnership. A city or a polis, then, is described as a collection of human beings who are able to live together by creating laws that enable both community survival and individual flourishing. According to Aristotle, humans have the power of speech on their side, which is assumed to be a necessary ingredient of a polis. It is through speech that humans are able to figure out how to live together, as it is speech itself that reveals "the advantageous and the harmful and hence also the just and unjust" (Aristotle, 1998, 1253a8). For Aristotle, the fact that we are capable of speech and complex language, in part, explains human sociability.

It is often assumed, then, that the polis is an exclusively human institution and that nonhuman animals are not political; since they do not have speech, it is presumed that they are unable to understand what is good and bad and just and unjust.[1] Yet, it is pointed out that, in this discussion found in *Politics*, Aristotle also presents the claim that humans are *more* of a political animal than any kind of bee or any herd animal (Aristotle, 1998, 1253a8). That is, he does not make the stronger claim that humans are the *only* political animal. This, then, leaves open the possibility that some nonhuman animals might, to some degree, be political animals. And, interestingly enough, recent cognitive and behavioral research demonstrates that certain group-living nonhuman animals are in fact political animals in the Aristotelian sense. Namely, certain nonhuman animals are said to demonstrate that they have a sense of what is good and bad and just and unjust (Bekoff & Pierce, 2013). In addition, cognitive and behavioral research demonstrates that many intelligent and social animals, who live in community with others with a shared goal of species flourishing, demonstrate a remarkable level of sociability, providing additional evidence that nonhuman animals, indeed, are also political animals. In what follows, I will provide an exposition of Aristotle's account of the "political animal" while demonstrating that many groups of animals can satisfy Aristotle's account. Furthermore, I will challenge Aristotle's claim that humans are *more* political than nonhuman animals by illustrating that certain highly social nonhuman animals have a sense of justice in the Aristotelian sense.

"POLITICAL ANIMALS": A COMMON MISCONCEPTION

Perhaps one of the most well-known phrases from Aristotle's *Politics* is the proposition that "man is a political animal." While this is often taken to mean that humans, and not nonhuman animals, are political in nature, David Depew (1995) remarks that one of the worst mistakes to make when reading Aristotle's discussion of the "political animal" is to assume that the phrase "'political animal' picks out the defining essence of human kind" (p. 162).[2] This is because a close reading of Aristotle's biological work reveals an acceptance of the continuity between humans and nonhuman animals. As R. G. Mulgan (1974) points out, while there are various senses of "political animal" found within Aristotle's work, one foundational sense is the biological (or zoological) account of the "political animal," which, according to Aristotle, many nonhuman animals, including some social insects, satisfy.

Larry Arnhart (1990) suggests that "Aristotle's proposition that man is by nature a political animal is fundamentally a proposition of biology and one essential to the grounding of his political science in biological science" (pp. 481–482). According to Arnhart, Aristotle's account of the political animal stems from a consideration of human nature and natural human needs, and we should judge a practice, such as politics, in light of how it promotes and/or satisfies our natural needs (Arnhart 1990, p. 482). Keeping this in mind, a number of Aristotelian scholars suggest that, in order to come to an informed understanding of Aristotle's account of the "political animal," we should first turn to Aristotle's biological (or zoological) description of the "political animal," which is found in the *History of Animals*, rather than focusing exclusively on Aristotle's discussion in the *Politics* (Arnhart, 1990, Depew, 1995; Mulgan, 1974; Kullman, 1991).

"POLITICAL ANIMALS": A BIOLOGICAL DEFINITION

In the *History of Animals*, which is perhaps one of Aristotle's oldest biological works, Aristotle draws a distinction between different types of animals. He claims there are solitary and gregarious animals and then there are scattered and political animals, whereby political and scattered animals are subcategories of gregarious animals. Aristotle defines political animals as those who live together for some common function. Specifically, he writes that "animals that live politically are those that have any kind of activity in common, which is not true of all gregarious animals. Of this sort are: man, bee, wasp and crane" (Aristotle, 1955, 1.1. 487 b33ff). According to this definition, being a political animal is not limited to human beings. Rather, any species of animals can be characterized as "political," so long as they have an essential work that its members all engage in together in the pursuit of a common goal, such as species survival or reproduction. As Arnhart (1990) points out, "Aristotle was impressed by the politics of the social insects, and particularly honeybees" (p. 489). Specifically, Aristotle observed that both bees and ants engage in complex forms of interaction and cooperation and that they are able to adapt to changes in the environment in order to maintain good social order, leading him to conclude that they, too, are "political animals."

From Aristotle's biological or zoological discussion of political animality in the *History of Animals*, we can conclude that "political animals" are those animals who are not self-sufficient and, rather, need to form partnership and cooperate with others in order to achieve a common goal, such as species survival or reproduction. Political animals, then, are those who engage in cooperative activity in order to achieve a common goal, such as future reproduction success. Keeping this in mind, Arnhart (1990) suggests that Aristotle adopts a "cybernetic definition" of politics, which presupposes that politics involves a steering process for "setting collective goals, organizing collective behavior to pursue those goals, and then altering both the goals and behavior in response to the experience" (p. 489).

This sort of cooperative behavior that Aristotle describes is observed in a variety of animals, including those without sophisticated cognitive capacities. For instance, entomologists point out that insects with the highest level of social organization, including ants, bees, and wasps, which are referred to as "eusocial insects," have the following three traits: (a) cooperative care of the young, (b) reproductive division of labor, and (c) overlap between generations so offspring can assist parent insects (Wilson, 1971). Furthermore, many insects, such as ants and bees, engage in "self-sacrificial" behavior in order to benefit their group. In this case, insects act politically, according to Aristotle's biological account, because (a) they form a partnership and cooperate with one another in order to (b) achieve a common goal, such as future reproductive success.

ARISTOTLE'S ACCOUNT OF THE "MORE POLITICAL ANIMALS"

Despite that, in the *History of Animals*, Aristotle seems to suggest that some nonhuman animals, including insects, can satisfy the conditions of being a "political animal," in *Politics*, we find that Aristotle's discussion of the "political animal" focuses on a so-called uniqueness of humans, which is said to affect their status as a political animal. In the following passage, Aristotle (1998) identifies the features he believes set human "politicalness" apart from nonhuman animal "politicalness":

> That man is much more a political animal than any kind of bee or any herd animal is clear. For, as we assert, nature does nothing in vain, and man alone among the animals has speech... Speech serves to reveal the advantageous and the harmful and hence also the just and unjust. For it is peculiar to man as compared to the other animals that he alone has a perception of good and bad and just and unjust and other things of this sort; and partnership in these things is what makes a household and a city. (1253a)

According to Arnhart (1990, p. 482), a number of scholars suggest that the above passage is at odds with Darwinian biology, which challenges the claim that humans are uniquely rational and political animals. According to Darwinian biology, one of the governing principles of evolutionary biology is the principle of "evolutionary continuity," which states that all differences between species are differences in degree and not in kind (Darwin, 1871). This entails that whatever capacities or powers humans have, some nonhuman animals will have to *some* degree. As evolutionary biologists point out, there is a continuum between human and nonhuman animals and, since Aristotle assumes that there are certain capacities that are "peculiar" to man, his account of the "political animal" in *Politics* is an indication of bad science and bad biology.

Aristotle seems to reject the idea that there is a psychic continuity between humans and animals, as he argues that the political life of humans is intensified due to their unique capacities, such as their capacity for speech or their capacity for rationality (Cooper, 1993; Kullman. 1991). So, what we find in the above passage is (a) the claim that humans are *more* of a political animal than any bee or other herd animal and (b) a possible explanation as to *why* humans are more of a political animal, which involves an account of "human uniqueness." Namely, humans are assumed to be more of a political animal because they: (a) have the capacity for speech, and (b) have perceptions about the good, bad, just, and unjust (and this sense of good, bad, just, and unjust stems from the capacity for speech).[3]

IS THERE A "MORE POLITICAL ANIMAL"?

Aristotle's claim that humans are more political than other nonhuman animals depends upon his assumption that humans have extrabiological features, such as reason, language, and the perception of the just and the unjust, in addition to humans being biologically political like other nonhuman animals (Kullman, 1991). As Kullman points out, on this account, humans possess greater "politicalness" due to the fact that their "politicalness" goes beyond what might be referred to as "biological politicalness." Thus we might conclude that, in addition to possessing "biological politicalness," humans also possess "nonbiological politicalness."

Arnhart (1990) points out that, according to Aristotle, human politics is unique insofar as only humans, and not nonhuman animals, can make judgments of goodness and justice. Having a conception of justice is an important part of the political because "the virtue of justice is what is political, and justice is the basis on which the political association is ordered, and the virtue of justice is a judgement about what is just" (Aristotle, 1998, 1253a33–5). Yet, important to keep in mind is that two different notions of "justice" are found within Aristotle's ethical and political philosophy (specifically, in Book V, Chapters 1 and 2 of the *Nicomachean Ethics*). First, there is what Aristotle refers to as "general justice," which refers to merely following the laws. Aristotle suggests that since laws are supposed to aim at the common advantage, citizens end up promoting the common good when they follow the law. According to this account of justice, possessing the virtue of general justice amounts to following the law and, as a consequence, "all lawful acts are in a sense just acts" (Aristotle, 1908, Book V.1).

Aristotle also writes about "special justice" (sometimes called "particular" justice), which refers to "justice as fairness." According to Aristotle, there are two forms of special justice: *distributive justice*, which involves having the right attitude toward natural goods and only taking what one is owed, and *corrective justice* (also referred to as rectificatory justice), which involves taking "remedial action when unfairness has occurred as a result of an injustice involving two people" (Sekine, 2005, pp. 95–96). Corrective justice, then, entails rectifying unjust distributions (gains or losses) between persons. Thus, someone who possesses the virtue of special justice is one who cares about and promotes fair outcomes. It is unclear which sense of justice Aristotle refers to when he writes that having a conception of justice is an important part of the political. Yet, whatever sense of justice Aristotle (1998, 1253a) had in mind in the passage found in *Politics*, one thing is clear: He assumes that nonhuman animals do not have a perception of it, and therefore, they are not *as political* as human beings.[4]

As Arnhart (1990) points out, Aristotle maintains that a full political life "emerges at the end of historical development, moving from isolated families, to villages, and finally to the *polis*" (p. 488). The partnership of the household is assumed to naturally arise for the sake of procreation, security, and basic survival. Villages, which are groups of related households, are a second type of partnership that arise for the sake of mutual defense and securing goods more efficiently. Finally, a community of several villages forms the highest partnership known as the polis. In the polis, human communities become completely self-sufficient and are not only able to live, but they are able to live well. It is through man's capacity for speech and conception of the just and the unjust that he is able to enter into the partnership of the polis. This is because Aristotle assumes that it is through the use of reason and speech that we are able to discover justice, determine the best way to live together, and create laws that both enable human communities to thrive and empower the individuals within these communities to live virtuous lives.

Keeping this in mind, we might summarize Aristotle's argument in the following way:

1. A city/ polis (i.e., a political community) is a partnership in what is good and bad and just and unjust.
2. One must have speech if one is to have a perception of what is good and bad and just and unjust.
3. Animals do not have speech.

4. Therefore, animals do not have a perception of what is good and bad and just and unjust.
5. Therefore, animals are not able to form a polis.[5]

Aristotle's claim that humans are more political than animals fundamentally rests on an argument from speech. According to him, it is through speech that humans come to an understanding of what is good and bad, what is advantageous and harmful, and what is just and unjust (Aristotle, 1998, 1253a). By having this perception of justice, injustice, and other moral qualities, we can establish and abide by just laws (i.e., laws that enable community flourishing). And, according to this logic, since nonhuman animals do not have speech, they are unable to perceive what is good or bad, right or wrong. So, while nonhuman animals can cooperate with one another in pursuit of a common goal, Aristotle denies that they have a conception of justice. And, since it is through "partnership in these things [a perception of the good and bad and just and unjust] is what makes a household and a city" (Aristotle, 1998, 1253a8), nonhuman animals are unable to enter certain partnerships, such as the polis.

CHALLENGING ARISTOTLE

Contemporary research in cognitive ethology concludes that some highly social nonhuman animals do in fact have a sense of justice, although there might be differences in degree between nonhuman animal and human justice. While a number of "justice" studies focus on nonhuman primates (see Sussman, Garber, & Cheverud, 2005), Bekoff and Pierce (2009) point out that "a sense of fairness or justice may function in chimpanzee society, and in a broad range of other animal societies as well" (p. 113). Robert Solomon (1995) likewise points out that

> Wolves have a keen sense of how things ought to be among them . . . justice is just this sense of what ought to be, not in some bone-in-the-sky theoretical sense but in the tangible everyday situations in which the members of the pack find themselves. Wolves pay close attention to one another's needs and to the needs of the group in general. They follow a fairly strict meritocracy, balanced by considerations of need and respect for each other's "possessions," usually a piece of meat. (p. 141)

Keeping this research in mind, in what follows, I will illustrate that there are nonhuman animals who do, in fact, possess the capacity that supposedly make humans "more of a political animal": a perception of the just and unjust. Specifically, I will demonstrate that highly social and cooperative nonhuman animals have demonstrated that they possess a perception of both general and special justice, leading us to challenge Aristotle's claim that "man is the most political animal."

GENERAL JUSTICE AND NONHUMAN ANIMALS

Recall that, according to Aristotle, general justice merely refers to following rules or laws of one's polis. The assumption, then, is that laws aim at the common advantage and thus, by following the laws, people will act in ways that promote the common good. Someone who has the virtue of general justice, then, is someone who follows the laws, even when doing so goes against one's own self-interest.

Like human beings, certain nonhuman animals are also lawful. That is, certain nonhuman animals understand and follow the codes of conduct that govern their communities, even when these rules only serve the common good and are not for one's benefit (Bekoff & Pierce, 2009). As Robert Sussman and Audrey Chapman (2004) point out, a number of group-living animals are willing to compromise their freedoms for the sake of the rules of their group, even when doing so goes against their self-interest. According to Bekoff and Pierce (2009) the codes of social conduct, which many nonhuman animals living in tight social groups develop and adhere to throughout their lives, "regulate actions that are and aren't permissible" (p. 125). These rules or "codes of conduct," which include both prohibitions against and expectations about certain actions and behaviors, foster harmonious and peaceful coexistence (Bekoff & Pierce, 2009, p. 5). The development of such rules or codes, then, is said to be an adaptive strategy for social living that is found in both human and nonhuman communities, as prosocial behavior decreases the likelihood of conflict and increases productivity (Bekoff & Pierce, 2012, p. 124). Bekoff and Pierce refer to this complex prosocial behavior as "wild justice": The sense of morality found in communities of highly social animals. As they point out, "behavior becomes immoral when it goes against socially established expectations" (Bekoff & Pierce, 2009, p. 16). For instance, biting too hard or trying to mate during play are punishable offenses in many coyote communities, and arriving late to dinner is a punishable offense in some primate communities. Thus, what animals ought to do, that is, the right or acceptable thing for nonhuman animals to do, is to follow the rules of their communities, which often vary from one social group to another (Bekoff & Pierce, 2009, p. 129).

Important to note is that the rules of conduct in nonhuman animal communities serve a similar function to the laws of the polis. While the laws of the polis aim at promoting the common good, so too do the rules of conduct in nonhuman animal communities. For instance, through the creation of codes of conduct concerning cooperation, nonhuman animals can "accomplish much more than they could alone, as for example in cooperative hunting, vigilance, and care for the young" (Bekoff & Pierce, 2012, p. 124). In addition, just as an individual member of the polis has a better chance of flourishing as a member of a political community, certain individual nonhuman animals also "benefit from the collective environment of living in stable social groups" (Sussman et al., 2005). So, just as Aristotle maintains that a just human (in the sense of general justice) is someone who is lawful, we might conclude that a just nonhuman animal is one who follows the code of conduct of his community.

Finally, Aristotle suggests that "right conduct" is conduct that conforms to the laws of the polis. The laws of the polis are said to specify which harms are wrongs, and one of the reasons why Aristotle assumes that humans are the highest political animal is because humans understand that what is lawful and unlawful is what is right and wrong. Likewise, the concept of right and wrong is said to play "an important role" in the social interactions of highly social nonhuman animals (Bekoff & Pierce, 2009, p. x). Right or good behavior for highly social nonhuman animals, then, is that behavior that conforms to the codes of conduct within one's community. The codes of conduct in nonhuman animal communities, then, designate which harms are wrongs. For instance, the code of conduct concerning "fair play" in a coyote community designates that the harm of aggressiveness during play is wrong.

SPECIAL JUSTICE AND NONHUMAN ANIMALS

According to Aristotle, the virtue of special justice is connected to the notion of fairness, merit, and moral desert. A just person, then, is one who has the right attitude toward natural goods and is concerned with promoting fair and equitable outcomes. This sense of justice is observed in nonhuman animal communities where animals "behave according to implicit rules about who deserves what and when" (Bekoff & Pierce, 2009, p. 5). For instance, Bekoff and Pierce (2009, pp. 120–124) discuss how a sense of fairness in animals is observed in social play. During social play, wolves, coyotes, and dogs demonstrate a concern for neutralizing inequalities (such as the inequality of strength, size, or social rank) when they engage in the practice of "role-reversal" and "self-handicapping." Essentially, strong, large, and dominant animals continually inhibit their aggressive tendencies and act submissively when playing with other animals who are smaller, weaker, and more subordinate to them. The purpose of role-reversal and self-handicapping is to make play fair and to ensure that there are no unfair outcomes: to set aside inequalities and to refrain from taking advantage of one's superior strength or status (Bekoff & Pierce, 2009, p. 121). One rule of conduct, then, in most coyote, wolf, and dog communities is that the norms of fair play must be abided. When community members violate these rules of play, they are often completely ostracized from the group.

Furthermore, Sarah Brosnan and Frans de Waal (2003) argue that a number of primates, such as capuchin monkeys, have a sense of fairness because they demonstrate an aversion to inequity. During one study, two capuchin monkeys (who were trained to exchange a rock for a piece of food) were positioned in two different cages that were situated right next to each other, and they were then asked to give an experimenter their rock in exchange for a piece of food. When the first monkey handed his rock to the experimenter, he was rewarded with a piece of cucumber, which he happily devoured. Yet, when the second monkey handed his rock to the experimenter, he was given a grape in return (which is much more desirable, in the eyes of a monkey, than a cucumber). When the first monkey continued to receive cucumbers in exchange for his rocks *after* he saw the second monkey receive a grape, he began to refuse to participate in the exchange and would throw the cucumbers back at the experimenter. The takeaway point is that the capuchin monkeys "expected to be treated fairly" (Bekoff & Pierce, 2009, p. 127). After measuring and comparing the reward that the neighboring monkey received, the monkey who continued to receive cucumbers in exchange for his rock become outraged due to his perceived sense of injustice. While this example arguably demonstrates that the capuchin monkeys have a sense of distributive justice, in that they can evidently understand that it was unfair that they received an unequal reward for performing the same task as other monkeys, nonhuman animals can also be said to have a sense of corrective justice. Cognitive ethologists have observed that it is common for group-living animals to punish others when they breach rules of fairness, for instance, through physical retaliation or social ostracism (Bekoff & Pierce, 2009; Clutton-Brock & Parker, 1995).

CONCLUDING REMARKS ABOUT JUSTICE IN NONHUMAN ANIMALS

The claim that nonhuman animals have a sense of justice stems from an evolutionary perspective that stresses continuity. Since research in biology, psychology, anthropology, and economics support the claim that a sense of justice is innate in humans, it would follow, then, that some nonhuman animals also have a sense of justice, although that sense of justice might differ in *degree* from that of a human sense of justice (Bekoff & Pierce, 2009, p. 114).[6] As Bekoff and Pierce (2009) point out, "the principles of parsimony suggests the following hypothesis: a sense of justice is a continuous and evolved trait" (p. 115). Whether it be general justice (law abidingness) or special justice (having the right attitude toward distribution of goods), it is apparent that some highly social nonhuman animals have a perception of what is just and are able to communicate this despite not having the capacity for speech.

Too often do philosophers and scientists cite a nonhuman animal's so-called inability to speak or use human language in order to justify denying certain higher capacities to them, such as the capacity to foster a sense of justice. And, since nonhuman animals cannot speak the language of humans, they are unable to defend themselves against claims of anthropodenial.[7] Unfortunately for those who go out of their way to endorse anthropodenial, the *behavior* of highly social nonhuman animals is quite telling—it tells of a rich and complex mental life that demonstrates a significant concern with following rules of conduct and abiding by norms of justice in one's community. Thanks to cognitive ethologists—such as Marc Bekoff and Frans de Waal, who have dedicated their careers to exploring, observing, and documenting the behavior of nonhuman animals we can no longer deny the rich social, moral, and political lives of nonhuman animals by pointing to their so-called inability to speak our language, as their lives have been shown to have complex emotional, social, and moral aspects.

OBJECTION

One might argue that Aristotle's distinction between animal and human agency and action speaks to a significant gap between the moral and social lives of nonhuman animals and rational human beings. Because human beings have a complex language and the ability to speak, we are able to engage in a discussion about what is good and bad, right and wrong, just and unjust. This possibility for debate and discussion furthermore entails that we can disagree with one another and attempt to persuade or convince each other of our own conception of morality. Furthermore, the capacity for discussion provides us with the possibility to change our conception of what we believe to be right or wrong.[8]

So, even if nonhuman animals have a perception of justice, there is still a significant gap between the moral, social, and political lives of humans and nonhuman animals because nonhuman animals are unable to communicate this perception of justice to others through the use of language.

In responding to this objection, we might pause to consider the principle of *evolutionary parsimony*, which states that "if closely related species act the same, the underlying mental processes are probably the same" (de Waal, 2009, p. 62). Taking this principle seriously has led some evolutionary biologists, such as Margoliash and Nusbaum (2009), to defend an evolutionary account of language, which lends support to the thesis that some nonhuman animals do in fact have language, and thus "human language" is not completely unrelated to "animal communication." And, in fact, there is a significant amount of compelling research that some animals, like the great apes, can learn sign language (see Gardner & Gardner, 1969; Patterson, 1978; Savage-Rumbaugh, Shanker, & Taylor, 2001; and Slobodchikoff, 2012).

Yet, even if there is no conclusive evidence for the claim that nonhuman animals possess language, this does not entail that nonhuman animals are unable to have a conception of justice or that they are unable to communicate this conception. If we take seriously the principle of evolutionary continuity, we are committed to the following view: If humans have a sense of justice and are able to communicate this conception to one another, then nonhuman animals, too, have a sense of justice and the capacity to transmit information about the good, bad, just, and unjust to one another, such as through socially transmitted behavior. For instance, when nonhuman animals are accepted into a social community, they often learn the "just" rules of the group by observing the behavior of others in the group and by becoming aware of what type of behavior is rewarded and what behavior is punished. Thus, in learning about what is permitted by their group and, in response, adjusting their behavior so it coincides with the norms of their community, these animals very well might be said to be "convinced" of what they ought to do, or they might come to a new understanding of what is good and bad. Likewise, older members of the group are often observed teaching younger or newer members about the rules of the group, such as by punishing them for violating the group rules, without completely ostracizing them altogether. This could very well be characterized as an attempt to "convince" younger or newer community members about what is right and wrong. And, finally, the behavior of nonhuman animals provides us with evidence that they can disagree with, or at least dislike, the established rules, such as when a female baboon uses deceptive behavior in order to "prevent the alpha male from discovering that she is engaging in a sexual act with a subordinate male"—an act which violates the rules of her community (Abbate, 2014, p. 15). Thus, even if nonhuman animals do not have language, it does not follow that they are unable to exchange information about morality.

CONCLUSION

Aristotle rightly points out that many nonhuman animals, including some insects, are political in the biological sense due to their observed prosocial behavior (i.e., behavior that promotes the welfare of others). He, furthermore, rightly points out that certain nonhuman animals, such as insects, do not have the same degree of politicalness as humans because they are unable to have perceptions about what is right, wrong, just, and unjust. Yet, where Aristotle goes wrong is in his failure to take into account other social nonhuman animals, such as wolves, dogs, coyotes, and primates, who arguably have heightened cognitive capacities, over and above the limited capacities of insects. As Bekoff and Pierce (2009) have demonstrated in *Wild Justice*, certain highly social mammals have a high

> level of complexity in social organization, including established norms of behavior to which attach strong emotional and cognitive cues about right and wrong; a certain level of neural complexity that serves as a foundation for moral emotions and for decision making based on perceptions about the past and the future; relatively advanced cognitive capacities (a good memory, for example); and a high level of behavioral flexibility. (Bekoff & Pierce, 2009, p. 13)

And, it is the complex sociality of these animals that challenges the idea that humans are "more political" than nonhuman animals.

If having the highest level of politicalness depends on having a perception of what is good, bad, just, and unjust, then contemporary research in ethology stands to challenge the proposition that humans are the "most political animals." Many group-living, socially complex nonhuman animals (a) create and abide by laws that enable community survival and individual flourishing, (b) employ their sense of justice to establish such laws, and (c) understand actions that violate the codes of their community to be bad. Thus, we have reason to believe that some nonhuman animal communities are highly political communities and, as such, are relevantly similar to Aristotle's polis.

ACKNOWLEDGMENT

The author would like to thank Mitzi Lee for her feedback on an earlier draft of this paper.

Notes

1. In this article, I will, at times, refer to nonhuman animals as just "animals," as it can be cumbersome to use the term "nonhuman" in certain passages.

2. For instance, Justin Smith (2014), a professor of history and the philosophy of science, wrote an essay titled "We Are Not the Only Political Animals," where he argues that Aristotle implicitly claims that animals are not, to any degree, political.

3. Arnhart (1990, p. 507) points out the two so-called unique human powers of (a) conceptual abstraction and (b) symbolic speech, as denoted by the word *logos*.

4. One might plausibly argue that, in this passage, Aristotle is only concerned with general justice, since the polis is described as a collection of human beings who are able to live together by *creating and following laws* that enable both community survival and individual flourishing. Yet, since Aristotle does not specify which conception of justice he has in mind, I will leave open the possibility that he might also have special justice in mind.

5. Note that there is a distinction to be made between the concepts of speech, language,

and communication. While it is generally accepted that nonhuman animals can communicate with one another, there is significant doubt as to whether nonhuman animal communication, which involves the transmission of signals or information, should be characterized as a "language," which involves applying grammar (syntax) to a finite number of words in order to create an infinite number of new, meaningful combinations (semantics), including combinations that refer to things that aren't present (displacement). Thus, some linguists, such as Hockett (1960) and Chomsky (1957) draw a distinction between "animal communication" and "human language."

On the other hand, speech refers to the vocalized form of human communication or spoken human language. Important to note is that, even if some nonhuman animals like chimpanzees and gorillas, can be said to possess language, as evident by their ability to imitate signs, combine them, and use them in varying contexts, it is unlikely that they will ever be capable of "speech," due to the structure of their vocal organs (see Savage-Rumbaugh, Shanker, & Taylor, 2001 and Gardner & Gardner, 1971, 1978 for a defense of the view that apes possess language and Slobodchikoff, 2012 for a defense of the view that a number of nonhuman animal species have language or something close to language). In this article, I will not take up the complex question of whether nonhuman animals can be said to have language, as my argument about the politics of nonhuman animals can be made independently of a discussion about animal language.

6. Note that there is a minority effort, led by Huxley and Ruse (2009) and supported by Williams (1988), that seeks to reject an evolutionary account of human morality. According to Huxley's view, which de Waal (2009) refers to as "veneer theory," humans are, by nature, nasty and selfish. Morality, then, is said to be a thin "veneer" over an otherwise nasty human nature. Since de Waal has thoroughly responded to and debunked this view, I will not take it up in this article.

7. Anthropodenial is a term coined by Frans de Waal (1997) that entails a "blindness to the humanlike characteristics of other animals, or the animal-like characteristics of ourselves."

8. Thank you to Mitzi Lee who suggested this objection during a personal conversation in May 2015.

References

Abbate, C. (2014). Nonhuman animals: Not necessarily saints or sinners. *Between the Species*, 17(1), 1–30.
Aristotle. (1908). *Nicomachean ethics* (W. D. Ross, Trans.). Oxford, England: Clarendon Press.
Aristotle. (1955). *Historia animalium* (A. L. Peck, Trans.). Cambridge, MA: Loeb Classical Library.
Aristotle. (1998). *Politics*. (C. D. C. Reeve, Trans.). Indianapolis, IN: Hackett.
Arnhart, L. (1990). Aristotle, chimpanzees and other political animals. *Social Science Information*, 29 (3), 477–557.
Bekoff, M., & Pierce, J. (2009). *Wild justice*. Chicago, IL: University of Chicago Press.
Bekoff, M., & Pierce, J. (2012). Wild justice redux: What we know about social justice in animals and why it matters. *Social Justice Research* 25: 122–139.
Brosnan, S., & de Waal, F. (2003). Monkeys reject unequal pay. *Nature, 425*, 297–299.
Chomsky, N. (1957). *Syntactic structures*. Berlin, GA: De Gruyter Mouton
Clutton-Brock, T., & Parker, G. (1995). Punishment in animal societies. *Nature, 373*(19), 209–216.
Cooper, J. (1993). Political animals and civic friendship. In N. Kapur Badhwar (Ed.), *Friendship: A philosophical reader*, (pp. 303–326). Ithaca, NY: Cornell University Press.
Darwin, C. (1871). *Thex descent of man* (1st ed.). London, England: Murray.

Depew, D. (1995). Humans and other political animals in Aristotle's history of animals. *Phronesis, 40*(2), 156–181.

de Waal, F. (1997). *Are we in anthropodenial?* Retrieved from http://discovermagazine.com/1997/jul/areweinanthropod1180

de Waal, F. (2009). *Primates and philosophers: How morality evolved.* Princeton, NJ: Princeton University Press.

Gardner, R. & Gardner, B. (1969). Teaching sign language to a chimpanzee. *Science, 165,* 664–672.

Gardner, B., & Gardner, R. (1971). Two-way communication with an infant chimpanzee. In A. M. Schrier & F. Stollnitz (Eds.), *Behavior of nonhuman primates*, (pp. 117–184). New York, NY Academic Press.

Gardner, R., & Gardner, B. (1978). Comparative psychology and language acquisition. *Annals of the New York Academy of Sciences, 309*: 37–76.

Hockett, C. (1960). Logical considerations in the study of animal communication. In W. Lanyon & W. Tavolga (Eds.), *Animal sounds and animal communication*, (pp. 392–430). Washington, DC: American Institute of Biological Sciences.

Huxley, T., & Ruse, M. (Ed.). (2009). *Evolution and ethics*. Princeton, NJ: Princeton University Press. (Original work published 1983).

Kullman, W. (1991). Man as a political animal. In D. Keyt & F. D. Miller (Eds.), *A companion to Aristotle's Politics*, (pp. 94–117). Oxford, England: Blackwell.

Margoliash, D., & Nusbaum, H. (2009). Language: The perspective from organismal biology. *Trends in Cognitive Science, 13*(12), 505–510.

Mulgan, R. G. (1974). Aristotle's doctrine that man is a political animal. *Hermes, 102*(3), 438–445.

Patterson, F. (1978). The gestures of a gorilla: Language acquisition in another pongid. *Brain and Language, 5,* 72–97.

Savage-Rumbaugh, S., Shanker, S., & Taylor, T. (2001). *Apes, language, and the human mind.* Oxford, England: Oxford University Press.

Sekine, S. (2005). A comparative study of the origins of ethical thought: Hellenism and hebraism. Lanham, MD: Rowman & Littlefield.

Slobodchikoff, C. (2012). *Chasing doctor Dolittle: Learning the language of animals*. New York, NY: St. Martin's Press.

Smith, J. (2014, November 2). We are not the only political animals. *New York Times*. Retrieved from http://opinionator.blogs.nytimes.com/2014/11/02/we-are-not-the-only-political-animals/?_r=0

Solomon, R. (1995). *A passion for justice*. Lanham, MD: Rowman & Littlefield.

Sussman, R. & Chapman, A. (2004). *The origins and nature of sociality*. New York, NY: Aldine De Gruyter.

Sussman, R., Garber, P., & Cheverud, J. (2005). Importance of cooperation and affiliation in the evolution of primate sociality. *American Journal of Physical Anthropology, 128,* 84–97.

Williams, G. (1988). Reply to comments on Huxley's evolution and ethics in sociobiological perspective. *Zygon, 23*(4): 437–438.

Wilson, E. (1971). *The insect societies*. Cambridge, MA: Harvard University Press.

Augustine of Hippo on Nonhuman Animals

CHRISTINA HOENIG
Independent Scholar

Abstract: This article presents a cross-contextual examination of St. Augustine's views concerning nonhuman animals. It aligns seemingly disparate conclusions of previous studies by considering both material and metaphorical nonhuman animals across Augustine's writings and by integrating the role he assigns to them into his broader metaphysical framework. While Augustine is found to assign instrumental value to all aspects of material creation, nonhuman animals are shown to carry a particularly complex significance due to their proximity to humans in his hierarchical account of creation.

Key Words: St. Augustine, history of animal ethics, nonhuman animals/animality, moral consideration, emotions, rationality, relative/instrumental value, cosmic hierarchy, Manichaeans, metaphor, pastoral exegesis

THE QUESTION OF AUGUSTINE'S LEGACY

St. Augustine of Hippo's statements concerning nonhuman animals have attracted negative attention. Frequently cited in historical accounts of animal ethics is *City of God* (*civ.*) 1.20. With regard to the commandment "You shall not kill," he notes that

> we do not understand this to apply to the plants, since they have no sensation, nor to the irrational animals . . . since they do not share with us the faculty of reason. . . . [T]herefore, by the creator's most just decree, their life and death are subject to our use.[1]

Similarly, *On the Catholic and Manichaean Ways of Life* (*mor.*) 2.17.54–59:

> Christ . . . shows that we have no community of rights [*societas iuris*] with beasts and trees. . . . We see and hear from their cries that animals die in pain. Man disregards this in beasts since, given their lack of a rational soul, we have no community of laws [*societas legis*] with them.

Unsurprisingly, it has been concluded that, for Augustine, "animals, animal behavior, and animal suffering are all for the physical or spiritual benefit of human beings" (Clark,

1999, p. 78). More generally speaking, Augustine's adaptation of the Stoic outlook[2] reflected in the above statements, which denied nonhuman animals moral consideration due to their assumed lack of a rational soul, is thought to have shaped subsequent perspectives in Western Christianity and the broader intellectual tradition (for instance, Calarco & Atterton, 2004, pp. xi-xiv; Clark, 1999; Linzey & Yamamoto, 1999, p. xiii; Linzey & Cohn-Sherbok, 2004, pp. 59–60; Sorabji, 1993, pp. 195–207; Steiner, 2010, pp. 2, 38). A reappraisal of Augustine's position is offered by Cox Miller (2018) in her recent study of ancient Christian engagement with animals and animality. Cox Miller, who places her contribution into the framework of the academy's so-called animal turn, complicates such negative accounts by arguing that Augustine expresses an ambiguous, at times undeniably appreciative, attitude toward metaphorical nonhuman animals in Scripture that frees them from the subordinate position they occupy in the material world.[3] Cox Miller's conclusions would appear to lend welcome reinforcement to, or at least make for a friendly dialogue with, analyses that emphasize the positive significance in Augustine's thought of material creation at large (e.g., Cipriani, 2006; Hanby, 2003; Harrison, 1992; Williams, 1994), against others from which he emerges as reiterating and cementing a contempt for all things material.[4] Yet, nonhuman animals, both material and metaphorical, have been strangely neglected in accounts of Augustine's relationship with the physical world.[5]

There appears, then, a lack of integration between the varying accounts of Augustine's position. Further analysis is needed to negotiate his, at face value, disparate views concerning material and metaphorical nonhuman animals and to integrate the role he assigns to them into his broader account of material creation. To do so, I will first examine Augustine's concept of a cosmic hierarchy that will allow us to locate nonhuman animals within the Augustinian metaphysical framework. I will then examine several contexts in which nonhuman animals emerge as a constant and crucial point of reference: Augustine's account of animal relationships in the postlapsarian material world and the role of metaphorical animals and animality in his human psychology and his pastoral exegesis. While no more than preliminary outlines of the complex roles Augustine assigns to nonhuman animals in these contexts can be given, this cross-contextual inquiry will direct us toward a more complete and integrated picture of the relationships he constructs between humans, other animals, and the world at large.

HIERARCHICAL CREATION

A useful framework for present purposes is Augustine's conception of a cosmic hierarchy[6] that orders creation into a coherent whole. He frequently alludes to his version of a "Great Chain of Being" in which a creature's position is determined by its associated mode of existence (for instance, *ord.* 2.48; *lib. arb.* 1.18, 2.7.13; *vera rel.* 13.52ff., 109ff.; *trin.* 15.7; *Gn. litt.* 7.21.27–31, 8.23.44; *doctr. Chr.* 1.8; *conf.* 7.23; *civ.* 7.3, 8.6, 11.16.28; *en. Ps.* 102.3, 144.13, 148.3). It is a creature's soul that determines this mode of existence (*civ.* 7.23.29; *an. quant.* 70–76), with Augustine distinguishing a vegetative (plants), a sensory (nonhuman animals), and a rational (human animals, angels) type of soul. What is without soul is without life, merely exists, and is placed at the bottom of the hierarchy.

Augustine's hierarchy exhibits continuity in its overall orientation toward the creator. In his exposition of Ps. 144, he describes creation as a "fabric" or "web" (*contextio*), a "most orderly beauty, ascending from the lowest to the highest, descending from the highest to the lowest, disrupted at no point, but balanced by its differences" (*en. Ps.* 144.13) that, in its entirety, praises God (see also *s.* 214.2, *civ.* 12.22). Within this "arrangement that distributes equal and unequal things each to own their proper position" (*civ.* 19.13.1; see also *ord.* 1.18, 2.17),[7] a creature's value derives from its "orderliness" or adherence to its assigned mode of existence within the order at large. Augustine explicitly removes from a human framework the relative value of nonhuman creatures as representatives of their assigned position within God's intended order: "Nature glorifies its artificer as seen in her own light, not with respect to our convenience or inconvenience. . . . [A]ll natural creatures, inasmuch as they exist and, therefore, have their own mode of existence, design, and inner harmony, are certainly good" (*civ.* 12.4–5, following a reference to the creatures of the plague at Exod. 8 and 10. See also *c. Faust.* 21.5). What is more, each individual creature possesses beauty, analyzed by Augustine as "measure, number, and order,"[8] the result of God's ordering design: "I see that all things are beautiful in their kind . . . for I observe the body and members of no living thing in which I do not find that measures, numbers, and order contribute to its harmonious unity" (*Gn. adv. Man.* 1.16.25, trans. Teske, 1991). We will return to this passage in due course.

Alongside Augustine's appreciation of material creation, including nonhuman animals, qua manifestation of God's orderly design, however, his description of it is not in terms of ecological kinship but in terms of a hierarchy in which the possession of rationality acts as a boundary line. Accordingly, his continued exposition of Ps. 144 emphasizes the differences between the modes of existence:

> God ordered and created everything: to some creatures, such as the angels, he gave sense perception, intellect, and immortality; to others, such as humans, he gave sense perception and intellect along with mortality. To others still, such as the beasts, he gave the bodily senses, but neither intellect nor immortality. But to others, he gave neither the senses, nor immortality, such as to plants, trees, and stones. (*en. Ps.* 144.13)

Rationality is introduced as a line of demarcation between human and nonhuman animals, thus deemphasizing their kinship while elevating human existence to a level "midway between that of angels and of beasts" (*Io. ev. tr.* 18.7; see also *Gn. litt.* 5.12, *lib. arb.* 2.3–6, *ep.* 177, *civ.* 5.11).[9] The difference between rational and irrational creation on earth articulates itself in distinct psychic activities.[10] The rational mind's ability to ascend beyond the material sphere is the signpost of discontinuity between humans and all lower-level creation, aligning the former, despite their corporeality, more closely with the divine:

> Although the divine being is beyond words . . . he who made us is nearer to us than many things that have been made. . . . But most creatures are inaccessible to our mind

because, being corporeal, they are of a different nature, and our mind is unable to see them in God. . . . For the foundations of the earth are beyond the range of our eyes but he who founded it is near our minds. (*Gn. litt.* 5.16.34; trans. J. H. Taylor, 1982, with minor alterations)

In this section, I have drawn attention to two dominant motifs in Augustine's discussions of nonhuman animals that will be of relevance to the remainder of our analysis: his hierarchical ranking of creation according to rationality and his insistence that all creatures possess value as illustrations of, and participants in, God's orderly design. While these perspectives are not incompatible, it is easy to understand how they may lead to disparate conclusions concerning his overall position without further contextualization. In the subsequent sections, I explore in greater detail how Augustine develops and negotiates between these perspectives in various contexts, thereby attempting to add both complexity and consistency to our understanding of his relationship with nonhuman animals.

MATERIAL ANIMALS: AUGUSTINE'S ANTI-MANICHAEAN POLEMICS

Augustine finds himself most pressed to engage with nonhuman animals in the physical world when countering Manichaean attacks against Christian doctrine. His notorious appeal to a lack of common rights and laws between human and nonhuman creation appears in his *On the Catholic and Manichaean Ways of Life*, a treatise that lays out the "true" Christian doctrine alongside the "falsehoods" of the Manichaean sect. To review the statement:

> Christ . . . shows that we have no community of rights [*societas iuris*] with beasts and trees. . . . We see and hear from their cries that animals die in pain. Man disregards this in beasts since, given their lack of a rational soul, we have no community of laws [*societas legis*] with them. (*mor.* 2.17.54–59)

While the preeminence of human rationality is a constant refrain in Augustine, the specific notion of a "community of rights/law" that result from its possession only features in anti-Manichaean contexts of his writings.[11] The rationale behind Augustine's appropriation of Stoic doctrine in these contexts lies in the details of his anti-Manichaean agenda. A constant target is the sect's dualistic materialism that divides the cosmos into a "good" and an equally powerful "evil" substance. Relevant for present purposes is the assumption that good divine soul had mixed with evil material bodies. More specifically, Augustine's disregard for nonhuman animal life at *mor.* 2.17 is part of his attack on the sect's prohibition against the killing of animals and plants, a consequence of their belief that particles of divine soul had been entrapped in these bodies (see also Sorabji, 1993, pp. 196–198). This tenet is unacceptable to Augustine since the mingling of divine reason with material creation would represent an obscene subversion of the hierarchy of being (let alone a metaphysical impossibility) and since God's material creation in its entirety is "good." The Stoics shared with the Manichaeans the basic tenet of corporealism, according to which a divine mind is diffused throughout the material world, but maintained for their divine Logos hierarchically ordered modes of material manifestation that withheld rationality from nonhuman animals.[12] Augustine's argumentative strategy in the above passage was likely motivated by his aim to invalidate the association of the divine with the material realm by appealing to a system of thought that, at face value, overlapped with the Manichaean outlook but differed from it in relevant aspects, thereby exposing its confusion. His refusal to grant nonhuman animals moral consideration, which would develop into an ideological signpost for subsequent centuries, arises in the specific context of invalidating the Manichaean prohibition against the killing of nonhuman life on earth. This context compels Augustine to stress nonhuman animals' lack of rationality and thus to highlight the discontinuity between the two animal kinds.

Countering a different Manichaean challenge elsewhere, Augustine is rather more interested in highlighting the positive value of nonhuman animals and adjusts his emphasis accordingly. At *Gen. adv. Man.* 1.16.25, he responds to the question of why a supposedly good creator would create animals who are hostile or, at best, superfluous from a human perspective. The motivation underlying this challenge is the Manichaean tenet of evil inherent in the material world, a tenet that would appear to be supported by humanity's exposure to such animals while exiled from Eden, according to Christian belief. In response, Augustine constructs a relationship between human and nonhuman animals that lends continuity to pre- and postlapsarian conditions, thereby safeguarding both creator's and creation's goodness.

> I admit that I do not know why mice and frogs were created, or flies or worms. Yet I see that all things are beautiful in their kind, though on account of our sins many things seem to us disadvantageous. For I observe the body and members of no living thing in which I do not find that measures, numbers, and order contribute to its harmonious unity. . . . Surely all living things are either useful for us, or harmful, or superfluous. [The Manichaeans] have nothing to say against the useful things. From the harmful we draw punishment or training or fear. As a result we do not love and desire this life that is subject to many dangers and toils, but another better life where there is supreme security. . . . Hence, make use of what is useful, watch out for what is harmful, leave what is superfluous. When you see measures, numbers, and order in all things, seek their maker. (*Gn. adv. Man.* 1.16.25, trans. Teske, 1991)

All nonhuman animals emerge from Augustine's account as elements of God's providential care for humans. Some, presumably domesticated ones, bear a straightforward instrumental value and are described as "useful" to humans. Those hostile or harmful toward humans are, likewise, assigned instrumental value, since their behavior benefits humans by fostering their moral improvement and a detachment from an earthly life. Mirroring human disobedience as a subversion of God's order that must be restored, these hostile animals play a soteriologically crucial role (see Pollmann, 2010, p. 85). Mice, frogs, and other seemingly "superfluous" animals, in turn, despite appearance to the contrary, exhibit the aesthetics of God's ordering agency, "measure, number, and order." In our previous discussion, this passage allowed us to infer a relative value for all creatures as illustrations of God's orderly design. Further contextualization, however, reveals an additional instrumental value: All creatures are useful to humans by communicating to them God's ordering agency *with the specific purpose* of compelling them to "seek their maker"[13] (i.e., to ascend beyond the material sphere). Augustine's understanding of material creation's instrumental value to humans is set out in his *On the Christian Doctrine*. There, he assigns different types of human psychological conditions to their ontologically appropriate objects. Only God may be truly loved, or "enjoyed" (*frui*), while the appropriate emotional response to creation's beauty is a kind of love that is exclusively in relation to, or for the sake of, God. To love creation in this manner means, in Augustine's terms, to "use" it:

> The whole temporal creation was made by divine providence for the sake of our salvation. We should use [*uti*] it, not with an abiding, but with a transitory love and delight . . . so that we love that by which we are carried along for the sake of that toward which we are carried. (*doctr. Chr.* 1.35.39)

Returning to Augustine's dispute with the Manichaeans, all postlapsarian nonhuman animals are shown to be "useful" to humans, whether through their beauty—intended to elicit a transitory love that facilitates a rapprochement between humans and their creator—or their hostility, to which humans respond by fear or violent subjugation,[14] activities that entail moral improvement and are thus, likewise, conducive toward their salvation.

In this section, I have examined how Augustine develops the familiar motifs of continuity and discontinuity between human and nonhuman animals in the physical world, against the specific background of his anti-Manichaean polemics. We saw how this background motivated him to develop his notorious denial of moral considerability to nonhuman animals. At the same time, it emerged that the relative value Augustine assigns to all creation as tokens of God's ordering agency, in the case of nonhuman animals, translates into an instrumental role that, reinforced by other types of animal behavior, is intended to facilitate humanity's reconciliation with its creator. Both the subordinate and the auxiliary roles of Augustine's nonhuman animals are mirrored and developed by him with greater complexity on the metaphorical level.

METAPHORICAL ANIMALS

Augustine's Human Psychology

Animal imagery plays a central part in Augustine's human psychology. The subjugation of unruly nonhuman animals in the material world is mirrored as a recurring theme in his theory of emotions, where the "beasts" to be tamed signify undue emotions of the human soul. At *conf.* 13.21.30, Augustine's readers are to restrain themselves "so that beasts may be tamed, cattle subdued, serpents rendered harmless. For these are the motions of the mind in allegory [*allegoria*]." The preeminence of human rationality in the physical world unfolds itself also on the psychological level, as shown at *Gn. adv. Man.*

1.20.31, where Augustine provides a "spiritual" or allegorical interpretation alongside the literal reading of Gen. 1.28:

> Apart from that interpretation according to which it is clear that man is master of all animals by reason, we can still understand this verse spiritually in the sense that we should hold in subjection all the affections and emotions of our soul, which are like those animals, and have mastery over them by temperance and modesty. For if we do not rule these emotions, they burst forth and turn into the foulest habits, carrying us off with all sorts of destructive pleasures and making us like every kind of beast. (trans. Teske, 1991)

Augustine's "beasts" thus carry a twofold significance, denoting both undue emotions and the humans experiencing them. What exactly does it mean for humans to become like "beasts"? Augustine distinguishes between the "lower" emotions, "perturbations, lusts, and desires," located in the appetitive part of soul, and "higher" emotions experienced by the rational mind, described by him as joys and holy "loves." He complicates this traditional distinction, however, by asserting that all human emotions are manifestations of the will (*civ.* 14.6), which, in turn, is identified with "love" understood as a specific, goal-directed longing. We recall the distinction drawn in Augustine's *On the Christian Doctrine* between love in the sense of an "enjoyment" that is suitably directed only toward God and love in the sense of "use," found to be appropriately directed toward all else (see earlier). If directed by reason toward its appropriate goal, love, entailing all relevant emotions, is good. A love that is left untamed by reason and attaches itself to an inappropriate goal is bad ("Right will, therefore, is good love and wrong will is bad love"; *civ.* 14.7).

This psychological framework is important for Augustine's interpretation of the Fall. By allowing undue emotions to go unchecked by reason—more specifically, by inappropriately directing enjoyment toward earthly matters—humans turn away from their role as creatures in "the image of God," a phrase interpreted by Augustine consistently in terms of rationality.[15] Humanity's turn away from rationality is a turn toward irrational, lower-level animality, as he explains in his *On the Trinity*:

> For the true honor of man is the image and likeness of God . . . but desiring to make trial of his own power. . . . [A]s a punishment, he is cast down from his own intermediate position to that which is lowest; that is, to those things in which beasts delight. And so, while his honor is the likeness of God, but his dishonor is the likeness of the beast, man does not abide in his honor. He is compared to the foolish beasts and is made like them. (*trin.* 12.11.16, with reference to Ps. 49.12)

Importantly, however, humans can merely become *like* nonhuman animals (see *Gn. litt.* 7.10.15). Throughout Augustine's psychology, the underlying hierarchy between the two animal kinds remains intact. Rational soul cannot change into irrational soul[16] since nonhuman animals lack a rational soul part (*div. qu.* 25; *en. Ps.* 101.1). Rather, for humans to become "like beasts," according to Augustine, means to have a nonrational love for a material life, those "things in which the beasts delight."

Human life oriented toward temporal, corporeal things is that of an "animal man" (*homo animalis*), or "outer man," (*homo exterior*), Latin Vulgate renderings for Paul's *anthrōpos psychikos* (1 Cor. 2.14), "man belonging to breath" or "man related to soul" (here referring to soul as the principle of life shared by human and nonhuman animals, opposed to *pneumatikos*, "spiritual," "belonging to rational soul"). Incidentally, Augustine's use of the Latin Vulgate rendering, *homo animalis*, allows him to capture, beyond the original Greek term, humanity's participation in the category of *animalia*, thereby imparting to the term a premonitory momentum. The animal man or outer man is distinguished from the "inner man" (*homo interior*), whose life as the *imago Dei* is the manifestation of rationality:

> When man is said to have been made to the image of God, these words refer to the inner man, where reason and intellect reside. From these, man also has power over the fish of the sea and the birds of heaven and all cattle and wild animals and all the earth and all reptiles which creep upon the earth. (*Gn. adv. Man.* 1.17.28, trans. Teske, 1991)

The failure to make appropriate use of reason, the very element that sets humans above other animals, entails an attachment to the material realm that is appropriate only for nonhuman animals, thereby threatening to blur the psychological boundary between the two animal kinds.

> Human soul, through use of reason and knowledge . . . removes itself as far possible from the body and gladly enjoys the delight of an inner life. The more it turns to the senses, the closer to the beast it renders man. (*an. quant.* 28.54)

Augustine's Pastoral Exegesis

In the context of Augustine's human psychology, nonhuman animality is negotiated exclusively in the negative terms of an attachment to the material world. This very attachment, however, acquires a rather positive exegetical significance in many of Augustine's pastoral writings. Of interest here is the distinction drawn in his *On the Christian Doctrine* between "things" (*res*) and "signs" (*signa*), the latter of which are defined as things that "are used to indicate something else" (*doctr. Chr.* 1.2.2). While this work warns that metaphorical language, including animal imagery, as one of such signs that may result in ambiguity (*doctr. Chr.* 2.10.15), Augustine elsewhere values its pedagogical potential for Scriptural exegesis over that of plain language:

> We accept metaphors (*similitudines*) . . . suited to illustrating holy things of the heavenly bodies, as of the whole creation, the winds, the sea, the earth, birds, fishes, flocks, trees, men. . . . If, however, these metaphors are drawn not only from heaven and the stars but also from the lower creation, and are adapted for the dissemination of the sacraments, the doctrine of salvation acquires a sort of eloquence that is suited to stir the emotions of its learners from visible to invisible, from corporeal to spiritual, from temporal to eternal things. (*ep.* 55, 7.13–11.21)

An instructive text in which nonhuman animal imagery guides believers toward Scripture's immaterial truths is Augustine's exposition of Ps. 42.[17] The deer mentioned in verse 1 of the Psalm, "as a deer longs for springs of water, so does my soul long for you, my God," represents, it will turn out, human soul seeking spiritual reunion with God. Initially, Augustine explores the deer in its familiar material realm, praising its speed and its apparently characteristic habit of killing snakes. Snakes, Augustine then explains, signify vice, thereby preparing his listeners for a metaphorical reading. Subsequently, the deer is replaced by human soul as the traveler whose journey begins amid the wonders of the material world but, since God is not found there (42.7), leads to the discovery of the immaterial realm (42.8). Augustine here aligns the contents of the Psalm with the methodological ascent from the visible to the invisible realm in Scriptural exegesis.

Cox Miller (2018) concludes from Augustine's initial lingering focus on the deer as a role model for his listeners that "the traditional position of human superiority is subverted by [Augustine's] exegetical mode [in his exposition of the Psalms]" and that "scriptural animals are freed from the debased position on the biological scale of being and took on a contemplative value that the ontological positioning of animals did not support" (p. 56). Against this view, I suggest that the deer's inferior position as a creature firmly anchored in the material world is crucial to Augustine's pedagogical exegesis. His change of focus from the deer, as a representative of the material world, to immaterial soul exemplifies the relationship between literal language and its metaphorical significance, thereby encouraging his listeners to appreciate the deer as a "sign" for the soul.

Augustine's pedagogical use of nonhuman animal imagery, I suggest, may have been inspired by passages such as 1 Cor. 2.14–15, "the animal man [*animalis homo*] does not receive the gifts of the Spirit of God, for they are folly to him, and he is not able to understand them because they are spiritually discerned," as well as 1 Cor. 3.1–3:

> But I, brothers, could not address you as spiritual men, but as men of the flesh, as little ones in Christ. I fed you with milk, not solid food; for you were not ready for it; and even yet you are not ready, for you are still of the flesh.

Augustine frequently alludes to these verses when describing those among the faithful who are capable merely of a literal reading of Scripture, referred to as "little ones" [*parvuli*], "carnal" [*carnalis*], and "animal" [*animalis*] men (*conf.* 12.27.37, 13.18.13; *en. Ps.* 8.10, 22.5, 49.27, 146.16; *Gn. adv. Man.* 1.17.27). Most illustrative is his interpretation of Ps. 104.[18] Analyzing verse 11: "All the beasts of the wood shall drink," Augustine points to a layered meaning:

> We see this also in the material creation, that beasts of the wood drink from springs. . . . [I]t has pleased God to hide his wisdom in the figures of such things, not to take it away from zealous learners, but to close it to those without care while opening it to those who knock. It has also pleased God our Lord to exhort you to this through us, that in all things that are spoken of as if belonging to the bodily and visible creation, that we may seek something hidden by spiritual meaning, in which, once found, we may rejoice. (*en. Ps.* 103 [3] 2)

Augustine subsequently compares the "hares" that drink from a spring with unlearned readers of Scripture who might be frightened by the "torrent" of more challenging prose, but who are confident to drinking from the gentle waters provided by a literal reading of the Psalm (*en. Ps.* 103 [3] 13). Unlearned readers are invited to access Scripture via nonhuman animal imagery that speaks to them as "animal men" still anchored within the material realm. Augustine's listeners at *en. Ps.* 42 begin their journey by accompanying the deer before setting off to a spiritual search for God. It is precisely their debased position on the cosmic scale that renders Scripture's nonhuman animals useful to humans.

In this section, I have described how Augustine explores nonhuman animal imagery in terms of an attachment to the material realm for rather different purposes. In the context of his human psychology, this attachment leads humans to become like "beasts." In the context of Augustine's pastoral exegesis, however, the association of nonhuman animals with the material world helps to make Scripture accessible to "animal men" by engaging them in their familiar habitat.

CONCLUSION

It has emerged that, on both the material and the metaphorical plane, nonhuman animals carry no intrinsic value as ends in themselves in Augustine's view. This, however, applies to all creation, which draws its value exclusively from participating in God's order. Nevertheless, nonhuman animals acquire a special significance in many contexts of Augustine's work due to their proximity to humans on the cosmic scale. Augustine responds to this proximity with both anxiety and pragmatism, either emphasizing the difference between human and nonhuman life with particular force or approaching animality as an intrinsic feature of human existence on Earth that must be navigated appropriately in order to be overcome. Accordingly, we witness him oscillating between two motifs that are continuous throughout both literal and metaphorical accounts of nonhuman animals: their subordinate ranking in a cosmic hierarchy arranged according to reason or their significance as fellow earthlings who are, however, consistently placed into an auxiliary role conducive to human salvation. Both motifs exploit the close association between nonhuman animals and the material world, either as a contrast to the rational life of the "inner man" or as a familiar habitat for those who are yet to ascend to this life. At all times, however, nonhuman animality remains for Augustine a point of reference for defining life on Earth as firmly centered around humans.

Notes

1. All translations follow the Latin text according to the *Library of Latin Texts Series A* (Brepolis), https://www.brepols.net/series/LLT-O, and are my own unless indicated otherwise. All abbreviations of Augustine's works follow Mayer (1986–1994).

2. As reported by Cicero's (fictional) Marcus Porcius Cato in the context of Stoic ethics at *On Ends* 3.67.

3. Discussed further below. See also the review in this journal by Langworthy (2020), who makes a case of the continued relevance of historical sources for contemporary discussions of animal ethics.

4. C. Taylor (1989) draws a connection between Platonic and Augustinian "inwardness" and the philosophy of Descartes (esp. pp. 139–158). Menn's (1998) study of Descartes's "reworking" of Augustinian thought underlines such an assessment by pointing, for instance, to Augustine's

desire to "fly from earthly things to [God]" (p. 74, with reference to Augustine, *Confessions* 3.4.8). Nussbaum (2001) and Dixon (2003) interpret Augustine's desire to flee from earthly things as indicating contempt for human material existence.

5. Harrison (1992) talks of material creation in general terms, while Hanby (2003) focuses on the role of Christ incarnate. Hart (2004), who goes as far as proposes Augustine as an inspiration for a renewed Christian ecotheology, credits him with a "call for respect for all creatures, even those not needed by humans, because they have some integrated role in creation" (p. 3 with n. 2) but does not explore his stance further. Elsewhere (Hart, 2006), he notes that Augustine "did not teach that earth and earth's creatures had an independent value beyond their utility for human well-being and the working of the universe" (p. 69), without attending to the apparent tension in Augustine's thought.

6. Augustine's version of the *scala naturae* is likely an amalgam of Greco-Roman, Neoplatonic, and early Christian thought. Saffrey and Westerink (1974, p. 86) point to a Neoplatonic source, likely Porphyry. See also König (1976, pp. 71ff.); O'Daly (1986–1994, pp. 315–340); and Baltes and Lau (1986–1994, pp. 356–374).

7. A similar notion of God's orderly creation is found also in Ambrose (e.g., *hex.* 1.7.26).

8. Sometimes "measure, number, and weight," with reference to Wis. 11:21. Du Roy (1945, especially pp. 279–281), remains an invaluable source on this triad as Augustine's reference to the Trinitarian structure of creation. See further, Harrison (1992, pp. 101–112) and below.

9. Clark (1999), who emphasizes the role of rationality in Augustine's view of nonhuman animals, notes that he rarely uses the term *animalia* to describe nonhuman animals, opting instead for terminology (e.g., *bestia*, *belua*) that underlines their distinction from humans (p. 68).

10. The ranking of psychic faculties is described in more detail in Augustine's *On the Magnitude of the Soul*, see esp. 70–76. Frequently, the distinction between these activities appears in the context of his interpretation of human's creation "in the Image of God" in terms of human rationality. See also below.

11. Similarly, *civ.* 1.20 (quoted above), attacks the Manichaean prohibition against the killing of nonhuman animals and plants as potential hosts to fragments of divine soul.

12. Unlike the Manichaean belief that fragments of divine soul are indiscriminately present in material bodies, the Stoics held that divine pneuma was present in the material world in various degrees and, for this reason, lent different qualities to different bodies. In both human and nonhuman animals, divine pneuma manifests itself as soul (*psychē*), but it bestows a rational "commanding faculty" (*hegemonikon*) only on humans. On the affinities between Stoic and Manichaean views as relevant from Augustine's perspective, see Menn (1998, pp. 89–129).

13. A notion inspired by Rom. 1:20: "For the invisible things of God, from the creation of the world are clearly seen, being understood by the things that are made, even his eternal power and Godhead."

14. An important parallel in Augustine's discussion at *Gn. adv. Man.* 1.13.19 and *Gn. litt.* 8.8–10 is the "behavior" of postlapsarian Earth, in particular the "thorns and thistles" of Gen. 3:18.

15. Examples abound: for instance, *trin.* 12.7; *civ.* 11.2; *Gn. litt.* 6.12.21; *Gn. adv. Man.* 1.23.40; *en. Ps.* 29.22. Ludlow (2010) stresses the prevalence among patristic writers to interpret the notion of the *imago Dei* in terms of human dominion. The relevance of such a reading among these authors must be acknowledged; see interpretations that ascribe to Augustine and others a predominantly allegorical exegesis, e.g., Harrison (1999, esp. p. 91).

16. Rationality is part of the human soul's substance; see, for example, *sol.* 2.22–24; *imm. an.* 8; *Gn. litt.* 6.12, 7.7, 7.9–11, 11.29.

17. Numbering according to the Revised Standard Version, which is based on the Hebrew text. Readers who wish to consult the Psalm should note that Augustine follows the Vulgate numbering, 41.

18. Ps. 103 according to the Vulgate numbering followed by Augustine. See previous note.

References

Ambrose of Milan. All Latin texts according to *Library of Latin Texts Series A* (Brepolis). Retrieved from:
https://www.brepols.net/series/LLT-O.
Hexaemeron (*hex.*)

Augustine of Hippo. All Latin texts according to *Library of Latin Texts Series A* (Brepolis). Retrieved from:
https://www.brepols.net/series/LLT-O. (Original works published between 386 and 430 BC)
City of God (*civ.*)
Confessions (*conf.*)
Eighty-three various questions (*div. qu.*)
Epistles (*ep.*)
Expositions on the Psalms (*en. Ps.*)
Homilies on the Gospel of John (*Io. ev. tr.*)
On Christian doctrine (*doctr. chr.*)
On order (*ord.*)
On the Catholic and Manichaean ways of life (*mor.*)
On the free choice of the will (*lib. arb.*)
On the immortality of the soul (*imm. an.*)
On the magnitude of the soul (*an. quant.*)
On the trinity (*trin.*)
On true religion (*vera rel.*)
Reply to Faustus the Manichaean (*c. Faust.*)
Sermons (*s.*)
Soliloquies (*sol.*)
The literal meaning of Genesis (*Gn. Litt.*)
Two books on Genesis against the Manichees (*Gn. adv. Man.*)

Baltes, M., & Lau., D. (1986–1994). Animal. In C. Mayer (Ed.), *Augustinus-Lexikon* (pp. 356–374). Basel, Switzerland: Schwabe.

Calarco, M., & Atterton, P. (Eds.). (2004). *Animal philosophy. Essential readings in continental thought*. London, England: Continuum Publishing Group.

Cipriani, N. (2007). Lo studio della natura e il lavoro umano in S Agostino. In *La cultura scientifico-naturalistica nei Padri della Chiesa, I-V sec. XXXV Incontro di Studiosi dellantichità christiana, 4–6 Maggio 2006. Studia Ephemeridis Augustinianum 101* (pp. 373–387). Rome, Italy: Institutum Patristicum Augustinianum.

Clark, G. (1999). The fathers and the animals: The rule of reason? In A. Linzey & D. Yamamoto (Eds.), *Animals on the agenda: Questions about animals for theology and ethics* (pp. 67–79). Urbana: University of Illinois Press.

Cox Miller, P. (2018). *In the eye of the animal: Zoological imagination in ancient Christianity*. Philadelphia: University of Pennsylvania Press.

Dixon, T. (2003). *From passions to emotions: The creation of a secular psychological category*. Cambridge, England: Cambridge University Press.

Du Roy, O. (1945). *L' intelligence de la foi en la Trinite selon Saint Augustin*. Paris, France: Etudes Augustiniennes.

Hanby, M. (2003). *Augustine and modernity*. London, England: Routledge.

Harrison, C. (1992). *Beauty and revelation in the thought of Saint Augustine*. Oxford, England: Oxford University Press.

Harrison, P. (1999). Subduing the earth: Genesis 1, early modern science, and the exploitation of nature. *Journal of Religion, 79*(1), 86–109.

Hart, J. (2004). *What are they saying about environmental theology?* Mahwah, NJ: Paulist Press.

Hart, J. (2006). Catholicism. In R. Gottlieb (Ed.), *The Oxford handbook of religion and ecology* (pp. 65–91). Oxford, England: Oxford University Press.

König, E. (1976). *Augustinus philosophus: Christlicher Glaube und Philosophisches Denken in den Frühschriften Augustins*. Munich, Germany: W. Fink.

Langworthy, O. B. (2020). Review of *In the eye of the animal: Zoological imagination in ancient Christianity* by P. Cox Miller. *Journal of Animal Ethics, 10*(2), 203–204.

Linzey, A., & Cohn-Sherbok, D. (2004). *After Noah: Animals and the liberation of theology*. London, England: Mowbray.

Linzey, A., & Yamamoto, D. (Eds.). (1999). *Animals on the agenda: Questions about animals for theology and ethics*. Urbana: University of Illinois Press.

Ludlow, M. (2010). Power and dominion: Patristic interpretations of Genesis 1. In D. Horrell & C. Hunt (Eds.), *Ecological hermeneutics. Biblical, historical, and theological perspectives* (pp. 140–153). London, England: T&T Clark.

Mayer, C. (Ed.). (1986–1994). *Augustinus-Lexikon*. Basel, Switzerland: Schwabe.

Menn, S. (1998). *Descartes and Augustine*. Cambridge, England: Cambridge University Press.

Nussbaum, M. (2001). *Upheavals of thought: Intelligence of the emotions*. Cambridge, England: Cambridge University Press.

O'Daly, G. (1986–1994). Anima, animus. In C. Mayer (Ed.). *Augustinus-Lexikon* (pp. 315–340). Basel, Switzerland: Schwabe.

Pollmann, K. (2010). Human sin and natural environment: Augustine's two positions on Gen. 3:18. *Augustinian Studies, 41*(1), 69–85.

Saffrey, H. D., & Westerink, L. G. (Eds.). (1974). *Proclus. Théologie Platonicienne 2*. Paris, France: Les Belles Lettres.

Sorabji, R. (1993). *Animal minds and human morals: The origins of the Western debate*. Ithaca, NY: Cornell University Press.

Steiner, G. (2010). *Anthropocentrism and its discontents: The moral status of animals in the history of Western philosophy* (2nd ed.). Pittsburgh, PA: University of Pittsburgh Press.

Taylor, C. (1989). *Sources of the self: The making of the modern identity*. Cambridge, England: Cambridge University Press.

Taylor, J. H. (1982). *Ancient Christian writers: St. Augustine. The literal meaning of Genesis*. New York, NY: Newman Press.

Teske, R. (Ed. & Trans.). (1991). *On Genesis: Two books on Genesis against the Manichees and on the literal interpretation of Genesis*. Baltimore, MD: Catholic University of America Press.

Williams, R. (1994). All good for nothing? Augustine on creation. *Augustinian Studies, 25*, 9–24.

"Mad Madge": The Contribution of Margaret Cavendish to Animal Ethics

LAUREN BESTWICK

Worcester College, Oxford, England

Abstract. In this article, I will be looking at the person and works of Margaret Cavendish (1623–1673), an aristocrat and author whose philosophical texts and poetry defended the rational capacity of nonhuman animals. Generally, society in 17th-century England did not consider nonhuman animals to have any intelligence or emotional capacity and treated them accordingly. In her works, Cavendish sheds a light on these commonly accepted views, providing arguments against them and indicating their inconsistencies.

Key Words: Margaret Cavendish, William Cavendish, women, rational hierarchy, privileged species, Cartesianism, Descartes, hunting, entertainment, dominion

In this article, I will be looking at Margaret Cavendish (1623–1673), whose experience as a female aristocrat and association at court provided her with a unique outlook that framed her philosophical works that defended the rational capacity of animals. Cavendish pointed out the inconsistencies of her class, especially how they viewed certain animals differently and treated them accordingly. I will consider some of her work related to animals and give evidence of the views that she held. Her work will be discussed in relation to the ambiguities around how animals were viewed and treated, especially among the higher classes. This is particularly significant as it was this aristocratic class that was the driving force behind the later animal rights movement that can be traced across the 19th and 20th centuries. For example, the Society for the Prevention of Cruelty to Animals was founded by a group of notable British men, such as Sir James Mackintosh, Lord Shaftesbury, and William Wilberforce in 1824. The society attained its royal status in 1835 when Princess (later Queen) Victoria became its first patron.

Cavendish was very privileged. She was born into the noble Lucas family, the youngest of eight siblings. Cavendish aspired to be a writer from a young age but was excluded from any formal academic or intellectual education, being taught only basic reading and writing (Whitaker, 2002, p. 16). Nevertheless, by the time she reached adulthood, she had "filled sixteen large notebooks, with observations and reflections, stories and poems" (Whitaker, 2002, p. 19).

Part II: Intellectual Figures

In 1645, she married a very reputable aristocrat, William Cavendish, Marquis of Newcastle. Her marriage, along with her presence at the royal court as one of the ladies in waiting to the wife of King Charles I (r. 1625–1649), provided her with an opportunity to establish herself as a writer. She made connections that allowed her to become more learned in areas that would usually have been inaccessible to women. The time she experienced in exile during the English Civil War (1642–1651), at the courts of France and the Netherlands, allowed her the time to reflect and write. She was aware of the limitations placed upon her because of her gender, writing how the lack of female education limited her potential. She suggested that otherwise, women could become just as intellectual, if not more so, than men. Cavendish expressed this in her message to the reader in her *Observations* (1668): "Many of our sex may have as much wit, and be capable of learning as well as men" (p. 11). She argued that the attitude that women were intellectually inferior to men, which was prevalent in the court especially, limited Cavendish's ability to partake in scientific and philosophical debate. The sense of exclusion Cavendish must have felt was furthered by the fact that she was not in the Queen's favor, especially since she could not speak French, and she was seen as an outcast by her fellow courtiers due to her "eccentricity." She was awarded the nickname "Mad Madge" by her contemporaries as a result. Samuel Pepys wrote that she was mad as well as a "conceited, ridiculous woman" (Narain, 2009, p. 70). She was aware of these opinions, as she apologized for her writings at the start of some of her works, such as in her *Poems and Fancies*, which readers still attacked (see Figure 1).

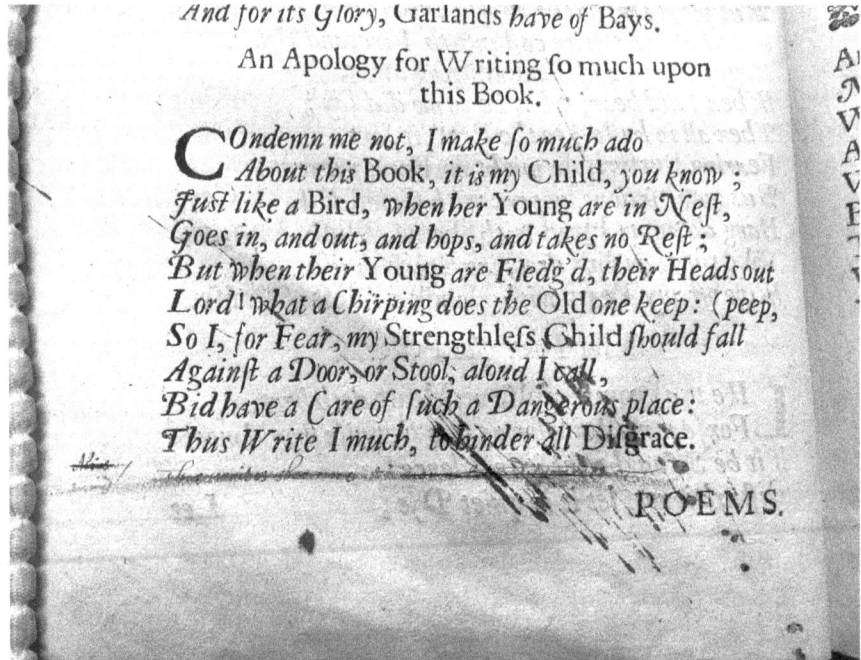

FIGURE 1. A photograph I took when visiting Cavendish's archives in University College, Oxford. A page from Cavendish's *Poems and Fancies* (1664). See here a jibe written by a reader, changing the final line to "Thus write she more, to accumulate disgrace," which was later crossed out.

The limitations placed upon Cavendish as a woman and the exploitation of nonhuman animals are linked. Cavendish herself made this connection in her writings. In her "Preface to the Reader" in *The Worlds of Olio* (1655), Cavendish stated how women were constrained by their lack of education and opportunities and so became what social prejudices made them:

> [Men] using us [women] either like Children, Fools, or Subjects, that is, to flatter or threaten us, to allure or force us to obey, and will not let us divide the World equally with them, as to Govern and Command, to direct and Dispose as they do; which Slavery hath so dejected our spirits, as we are become so stupid.

She then relates this to society's perception of "beasts": "Beasts are but a Degree below us [women], and Men use us but a Degree above Beast'" (Cavendish, 1655). Here, she was referring (knowingly or unknowingly) to the Thomist rational hierarchy (influenced by Aristotle), where the order of rationality was God, angels, man, woman, slaves, animals, and plants, which implies that she was aware of the prominence of this theology in 17th-century thinking (see a discussion in Linzey & Clarke, 1990, pp. xiii-xxii). Thus, in her writings, where she defended nonhuman animals, she was aware that these prejudices were similar to the prejudices against women.

Prejudices toward animals regarding their inferiority, lack of individuality, and intelligence were sometimes at variance with the keeping of "pets" by the higher classes. Dogs especially were a "privileged species" in terms of how they were seen as companions and not food. The trend of keeping dogs as "pets" probably began with the royal family during this period. King James I (r. 1603–1625) had two favorite dogs, Jowler and Jewel, and in 1617 was accused of loving his dogs "more than his subjects" (Thomas, 1994, p. 103). Similarly, King Charles II (r. 1660–1685) was known for his love of spaniels—hence the King Charles Cavalier that is still a popular breed. These attitudes were apparent across the aristocracy and shared by Cavendish and her husband. Their portrait in the Gardens at Ruben in Antwerp by Gonzales Coques (c. 1650s) portrays a positive relationship with a canine, who is captured frolicking around and looking back at them, with the couple seemingly gesturing toward the dog. Thomas (1994) explains how this love of dogs by the aristocracy was prevalent in the 1600s:

> A gentleman's hounds were treated with much indulgence. When masters returned from the hunt, observed an early Stuart commentator, they would often show "more care for their dogs than for their servants and make them lie down by them, and often the servant is beaten for the dog; you may see in some men's houses fair and fat dogs to run up and down and men pale and wan to walk feebly." (p. 104)

This attitude implies that some people saw their dogs as superior to some humans, which contradicts the accepted rational hierarchy. This hierarchy held that animals and women were inferior to men, as previously discussed, but this example shows that this also applied to servants. According to Katie Whitaker (2002), in Cavendish's youth, she disregarded the boundaries kept between servants and their masters, as she became lifelong friends with her personal maid, Elizabeth Chaplain (p. 16). While details of her later relationships with other servants are unknown, what we do know suggests that Cavendish did not see any humans, or nonhuman animals, as "inferior."

On one hand, these ambiguities about whether some humans were inferior to some animals suggest that the domestication of nonhuman animals created the opportunity for people to recognize an animal's individuality and intelligence. On the other hand, it also highlights the difference in attitudes that were held on an individual basis in 17th-century society. We can acknowledge the general consensus that animals were inferior to humans and that humans had the right to treat them how they wanted. Yet, it must be recognized that the extent of this belief differed according to each individual.

The mechanist theory of the French philosopher and scientist René Descartes (1596-1650) supported this consensus surrounding animals, as he "proved" that animals were inferior to humans through his experiments. Cavendish was aware of Descartes's theories as he was a member of the "Cavendish circle" with her husband and his brother, along with other prominent scientists and philosophers of the period, including intellectuals from across Europe (Whitaker, 2002, p. 96). Many of them, including Descartes, visited the Cavendish lodgings (Whitaker, 2002, p. 96). In her *Philosophical Letters* (1664), Cavendish particularly opposed the Cartesian theory that nonhuman animals did not possess souls and that they functioned like machines (see Descartes's 1649 letter to William Cavendish, extracted in Linzey & Regan, 1990, pp. 45–52). Descartes distinguished humans from animals by arguing that animal perception is a "purely mechanical process that involves no awareness at all" (Cooney, 2019, p. 646). He also argued that because they have no awareness, they do not feel pain, even though they may look as though they are experiencing pain. In stating this, Descartes claimed it was not so much cruel to animals as it was kind to humans "since it absolves them [humans] from the suspicion of crime when they kill or eat non-human animals" (Cooney, 2019, p. 646). He justified his theories with his language and rationality tests that animals reportedly failed. Cavendish (1664) wrote on the intelligence of nonhuman animals, explaining that because mankind does not understand their communication and behaviors does not make them unintelligent, but quite the opposite in fact:

> What man knows, whether Fish do not Know more of the nature of Water, and ebbing and flowing, and the saltness of the Sea? or whether Birds do not know more of the nature and degrees of Air, or the cause of Tempests? or whether Worms do not know more of the nature of Earth, and how Plants are produced? or Bees of the several sorts of juices of Flowers, then Men? And whether they do not make there Aphorismes and Theoremes by their manner of Intelligence? For, though they have not the speech of Man, yet thence doth not follow, that they have no Intelligence at all. (p. 40)

William Cavendish also challenged the Cartesian view. From his experience as a horse trainer, he stated,

> If he [the horse] does not think it would be impossible to teach him what he should do. But by the hope of reward, and fear of punishment; when he has been rewarded or punished, he thinks of it, and retains it in his memory (for memory is thought) and forms

a judgment by what is past of what is to come (which again is thought); insomuch that he obeys his rider not only for fear of correction, but also in hopes of being cherish'd. (as cited in Fudge, 2006, p. 7)

While Margaret Cavendish speaks more generally for all animal species, her husband speaks more specifically about horses, arguing that these animals have the capacity to think. This is an example of how the domestication and closeness of animals provided people with the opportunity to understand their intelligence and individuality and was helpful in the positive development of people's attitudes toward animals.

Cavendish wrote of her husband's love for horses as well as the horses' love for her husband: "They seemed to rejoice whensoever he came into the stables" (Cavendish, 1886, p. 101). Clearly then, William Cavendish was sympathetic to these horses and was evidently aware of their intelligence and possibly, by extension, other animals' intelligence. However, it appears William Cavendish enjoyed hunting, as it was documented that during the English Civil War he lost eight of his hunting parks (Whitaker, 2002, p. 243). It seems William had built a relationship with one species of animal but did not feel this empathy for the animals that he hunted. This was a common occurrence since hunting was a popular sport during this period. Contrastingly, Margaret Cavendish did feel compassion for these hunted animals. In her *Poems and Fancies* (1653), she wrote the poem "The Hunting of the Stag," which imagines how the hunted felt during the hunt. She portrays the stag as a conscious, intelligent being who tried all that he could to escape the dogs and men, but in the end failed.

> The Stag no hope had left, nor help espies
> His Heart so heavie grew, with Griefe, and Care
> That his small Feet his Body could not beare'
> Then Men, and Dogs do circle him about
> Some bite, some bark, all ply him at the Bay
> Where with his Hornes he tosses some away
> But Fate his thread had spun, so downe did fall
> Shedding some Teares at his owne Funerall. (Cavendish, 1653, p. 116)

The way that she wrote of the stag as having these emotions triggers sympathy from the reader. Similarly, in her poem "Dialogue of Birds," Cavendish (1653) wrote from the first-person perspective of a bird:

> But Men do strive with Nets us for to catch:
> With Guns, and Bowes they shoot us from the Trees,
> And by small shot, we oft our Lifes do leese,
> Because we pick a Cherry here, and there,
> When, God he knowes, we eate them in great feare.
> But Men will eat, untill their Belly burst,
> And surfets take: if we eat, we are curst.
> Yet we by Nature are revenged still,
> For eating over-much themselves they kill.
> And if a Child do chance to cry, or brawle,
> They strive to catch us, to please that Child withall:

> With Threads they tye our legs almost to crack,
> That when we hop away, they pull us back:
> And when they cry Fip, Fip, strait we must come,
> And for our paines they'l give us one small Crum. (p. 71)

This conveys Cavendish's opposition to the eating of birds as well as the keeping of them as companions. It portrays an empathy and understanding for these creatures and a recognition of the cruelty and injustice that they endure at the hands of humans. In both these poems, it seems as though Cavendish wanted the reader to understand this cruelty and feel guilty for the way in which animals are treated. This would have been a very radical opinion at a time when hunting was an accepted social recreation and a symbol of status that was highly important in her aristocratic world.

It is particularly interesting that these two poems especially targeted hunting, as her husband, a hunter, was part of the intended audience. Cavendish must have felt very strongly about this matter to have formed her independent opinion, not only against the influence of society but also her own husband. This goes against the idea that a woman had to identify and align herself with the beliefs and politics of her husband. It speaks to her strong relationship with her husband, who always supported her despite his own obvious disagreements. We know this from the countless love poems and letters that they wrote to each other (Whitaker, 2002, p. 310). William discussed philosophy and science with her, acting as her "only tutor" (Whitaker, 2002, p. 116). He had Margaret buried next to him in a tomb in Westminster Abbey, and the inscription penned by William read: "This Dutches was a wise wittie & learned Lady, which her many Bookes do well testifie" (Westminster Abbey, n.d.).

Even though she had the support of her husband, Cavendish (1664) acknowledged that she was alone in her opinions and wrote how this was because "*man*kind" (Cavendish focused on men especially) did not fully understand animals, "but the Ignorance of Men concerning other Creatures is the cause of despising other Creatures, imagining themselves as petty Gods in Nature, when as Nature is not capable to make one God, much less so many as Mankind" (p. 40).

This is a frontal attack on the anthropocentric view that *man*kind had dominion (understood in a negative sense) over all other creatures' lives and were thus allowed to act as gods on earth. Cavendish believed the view that *man*kind has the right to control animals, conceiving of themselves as "petty Gods in nature," led inevitably to their cruel treatment. Cavendish applied this also to the pursuit of hunting witches, which became very popular in the late 16th and early 17th centuries. She wrote:

> That there should be any such devilish witchcraft . . . I cannot readily believe. Certainly, I dare say, that many a good old honest woman hath been condemned innocently, and suffered death wrongfully, by the sentence of some foolish and cruel judges. (Cavendish, 1664, p. 298)

Here again, parallels can be drawn between the treatment of women and animals, going so far as to say that this treatment was unjust because the judges were "foolish and cruel." Cavendish identified a systemic problem in the way that order is kept in society.

Her views of course have to be understood in context. They are perhaps better understood when remembering the attempts at restructuring government systems during the English Civil War and Interregnum (the period from 1649–1660 when England was governed as a republic after the execution of King Charles I and before the restoration of King Charles II). No matter, the comments that Cavendish was making in defense of women and nonhuman animals were still very radical for their time.

It is interesting to note that in the 1600s, English law on punishing an animal who had caused injury or death to a human was different to that on the continent. In continental Europe, animal trials did take place. In contrast, in England, the animal was declared "deodand" (from the Latin "deo dandum"—given to God), meaning that the animal was regarded similarly to an object and not deemed capable of intent. This ordinarily meant that the "owner" of the animal was punished instead of the animal. The "owner" would sometimes have to pay a fine to retrieve the animal or the animal was killed. Animals in England during this period were viewed as mere property, and they still are in the modern day. However, some forms of "trial" (in another sense) did take place. These often involved some form of baiting to provide entertainment. An example of this occurred in 1609 when a toddler was mauled to death by a bear after being mistakenly locked in the bear enclosure at the Bear Garden in London, a space dedicated to "animal sports."

> The bear for killing the Child fell to the Lord of the soil, and was by the bearward redeemed for fifty shillings; and the bearwards told the mother of the child that they could not help it, (though some think it to be a design of that wicked house to get money) and they told the mother that the bear should be bated to death, and they should have half the money, and accordingly there were bills stuck up an down the city of it, and a considerable summe of money gathered to see the bear bated to death . . . they offer the woman three pound not to prosecute them. (Anonymous, 1665, p. 9)

This baiting took place in the form of a "trial" in the Tower of London when King James I was in attendance. The bear was placed up against a lion, which represented the law, and the ritual allowed the spectators to see "right overcome might" (Fudge, 2006, p. 24). However, on this particular occasion, the lion, as well as some dogs and a horse, failed to create the desired spectacle and the bear was unharmed. The king ordered the bear be baited to death on stage instead, with the master of the bears losing the value of the creature on its death and the compensation being paid to the mother out of the day's profit (Fudge, 2006, p. 25). This shows that the punishment of animals was not so different from that of humans in the sense that it was a public spectacle. The fact that it was called a "trial" is interesting as it suggests that some attempt at justice (however misguided) was taking place. However, there was no formal trial to decide who was to blame for the incident, and the "bearwards" were not considered to be held accountable. Further, it was not considered that the animal was being punished even though it was killed; it was the "keeper" of the animal who was being punished. This indicates how animals were viewed as unconscious beings, objects even, and mediums of entertainment. This links to what Cavendish said about *man*kind acting as gods, deciding the fate of animals, which was also the case with the punishment of innocent women accused of witchcraft.

Cavendish (1653) attacked the notion of eating meat, and in her poem "The Hunting of the Hare" linked it again to the belief that *man*kind has dominion over all other creatures. She wrote:

> When they do Lions, Wolves, Beares, Tigers see,
> To kill poore Sheep, strait say, they cruell be.
> But for themselves all Creatures think too few,
> For Luxury, wish God would make them new.
> As if that God made Creatures for Mans meat,
> To give them Life, and Sense, for Man to eat;
> Or else for Sport, or Recreations sake,
> Destroy those Lifes that God saw good to make:
> Making their Stomacks, Graves, which full they fill
> With Murther'd Bodios, that in sport they kill.
> Yet Man doth think himselfe so gentle, mild,
> When he of Creatures is most cruell wild.
> And is so Proud, thinks onely he shall live,
> That God a God-like Nature did him give.
> And that all Creatures for his sake alone,
> Was made for him, to Tyramize upon. (Cavendish, 1653, pp. 112–113)

Here Cavendish contrasts how animals were seen as "wild" and "savage" for the ways in which they killed their prey, whereas in fact men were the most cruel and "wild" of all. She drew on the interpretation of Genesis Chapter 1 that God gave humankind dominion over all other animals, which was thought to imply that *man*kind has the right to kill animals (despite Genesis 29–30, where God assigns a vegan diet to humans and animals). In rejecting the common view, Cavendish was obviously very radical for the period. In fact, it is remarkable that Cavendish held these views at all and that she felt strongly enough to publish them in her works. Thus, it is perhaps understandable that she was perceived as "mad" and "irrational" by her contemporaries.

The social pressure that Cavendish faced as an aristocrat and as a woman perhaps also limited her ability to implement her attitudes toward animals in her daily life. Aristocratic and court life heavily revolved around the use of animals for consumption and recreation. As was noted in Cavendish's letters, when she was in exile, entertainment in Antwerp consisted of "trained animals—'acting baboons and apes,' and 'strange erotica—dromedaries, camels and lions'" (Whitaker, 2002, p. 219). Furthermore, the food they ate was especially important during this period in exile. Cavendish noted that during a harsh winter, they had a dinner of "beef, cabbage, sausages, carrots, marrowbones, pork, mutton, veal, poultry" (Whitaker, 2002, p. 219). It is not specified whether Cavendish tried to avoid eating meat products or ate as little as possible, but with offerings such as the one described it seems as though eating meat was almost unavoidable. Similarly, since she was living on her husband's estates and hosting visitors, it would have been deemed ersatz, even rude, not to serve and eat meat or to refuse meat if offered. Therefore, implementing a vegetarian diet would have been very difficult in Cavendish's circumstances, whether she wanted to or not.

The works of Cavendish provide an interesting and useful insight, then, into how nonhuman animals were viewed and treated in 17th-century England. Her works portray what the commonly accepted attitudes toward animals were as well as provide arguments against these views, or point out the inconsistences within them. However, it must be acknowledged that Cavendish's writings are limited to the views and actions of the higher classes. Nevertheless, general attitudes held by the higher classes were often reflected in wider society in terms of how nonhuman animals were viewed as inferior creatures. This is especially because what was accepted in wider society was often determined by the aristocracy, especially as they were the driving force behind the later animal rights movements. Furthermore, conducting forms of animal "trials" and the fears surrounding witchcraft were important contextual factors regarding humankind's relationship with animals, applied to both the common people and the higher classes. Cavendish provides a rare example of a woman who was able to resist the popular attitudes and form her own opinion despite these apparent threatening contextual factors. Cavendish was successful with her publications, becoming "famous as an author" by her mid-40s (Whitaker, 2002, p. 293), and this implies that her opinions were of interest, even if they were dismissed as "mad." Either way, Cavendish was having an influence on people, spreading messages of animal advocacy, and providing a voice for nonhuman animals.

References

Anonymous. (1665). *Newes from More-lane*. London, England: William Gammon. https://www.proquest.com/docview/2240873571/99827900

Cavendish, M. (1653). *Poems, and fancies written by the Right Honourable, the Lady Margaret Newcastle*. London, England: J. Martin and J. Allestrye. https://www.proquest.com/docview/2240863254

Cavendish, M. (1655). *The worlds of Olio*. London, England: A. Maxwell. https://www.proquest.com/docview/2240953569?&imgSeq=1

Cavendish, M. (1664). *Philosophical letter or, modest reflections upon some opinions in natural philosophy*. London, England: (n.p). https://www.proquest.com/docview/2240875599/11765757

Cavendish, M. (1886). *The life of William Cavendish, duke of Newcastle: To which is added the true relation of my birth, breeding and life*. New York, NY: Scribner & Welford. https://babel.hathitrust.org/cgi/pt?id=hvd.32044010673606&view=1up&seq=13&skin=2021

Cooney, H. (2019). Cavendish vs. Descartes on mechanism and animal souls. In S. Nadler, T. M. Schmaltz, and D. Antoine-Mahut (Eds.), *The Oxford handbook of Descartes and Cartesianism* (pp. 643–657). Oxford, England: Oxford University Press. https://www.oxfordhandbooks.com/view/10.1093/oxfordhb/9780198796909.001.0001/oxfordhb-9780198796909-e-40

Descartes, R. (1990). Animals are machines. In A. Linzey and T. Regan (Eds.), *Animals and Christianity: A book of readings* (pp. 45–52). New York, NY: Crossroad.

Fudge, E. (2006). Two ethics: Killing animals in the past and the present. In The Animal Studies Group (Eds.), *Killing Animals* (pp. 99–119). Urbana: University of Illinois Press.

Gibson, M. (2000). *Early modern witches: Cases in contemporary writing*. London, England: Routledge.

Linzey, A., & Clarke, P. B. (1990). *Animal rights: A historical anthology.* New York, NY: Columbia University Press.

Narain, M. (2009). Notorious celebrity: Margaret Cavendish and the spectacle of fame. *Journal of the Midwest Modern Language Association, 42*(2), 69–95.

Thomas, K. (1994). *Man and the natural world.* London, England: Penguin Books.

Westminster Abbey. (n.d.). William and Margaret Cavendish. *Westminster Abbey.* Retrieved from: https://www.westminster-abbey.org/abbey-commemorations/commemorations/william-margaret-cavendish#i14922

Whitaker, K. (2002). *Mad Madge.* London, England: Chatto & Windus.

Frances Power Cobbe and the Philosophy of Antivivisection

ALISON STONE

Lancaster University, United Kingdom

Abstract: Frances Power Cobbe led the Victorian movement against vivisection. Cobbe is often remembered for her animal welfare campaigning, but it is rarely recognized that she approached animal welfare as a moral philosopher. In this article, I examine the philosophical basis of Cobbe's antivivisectionism. I concentrate on her 1875 article "The Moral Aspects of Vivisection," in which Cobbe first locates vivisection within the historical movement of Western civilization and the tendency for science to supersede religion and then endeavors to refute the defenses of vivisection one by one. I emphasize the philosophical considerations that led Cobbe to oppose animal experimentation on a reasoned basis.

Key Words: animal experimentation, Frances Power Cobbe, science, sympathy, vivisection

Frances Power Cobbe (1822–1904) was the leader of the antivivisection movement in 19th-century Britain and an inspiration for animal welfare campaigners around the world.[1] She began to be concerned about vivisection in the early 1860s, after reading press reports about the routine use of animal experiments without anesthetics in European medicine and science.[2] Vivisection was becoming more mainstream in British science at the time, and so Cobbe started to campaign and influence public opinion in favor of regulatory legislation. She was the central driving force behind the introduction of the 1876 Cruelty to Animals Act, the first-ever set of laws regulating the scientific use of live animals, which remained the basis of British legislation right up until 1986. While one might think this an impressive achievement on Cobbe's part, she herself judged the 1876 act in its final form to be watered down to the point of uselessness. Despairing of any possibility of effective regulation, she started to advocate that vivisection must be abolished outright.[3]

Cobbe is commemorated by the two antivivisection organizations she founded—the National Anti-Vivisection Society (originally called the Victoria Street Society) and Cruelty Free International (originally called the British Union for the Abolition of Vivisection)—and she is often remembered in histories of animal welfare and antivivisection activism.[4] It has been recognized much less often that Cobbe argued against vivisection and other forms of cruelty to animals on a philosophical basis.[5] She came to issues of animal welfare having already developed her moral theory in her 1855–1857 *Essay on Intuitive Morals*. Although Cobbe approached animal welfare as a moral philosopher, it remains surprisingly rare for animal ethicists, even feminist animal ethicists, to remember Cobbe's pioneering work in this domain.

My goal in this article is to help restore Cobbe, and the philosophical basis of her antivivisectionism, to our collective memory. This is important not only for historical accuracy and to capture women's contributions in the history of animal ethics but also because Cobbe's work is a mine of ideas, formulations, and insights regarding animals and ethics that contemporary scholars could tap.[6] Moreover, her work offers a window into the wider world of Victorian public debate about animal ethics, which was rich and heated, and of which she was at the center.

Since Cobbe wrote extensively on animal ethics over 40 years, and since her thinking underwent some significant shifts, I cannot encompass all of her thought on animal ethics in one article.[7] Instead I shall focus on her essay "The Moral Aspects of Vivisection," published in the *New Quarterly* in 1875 and subsequently repeatedly reissued as a pamphlet (Cobbe, 1875). This article provides a good way into Cobbe's wider thought because it tackles vivisection from two angles: In the first half, Cobbe locates vivisection within the whole historical direction of European civilization, and in the second, she endeavors to refute the "argumentative defences" of vivisection one by one. Because she draws on arguments and interpretations put forward in her other works, this article is something of a synthesis. I shall present Cobbe's arguments in the article, bringing out the reasoned and philosophical basis of her antivivisectionism and pulling in other works of hers where they provide further support. I concentrate on exposition more than evaluation. This is because Cobbe, like almost all women philosophers, has been excluded from the canon of "great philosophers" and from our narratives about the history of philosophy, so her standpoint is unfamiliar to us today. Our primary need is therefore to approach Cobbe's work with sympathetic understanding; criticism can mostly wait until later.[8]

Beginning "The Moral Aspects of Vivisection" with her historical analysis, Cobbe (1875) maintains that, across world history, a gradual progression has taken place in which humanity has become ever more sympathetic and compassionate (pp. 222–223). The ever-deepening and widening extension of our sympathies—not the growth of the intellect, knowledge, science, or technology—is the central measure of progress.[9] However, the line of progress is not even, and "counter-currents"—anti-sympathetic forces—threaten to pull us in a retrograde historical direction. This is where Cobbe places vivisection. Though it may appear to be a "comparatively insignificant" part of human life, it is actually central, because it condenses and discloses these counter-sympathetic forces and tendencies (Cobbe, 1875, p. 223).

What is the source of these counter-sympathetic forces? Vivisection of course arises out of science, which Cobbe (1875) defines simply as the "pursuit of physical Knowledge" (p. 223). Previously, truth was treated as just one value alongside such others as goodness, beauty, and faith; physical knowledge was regarded as just one kind of knowledge alongside the moral, aesthetic, and religious. But now, increasingly, science is driving all other values and kinds of knowledge out of the field (Cobbe, 1888, p. 4).

Even so, Cobbe (1875) remarks, one might have expected science to weigh in against vivisection. For scientists have learned a great deal about the bodily bases of feelings of pain and suffering (Cobbe, 1875, p. 226). In addition, in Darwin's wake, scientists see humans as having evolved out of other animals, thereby recognizing greater continuity between humans and other animals than ever before (Cobbe, 1875, pp. 226–227). On both counts, one might have expected scientists to abjure or feel cautious about vivisection, but on the contrary, most scientists support it. In historical fact, the bulk of scientists in Cobbe's time did favor vivisection, and Darwin and his supporter Thomas Henry Huxley were among the chief opponents of the tighter version of the Cruelty to Animals Act that Cobbe and her allies had sought to introduce.[10] "That the disciples of Darwin should themselves be the teachers [of vivisection] is . . . a portent of strange and threatening augury," Cobbe (1875) concludes (p. 227).

What this portent augurs, for Cobbe (1875), is as follows. Our evolutionary history has given us instincts to be competitive, aggressive, and trample the weak underfoot (Cobbe, 1872, p. 18). This is because evolutionary pressures have favored the "survival of the fittest," in Herbert Spencer's phrase. Darwin argued otherwise in *The Descent of Man* (1871), maintaining that, because we are group animals, selection pressures have favored our social and cooperative instincts. But Cobbe (1872), in her lengthy critique of *Descent*, is unconvinced, thinking that Darwin projects the cultured mores of the bourgeois gentleman back onto primitive hominids (pp. 20–23). She sees the pessimistic "survival of the fittest" analysis as more accurate. The only ethics that evolutionary theory can really supply or underpin, then, is one of "might makes right"—no real ethics at all. Those scientists who follow Darwin and believe that evolutionary theory *can* supply an ethics will only end up acting on "might makes right" and believing themselves vindicated in doing so. They have "adopted a moral theory of boundless application—namely, that the weak have absolutely no claims at all against the strong, but may be tortured *ad infinitum* even on the chance of discovering something interesting to the lordlier race" (Cobbe, 1875, p. 227). This is put into practice in vivisection.[11]

Vivisection, then, is the inevitable outcome of science's rise to ascendancy and its displacement of the moral and religious values that previously underpinned everyday ethics. In their place, scientists look to evolution to ground ethics, but for Cobbe (1875) the only "ethics" this grounds is one where the strong trample on the weak and feel legitimated in doing so. And so we get vivisection, in which the strong (scientists) dominate the weak (animals) to advance the interests of the stronger party.

To relate this back to Cobbe's (1874) account of the historical progression of sympathy, she claims that the various world religions, especially Christianity, have been crucial in educating and cultivating us in sympathy. These religious influences counteract our instincts toward aggression, domination, and cruelty. By ousting religion, science is undermining its power to instill sympathetic feelings in us, which gives our cruel instincts room to push forward, threatening to drag us down below the level of civilization we have reached. By no coincidence, vivisection is one of the main outlets for this newly resurgent cruelty, because vivisection is practiced by scientists and scientists have led the way in jettisoning religion with its softening influence (Cobbe, 1875, pp. 227–228).

For Cobbe (1875), then, vivisection is not a marginal issue but one that reveals a fault line in the historical process, where we stand at a dangerous fork in the road—with religion, sympathy, love, and respect for the sacredness of life in one direction and science, cruelty, heteropathy, and the survival of the fittest in the other.[12] Cobbe's interlocutor Vernon Lee conveys Cobbe's perspective well in her dialogue on vivisection, in which Lee's spokesperson, "Baldwin," converses with "Michael," who represents Cobbe:

> Modern civilization has a sort of mark of the beast—a something hideous and Moloch-like, even where it is most obviously subservient to our comfort and welfare. The angel of progress makes a sound with his wings, and has a sulphurousness in his breath which is oddly suggestive of hell. Vivisection somehow seems to fit very neatly into it. (Lee, 1886, p. 180)[13]

Cobbe's (1875) view of the world-historical significance of vivisection shows part of why she sees it as being of great moral concern. Some of her further reasons for thinking so emerge when she argues against the defenses of vivisection. Unleashing an arsenal of rejoinders to these defenses, she anticipates many criticisms and concerns that would be raised about animal experimentation over the 20th century and that remain widely shared by the British public.[14]

Cobbe (1875) begins with what she calls the "*tu quoque*" defenses, which appeal to "our bad conscience as regards various kinds of cruelty" (p. 229). Why single out vivisection from other forms of human mistreatment of animals, such as hunting and everyday acts of cruelty? Cobbe (1875) replies that these other practices are also wrong, and "one offence does not exculpate another" (p. 229). That said, Cobbe (1875) continues, vivisection does deserve special condemnation because (a) often those who, for example, whip their horses, or kick their dogs, or go hunting are ignorant of how much pain they cause—whereas the same cannot be said of scientists (p. 229); (b) vivisectors are from the social elite and so carry a special responsibility, for where they lead others will follow (p. 224), and neither can their actions be excused on the grounds they were afflicted by overwork, poverty, hunger, and so forth (p. 229); and (c) whereas the other forms of cruelty to animals have been with us for centuries, vivisection is new (p. 230). It is a typical product of modernity, distilling the competing tendencies of modern civilization as age-old customs like grouse shooting (wrong as they are) do not.

But what about meat-eating? Surely if vivisection is bad, meat-eating, which is much more widespread, must be as bad or worse? Cobbe (1875) responds that, again, if meat-eating were an offense, this still would not make vivisection right. But in any case, she claims, meat-eating is not actually wrong so long as the animals we raise and kill for meat are treated and killed humanely. This is the most we can do here, she claims, because meat-eating is an unavoidable necessity for humans (Cobbe, 1875, p. 229). Of course, we may object to Cobbe that meat-eating is not unavoidably necessary—an objection that Anna Kingsford was already pressing in Cobbe's time. Kingsford (1882, 1883, 1912) argued that a meat diet is neither necessary nor healthy for human beings and that meat-eating and vivisection are alike in that both are harmful, unnecessary, and should cease. But even though Cobbe (1875) is on weak ground in differentiating vivisection (unnecessary) from meat-eating (necessary), the obvious inference—as Kingsford (1882, 1883, 1912) saw—is not that vivisection is unproblematic but that meat-eating should be abandoned or reduced as well.

We now come to what Cobbe (1875) regards as the central defense of vivisection, which is utilitarian: That vivisection yields knowledge of the living body, and medical applications, which enable us to reduce human suffering, so that even though animals suffer in vivisection the practice reduces the net amount of suffering in the world. Cobbe ventures some doubts that scientists are genuinely motivated by concern for humankind (p. 231). Still, she remarks, "the motives which actually influence living vivisectors do not . . . determine the ethical lawfulness of the practice" (p. 232). For the practice to be ethically lawful, the end (reducing human suffering) would have to justify the means; and for this three conditions must be met: (i) the end must be "reasonably sure of attainment," (ii) it must be impossible to reach any other way, and (iii) the infliction of suffering must be kept to the minimum (p. 233). Cobbe questions whether vivisection ever satisfies these conditions. Its end is only hypothetical, possible, abstract, future, and long-term; but no utilitarian should prioritize merely hypothetical future reduction in suffering over present, definite, actual, concrete increases in suffering. The vivisector "is enthusiastically anxious to relieve the sufferings of unseen, and perhaps unborn, men and women, but . . . cares in comparison nothing at all for those agonies which are endured immediately under his eye" (p. 231). Plus, the promised medical benefits are often a mirage, she believes (1882); many medical treatments are either unnecessary—being promoted only out of profit and career motives or due to *idées fixes* on physicians' parts—or are positively harmful—not least in contributing to the cult of physical health instead of spiritual well-being, which she called "hygeiolatry."

However, Cobbe (1875) continues, vivisection's advocates weight the utilitarian scales in its favor by claiming that human pain and suffering count for more than those of animals (p. 233). Huxley, for example, had written to Cobbe that he would gladly sacrifice any number of dogs to save even one human. For Cobbe, utilitarianism should, in any case, be rejected as a moral theory, for reasons on which I will touch below (and see Cobbe, 1855, pp. 68–70, 148–149). But operating on utilitarian terms, Cobbe argues, a right action is one that reduces net suffering and/or increases net happiness. Suffering and happiness, equated with pain and pleasure, are the sole rubrics here. But all sentient beings feel pain and pleasure, so there are no grounds to privilege the pain or pleasure of human beings. To do so is merely a new form of "Race Selfishness" (Cobbe, 1875, p. 233). Cobbe (1874) uses this phrase deliberately, for she believes that there had been a long historical struggle for white people to overcome the "barrier of race" and extend their sympathies to Black people, an extension embodied in the abolition of slavery (pp. 199–200). Now Cobbe (1875) sees "Race Selfishness" reappearing in a new form, as an arbitrary privileging of the human species and its pains and pleasures. Cobbe thus anticipates Richard Ryder's critique of speciesism by a hundred years.[15]

Some of Cobbe's provivisection adversaries, notably James Paget, countered that animal pain counts for less because animals do not feel pain as acutely as humans.[16] On this view, there is a difference (either of degree or kind) between the pains and pleasures of humans and animals, which gives us grounds to privilege the former. In her 1882 essay "Vivisection: Four Replies," Cobbe observes that the testimony concerning animal pain behaviors and reactions given by many scientists, including Paget himself, contradicts this claim. Furthermore, vivisectionists use species of animals who are similar to humans in structure and function—otherwise their findings would have little bearing on the reduction of human suffering. By the same token, the animals being used must feel pain and pleasure very much as humans do; if they did not, there would be little point in using these animals for research. The very practice of vivisection tells against the claim that animals feel pain in a qualitatively different or diminished way compared to humans (Cobbe, 2004, p. 190).

What about John Stuart Mill's idea of higher pleasures? Perhaps these pleasures are uniquely human and should count for more than animal pleasures, so that humans weigh more heavily in the scales overall? Cobbe considers and rejects this argument, too, in her essay "The Higher Expediency," included in her collection *The Modern Rack: Papers on Vivisection* (1889, esp. p. 32). For us to experience the higher pleasures of doing good, and acting with kindness and compassion, we must shun vivisection—neither participating in it directly nor being complicit with it indirectly. Otherwise we are caught up in cruelty and wrongdoing and cannot experience the higher pleasures of virtuous action (Cobbe, 1889, pp. 32–34). This is not, for Cobbe, actually the right reason for opposing vivisection—she sees it as putting antivivisection on a basis of concern for *our* moral welfare as humans, whereas it should be based on concern for *animal* welfare (Cobbe, 1865, p. 241)—but still, for her, one cannot appeal to higher pleasures to vindicate vivisection.

The upshot of "The Moral Aspects of Vivisection," then, is that although the central defenses of vivisection are utilitarian, when properly understood, utilitarianism tells against vivisection in several ways: because actual present suffering trumps hypothetical future suffering; because the vaunted medical benefits are often doubtful; because human "Race Selfishness" is unwarranted; and, lastly, because higher pleasures fail to shore up the case for vivisection. The fact that vivisectionists still insist on counting human pleasures for more than animal ones shows that they are not really acting from a utilitarian calculation at all, Cobbe (1875, p. 234) infers. They are acting from the creed that might makes right and merely invoking utilitarianism to give themselves a veneer of legitimacy. Here Cobbe (1875) joins up the two halves of her essay, concluding: "As the main work of civilization has been the vindication of the rights of the weak, . . . the practice of vivisection . . . is a retrograde step in the progress of our race, a backwater in the onward flowing stream of justice and mercy" (p. 234).

We may yet wonder on what positive basis Cobbe (1875) herself considers vivisection wrong, if not a utilitarian one. The answer is that, for Cobbe, we have a fundamental duty of benevolence: to minimize the suffering and increase the happiness of all sentient beings, animals as well as humans. She makes this case in her 1863 essay "The Rights of Man and the Claims of Brutes." Cobbe regards the duty of benevolence as basic and intuitive; we cannot go any deeper than it, but it is bedrock and our other duties flow out of it. While this duty sounds rather like the utilitarian imperative to increase the general happiness, utilitarians in Cobbe's time generally argued for that imperative on empirical grounds, whereas for Cobbe, the duty of benevolence is known intuitively and not derived from any prior empirical facts.

Clearly, though, many of Cobbe's provivisection adversaries did not find the duty to treat animals with benevolence or kindness to be intuitive. To accommodate such cases, Cobbe (1874) distinguishes between the ground of the *obligation* to act with benevolence and the ground of our *motivation* to act with benevolence (p. lxxiii). The obligation is, ultimately, legislated by God, as are all moral laws; moral laws presuppose a moral legislator, and that legislator must be God. It cannot be we ourselves, as Kant thought, for then moral laws would not bind us absolutely (Cobbe, 1855, pp. 10–11). If we are motivated to act with benevolence, though, this must be from the emotion of sympathy; sympathy is the immediate motivating source of all benevolent moral action (Cobbe, 1874, p. 154). For Cobbe, then, it is the lack of sympathetic feeling for animals that leads vivisectionists to fail to act on the duty of benevolence to which, nonetheless, they remain subject. And, as we saw earlier, Cobbe believes that science and its erosion of religion are undermining sympathetic feelings for animals and giving our contrary instincts of cruelty and aggression a new outlet. The various strands of her moral thought thus interlock and support one another.

Cobbe does not make explicit whether she intends the arguments of "The Moral Aspects of Vivisection" to tell for the abolition of vivisection or only for stringent regulation. But in 1875, when the essay appeared, she was involved in intense political and parliamentary struggles over the Cruelty to Animals Act, so presumably she still favored stringent regulation. In that case, her essay can be read as suggesting that while vivisection is wrong, its wrongness can be reduced to the point where some limited use of it is permissible, if certain conditions are strictly adhered to (i.e., with some "higher" animals absolutely protected from experimental use, with experiments always performed under anesthesia, only performed at all when the medical benefits are certain and immediate, and with tightly enforced controls upon any exceptions to anesthesia). These were some of the conditions stipulated in her proposed more restrictive legislation. When the more permissive 1876 act was passed, Cobbe was so disappointed that she inferred that vivisectionists would never accept any restrictions on or ethical scrutiny of their activities. The only solution, she concluded, was abolition. From this perspective, her arguments in "The Moral Aspects of Vivisection" could be repurposed to suggest that, because vivisection is wrong, its abolition is required.

Either way, Cobbe was clearly not the hysterical sentimentalist that her adversaries, such as Cyon (1883), made out. She had a considered and closely argued position that was embedded in a comprehensive and far-reaching account of Western civilization and drew on her duty-based and intuitionist moral theory (although I have only briefly touched on this latter element here). Many of her points, such as her opposition to human "Race Selfishness"—or speciesism—have become important in animal ethics in the later 20th century, although it has seldom been acknowledged that Cobbe got there first. We may not accept all of Cobbe's arguments. But the first step is to acknowledge that she made them, and on reasoned philosophical grounds. As I hope I have begun to show, Cobbe deserves to be taken seriously, not only as a formidable activist, but also as a significant and historically influential philosopher of animal welfare.[17]

Notes

1. The practice that Cobbe and her contemporaries called "vivisection" is now more often called "animal experimentation." Animal experimentation sounds more morally neutral—Cobbe's critics complained that vivisection was a loaded term (see, e.g., Davis, 1885, p. 203)—while vivisection, if taken literally as "dissection of living beings," is too narrow to cover all forms of animal experimentation (see, again, Davis, 1885, p. 204). Nonetheless, Cobbe used the word more broadly, and I retain her usage to capture her views and the language employed in her time.

2. So Cobbe (1894) relates in her autobiography (see pp. 2:246–247).

3. For excellent accounts of Cobbe's antivivisection and animal welfare campaigning, her role in the 1876 act, and the political and parliamentary struggles around the latter, see Donald (2019), Hamilton (2004, 2013), and Hampson (1981).

4. See, for just a few examples, Simpson (2017), Traïni (2016), and Vyvyan (1969); also Cruelty Free International (n.d.) and National Anti-Vivisection Society (2012).

5. Donald (2019), however, emphasises Cobbe's philosophical background.

6. For instance, Cobbe's focus on sympathy anticipates the animal care ethics of Josephine Donovan (e.g., Donovan, 2007), while many of Cobbe's arguments against vivisection reappear in more recent critical analyses such as that of LaFollette and Shanks (1995).

7. On the development of Cobbe's philosophical thought, see Hamilton (2006), Mitchell (2004), Peacock (2002), Stone (2022), and Williamson (2004).

8. However, I cannot refrain from pointing out the problems of Cobbe's antivegetarianism, as they are so striking.

9. Cobbe (1874) argues for this view of history in her long essay "Heteropathy, Aversion, Sympathy," included in her book *The Hopes of the Human Race*.

10. To be fair, Darwin and Huxley did support regulation, but under a system less stringent than Cobbe wanted. On the contestive relations between Cobbe and Darwin, see Carvalho and Waizbort (2010), Feller (2009), and Harvey (2009). See also Boddice (2016) on how professional men of science reinvented themselves to circumvent accusations of cruelty.

11. Cobbe (1889) satirically remarks that for scientists: "Nature is extremely cruel, but we cannot do better than follow nature; and the law of the Survival of the Fittest, applied to human agency, implies the absolute right of the Strong (i.e., those who can prove themselves 'Fittest') to sacrifice the Weak and Unfit" (p. 66). For discussion, see Gates (1998).

12. On the sacredness of all life, which Cobbe counterposes to evolutionism and the eugenicism of Francis Galton, see Cobbe (1874, p. lxxiv).

13. Lee opposes vivisection but argues, contra Cobbe, that evolutionism tells against vivisection. For Lee, the evolutionary process has given us impulses toward nobility and humaneness to which vivisection does violence.

14. See YouGov (2021): British people oppose animal testing of completed medicines (by 41%), ingredients (44%), and cosmetic products (73%). This compares to just 37% who support animal testing of even completed medicines.

15. Cobbe's critique of "Race Selfishness" may indirectly have influenced Ryder in formulating the concept of speciesism, through the legacy of her arguments in the National Anti-Vivisection Society, to which Ryder belonged. For instance, Ryder conceives of speciesism by analogy with racism, as Cobbe did. He discusses Cobbe in *Victims of Science* (1975), but as an activist more than a theorist.

16. Nietzsche (1887/2006) makes the same claim, picking up and reversing the link Cobbe made with racial slavery: Pains

> that would drive the European . . . to distraction . . . do *not* do that to Negroes. . . . I do not doubt that in comparison with one night of pain endured by a single, hysterical blue stocking, the total suffer-

ing of all the animals . . . interrogated by the knife in scientific research is as nothing." (Nietzsche, 1887/2006, p. 44)

Nietzsche's remarks place him among the most sexist, racist, and reactionary of Cobbe's opponents—yet it is far more common for animal philosophers today to draw on Nietzsche's work than that of Cobbe (see, for instance, Acampora & Acampora, 2004, Calarco, 2021, Lemm, 2009, and Oliver, 2009).

17. My thanks to Clare Palmer for her very helpful comments on an earlier draft of this article.

References

Acampora, C. D., & Acampora, R. R. (Eds.). (2003). *A Nietzschean bestiary: Becoming animal beyond docile and brutal*. Lanham, MD: Rowman & Littlefield.

Boddice, R. (2016). *The science of sympathy: Morality, evolution, and Victorian civilization*. Champaign: University of Illinois Press.

Calarco, M. (2021). *The boundaries of human nature: The philosophical animal from Plato to Haraway*. New York, NY: Columbia University Press.

Carvalho, A. L. de Lima, & Waizbort, R. (2010). Pain beyond the confines of man: A preliminary introduction to the debate between Frances Power Cobbe and the Darwinists with respect to vivisection in Victorian England (1863–1904). *Hist. cienc. saude-Manguinhos, 17*, 577–605.

Cobbe, F. P. (1855). *An essay on intuitive morals, volume one: Theory of morals*. London, England: Longmans.

Cobbe, F. P. (1865). The rights of man and the claims of brutes. In F. P. Cobbe, *Studies new and old of ethical and social subjects* (pp. 211–260). London, England: Trübner.

Cobbe, F. P. (1872). *Darwinism in morals, and other essays*. London, England: Williams & Norgate.

Cobbe, F. P. (1874). *The hopes of the human race*. London, England: Williams & Norgate.

Cobbe, F. P. (1875, April). The moral aspects of vivisection. *New Quarterly, 4*, 222–237.

Cobbe. F. P. (1882). Hygeiolatry. In F. P. Cobbe, *The peak in Darien: An octave of essays* (pp. 77–88). London, England: Williams & Norgate.

Cobbe, F. P. (1888). *The scientific spirit of the age*. London, England: Smith & Elder.

Cobbe, F. P. (1889). *The modern rack: Papers on vivisection*. London, England: Swan Sonnenschein.

Cobbe, F. P. (1894). *Life of Frances Power Cobbe* (2 Vols.). London, England: Bentley & Son.

Cobbe, F. P. (2004). Vivisection: Four replies. In S. Hamilton (Ed.), *Animal welfare and antivivisection 1870–1910: Vol. 1. Frances Power Cobbe* (pp. 186–202). London, England: Routledge. (Original work published 1882)

Cruelty Free International. (n.d.). *Our history*. Retrieved from: https://crueltyfreeinternational.org/what-we-do/our-history

Cyon, E. de. (1883). The anti-vivisectionist agitation. *Contemporary Review, 43*, 498–510.

Darwin, C. (1871). *The descent of man, and selection in relation to sex.* (2 Vols.). London, England: Murray.

Davis, N. K. (1885). The moral aspects of vivisection. *North American Review, 140*, 203–220.

Donald, D. (2019). *Women against cruelty: Protection of animals in nineteenth-century Britain*. Manchester, England: Manchester University Press.

Donovan, J. (2007). Attention to suffering: Sympathy as a basis for ethical treatment of animals. In J. Donovan & C. J. Adams (Eds.), *The feminist care tradition in animal ethics* (pp. 174–197). New York, NY: Columbia University Press.

Feller, D. A. (2009). Dog fight: Darwin as animal advocate in the antivivisection controversy of 1875. *Studies in the History and Philosophy of the Biological and Biomedical Sciences, 40*(4), 265–271.

Gates, B. T. (1998). *Kindred nature: Victorian and Edwardian women embrace the living world*. Chicago, IL: University of Chicago Press.

Hamilton, S. (2004). Introduction. In S. Hamilton (Ed.), *Animal welfare and anti-vivisection 1870–1910: Vol. 1. Frances Power Cobbe*. London, England: Routledge.

Hamilton, S. (2006). *Frances Power Cobbe and Victorian feminism*. London, England: Palgrave.

Hamilton, S. (2013). *On the Cruelty to Animals Act, 15 August 1876*. BRANCH: Britain, Representation and Nineteenth-Century History. Retrieved from: https://branchcollective.org/?ps_articles=susan-hamilton-on-the-cruelty-to-animals-act-15-august-1876

Hampson, J. E. (1981). *History of animal experimentation control in the U.K.* WellBeing International. WBI Studies Repository. Retrieved from: https://www.wellbeingintlstudiesrepository.org/cgi/viewcontent.cgi?article=1002&context=acwp_all

Harvey, J. (2009). Darwin's "angels": The women correspondents of Charles Darwin. *Intellectual History Review, 19*, 197–210.

Kingsford, A. (1882). The uselessness of vivisection. *The Nineteenth Century, 11*, 171–183.

Kingsford, A. (1883). *Unscientific science: A lecture*. Edinburgh, Scotland: Andrew Elliot.

Kingsford, A. (1912). *Addresses and essays on vegetarianism* (S. H. Hart, Ed.). London, England: J. M. Watkins.

LaFollette, H., & Shanks, N. (1995). Utilizing animals. *Journal of Applied Philosophy, 12* (1), 13–25.

Lee, V. (1886). *Baldwin: Being dialogues on views and aspirations*. Boston: Roberts Brothers.

Lemm, V. (2009). *Nietzsche's animal philosophy: Culture, politics, and the animality of the human being*. New York, NY: Fordham University Press.

Mitchell, S. (2004). *Frances Power Cobbe: Victorian feminist, journalist, reformer*. Charlottesville: University of Virginia Press.

National Anti-Vivisection Society. (2012). *The history of the NAVS*. Retrieved from: https://www.navs.org.uk/about_us/24/0/299/

Nietzsche, F. (2006). *On the genealogy of morality* (C. Diethe, Trans.) Cambridge, England: Cambridge University Press. (Original work published 1887)

Oliver, K. (2009). *Animal lessons: How they teach us to be human*. New York, NY: Columbia University Press.

Peacock, S. J. (2002). *The theological and ethical writings of Frances Power Cobbe, 1822–1904*. Lewiston, NJ: Edwin Mellen.

Ryder, R. (1975). *Victims of science*. London, England: National Anti-Vivisection Society.

Simpson, M. (2017). In defence of Frances Power Cobbe. *Voice for Ethical Research at Oxford*. Retrieved from: https://voiceforethicalresearchatoxford.wordpress.com/2017/08/01/in-defence-of-frances-power-cobbe/

Stone, A. (Ed.). (2022). *Frances Power Cobbe*. Cambridge, England: Cambridge University Press.

Traïni, C. (2016). *The animal rights struggle*. Amsterdam, Netherlands: Amsterdam University Press.

Vyvyan, J. (1969). *In pity and in anger*. London, England: Michael Joseph.

Williamson, L. (2005). *Power and protest: Frances Power Cobbe and Victorian society*. London, England: Rivers Oram Press.

YouGov. (2021). *Where do Britons stand on animal testing?* Retrieved from: https://yougov.co.uk/topics/health/articles-reports/2021/11/17/where-do-britons-stand-animal-testing

PART III

Historical Controversies: Meat Eating

Biblical Veganism: An Examination of 1 Timothy 4:1–8

MARCELLO NEWALL
University of Leeds, England

Abstract: 1 Timothy 4:1–8 is often used as a proof text against veganism; this is especially true among certain fundamentalist Christian groups and conspiracy theorists. This article argues that a closer look at its linguistic, historical, and theological context reveals that Paul is in reality seeking to uphold the goodness of creation, as described in the first chapters of Genesis, against the dualistic proto-Gnostic creation story that saw the material world as evil. In this sense, 1 Timothy 4:1–8 appears to be a point-by-point rebuttal of the proto-Gnostic view of creation, which is contrasted with the account in Genesis. In particular, the apostle is denouncing a harsh asceticism, and food restriction/deprivation, described as "bodily exercise," which by severely mortifying the body sought deliverance from the material world. The article goes on to analyze ancient forms of asceticism as well as dietary patterns in the ancient Mediterranean in order to show how contemporary veganism differs sharply from the kind of mortification that is being condemned. 1 Timothy 4:1–8 highlights how food, generally understood, and creation should be received with thanksgiving as they are both gifts from God, which were pronounced good. Furthermore, 1 Timothy underlines that true Christian holiness does not consist in the harsh mortification of the body but in an inner holiness based on love and faith in the incarnation, death, and resurrection of Christ. Ultimately, veganism, far from being anti-Christian, as God's original ideal, can be seen as a sign of hope pointing to the coming of the Kingdom of God and the restoration of creation beyond all violence, suffering, and death.

Key words: veganism, 1 Timothy 4, vegetarianism, asceticism, food restriction, Christianity, Bible, Gnosticism, animals, meat-eating, dualism, creation

1 Timothy 4:1–8 is often used to denounce veganism as being anti-Christian and even demonic. This is a favorite theme for many hardline fundamentalists, but it is also used by conspiracy theorists. In contrast, I argue that a closer examination of the passage in question, and its context, shows that Paul is *clearly* not referring to anything similar to contemporary veganism but to a *harsh* form of asceticism based on an unbiblical view of

creation. In fact, after analyzing the King James Version (KJV) of the Bible, it becomes apparent that some of the confusion over this matter is *simply* linked to the use of "meats" in 17th-century English, which does *not* mean "animal flesh" like its present-day equivalent.

Far from denouncing veganism, I hold that Paul is upholding the creation account given in Genesis Chapters 1 and 2. His polemic was and is against those who deny the incarnation of Christ, the goodness of God's creation, and promote dualism and *severe forms of asceticism* as a means of union with God and sanctification. Paul contends that *harsh bodily mortification and food deprivation* is useless and that Christians should be seeking true inner godliness instead. The misreading of 1 Timothy 4:1–8, ultimately, is an example of how the Bible can be used to help perpetuate worldviews and traditions that are beginning to be questioned in society; it also underlines how Scripture can become a pretext to promote false ideologies. As is the case with much poor exegesis, 1 Timothy 4:1–8 has been excluded from:

- its immediate context: both linguistic and conceptual
- the general context and message of 1 Timothy
- the rest of the New Testament
- the overall teaching and direction of Scripture
- history and knowledge from other fields of learning and common sense

THE AUTHORSHIP OF 1 TIMOTHY

There has been much discussion over the authorship of 1 Timothy—and more generally the Pastoral Epistles—with many contemporary scholars denying its Pauline authorship and believing that it is possibly pseudonymous, the work of one of Paul's disciples, or even of Timothy himself (Bauckham, 1988, p. 494). The various problems linked to Paul being the author include the different vocabulary and style used in the Pastoral Epistles compared to Paul's other letters, the apparent discrepancies between their account of Paul's ministry and the way it is chronicled in the book of Acts, and what appears to be an excessively developed church structure and organization for the first century. On the other hand, a minority of scholars believe in the Pauline authorship of 1 Timothy (Guthrie, 1957/1990, pp. 55–62; Klinker-De Klerck, 2008). It has been argued, for example, that 1 Timothy had always been considered an authentic letter of Paul by Church tradition up until the 19th century and seems to have been known, and viewed positively, by some of the earliest Church fathers like Polycarp, Tertullian, Ignatius of Antioch, Justin Martyr, Irenaeus, and possibly Clement of Rome, while it was purposely ignored by Marcion in his unorthodox canon.[1] It also appears strange that in the defining of the Christian canon, other texts, even ones perfectly in line with orthodoxy, would be excluded on the basis of their clear pseudonymity whereas the Pastoral Letters would be included. The early Church had, in fact, developed a fairly sophisticated series of tests in order to ascertain the authenticity of a text, and Jerome, for example, followed several criteria for understanding the genuineness of documents (Metzger, 1972, pp. 13–14). Likewise, while Metzger (1972) actually argued that *pseudepigrapha* may have made their way into the canon, he was forced to assert after analyzing the early Church's attitudes toward false documents and impersonation that "from the preceding examples it appears that patristic writers condemned pseudonymous works not merely on literary grounds but also, and sometimes primarily, on doctrinal grounds" (p. 15). Furthermore, the differences in style and lexicon could be explained by the use of amanuenses and secretaries on the part of Paul (Rom. 16:22; see also Richards, 2004), as well as a certain evolution in his ministry—now advanced—and the personal nature of the Pastoral Letters as opposed to others that were addressed to specific churches. Either way, while a Pauline authorship of 1 Timothy certainly makes what I argue stronger and places 1 Timothy more organically in the context of Paul's overall theology, life, and other letters, my thesis does not depend on it.[2]

CREATION AND GNOSTIC MYTHS

1 Timothy claims to have been written by the Apostle Paul to Timothy (1:1) in order to help his young pupil who was stationed in the church in Ephesus. Timothy was young (1 Tim. 4:12) and apparently fearful (2 Tim. 1:7). Paul at the start of the letter immediately underlines the purpose of his writing:

> As I urged you when I was going to Macedonia, remain at Ephesus so that you may charge certain persons not to teach any different doctrine, nor to devote themselves to myths and endless genealogies, which promote speculations rather than the stewardship from God that is by faith. The aim of our charge is love that issues from a pure heart and a good conscience and a sincere faith. Certain persons, by swerving from these, have wandered away into vain discussion, desiring to be teachers of the law, without understanding either what they are saying or the things about which they make confident assertions. (1 Tim. 1:3–7)

Paul wants Timothy to stop certain false teachers "who devote themselves to myths and endless genealogies" (see also Brown et al., 1992, pp. 277–283). These teachers also seem to act as if they are teachers of the "law," even though their interpretation of the Law of Moses is particularly heterodox: The Hebrew Scriptures appear to be only a starting point—and were normally turned completely upside down—from which they developed their convoluted theories and stories.[3] It may be that claiming to be "teachers of the law" was simply a pretense in order to infiltrate churches made up of many Jewish converts and Gentiles that had a high regard for Jewish monotheism; Paul certainly sees their interpretations as totally spurious (1 Tim. 1:7). Various scholars agree (Barker, 1995, pp. 1834, 1840; Kroeger & Kroeger, 1998, pp. 59–66, 117–125), and the internal evidence in the letter points to a form of *proto-Gnosticism* as being the error that Paul is attacking (Pearlman, 1935, pp. 48–53); in fact, Paul seems to directly mention proto-Gnosticism at the end of the letter: "O Timothy, guard the deposit entrusted to you. Avoid the irreverent babble and contradictions of what is falsely called 'knowledge [gnosis].'" The word for knowledge is *gnosis*, from which the word "Gnosticism" is derived. Moreover, the errors mentioned in the letter fit well with what we know about Gnosticism, even though this would develop *fully only in the next two centuries* (Tiessen, 2007, pp. 31–48; see also Jonas, 1958/2001).

While being a philosophy that encompassed various positions and contradicted itself in many doctrines, Gnosticism was essentially an esoteric and dualistic view of the world that believed that the physical creation was made by an inferior demiurge (Jonas, 1958/2001, pp. 42–44, 48–65; Moore & Turner, 2000, pp. 174–196; see also Kasper, 1974/1977, pp. 198–199). This lesser "god," whom the Gnostics identified with the Jewish God of the Old Testament, had trapped human beings in the inferior material creation. At the same time, a more spiritual god had sent Lucifer to aid humanity by opening its eyes and helping it to escape the bondage of the material realm. The Gnostic account of creation, which could be extremely complex and utilized long convoluted genealogies, contradicted almost entirely the biblical view (Barnstone & Meyer, 2009, pp. 2–3, 123–133, 200–202, 596–597; Meyer, 2007, pp. 191–218). The Gnostics also believed they possessed special "knowledge" that helped them escape the earthly realm of existence, and which would bring about their salvation. Despite their controversies, Gnostic groups tended to have four main areas of agreement:

> First, they believed in one God who is wholly transcendent, spiritual, and far removed from the fallen, material universe, which he did not create. The physical universe was created by an evil or demented lesser god (a "demiurge"). Second, human beings are sparks (or droplets) of the same material substance that God is and have somehow become trapped in physical bodies, which are like tombs to be escaped. Third, Gnostics all agreed that the "fall" that led to sin and evil is identical to the fall into matter. Creation and fall coincide. As long as spirits are trapped in physical bodies and materiality, they will be subject to sin, which is caused by ignorance of their nature and home. The fourth common feature of Gnostic belief was their vision of salvation. All Gnostics agreed that salvation is to escape from the bondage of material existence and travel back to the home from which souls/spirits have fallen. The possibility is initiated by the great Spirit, God, who wishes to draw back to himself the stray bits and pieces. God sends forth an emanation of himself—a spiritual redeemer—who descends through layers and layers of reality from pure spirit to dense matter and attempts to teach some of the divine sparks of Spirit their true identity and home. Once awakened, they are able to begin the journey back. Salvation is by knowledge—self-knowledge. Finally, all of the Gnostics (so far as anyone knows) considered themselves Christians and regarded Jesus as the human vehicle for this heavenly messenger, "Christ." All rejected the idea of God becoming incarnate, dying and rising bodily. Such beliefs were considered unspiritual and against true wisdom because they entangled spirit with matter (Olson, 1999, pp. 37–39).

As mentioned earlier, while in the first century Gnosticism was not the fully developed kind we find in the second and third centuries and it would be more appropriate to talk of *proto-Gnosticism*, many of the features of later Gnosticism are already present. The dualistic worldview of Gnosticism led to the *opposite* tendencies of extreme licentiousness and harsh forms of asceticism: This was because the body was of limited importance and had been transcended through special spiritual knowledge. Whereas letters like 1 John,

2 Peter and Jude—possibly together with parts of 1 Corinthians—lambast the libertine version of proto-Gnosticism, 1 Timothy and Colossians appear to address legalistic and especially the ascetic tendencies that brought about self-mortification. And yet it would seem that libertine teachings, and profound greed, may have been present even in the church of Ephesus and that Paul addressed some of them in 1 Timothy 6:5. Various Gnostic tendencies, whether legalism, asceticism, or libertinism, often coexisted in the churches as mixtures, or even in opposition to each other; many Gnostic sects and movements were in fact often an amalgam of legalism and asceticism as in the case of certain proto-Gnostics in the church of Colossae.[4]

THE TEXT OF 1 TIMOTHY 4

> But the Spirit explicitly says that in later times some will fall away from the faith, paying attention to deceitful spirits and doctrines of demons, by means of the hypocrisy of liars seared in their own conscience as with a branding iron, *men* who forbid marriage *and advocate* abstaining from foods which God has created to be gratefully shared in by those who believe and know the truth. For everything created by God is good, and nothing is to be rejected if it is received with gratitude; for it is sanctified by means of the word of God and prayer. In pointing out these things to the brethren, you will be a good servant of Christ Jesus, *constantly* nourished on the words of the faith and of the sound doctrine which you have been following. But have nothing to do with worldly fables fit only for old women. On the other hand, discipline yourself for the purpose of godliness; for bodily discipline is only of little profit, but godliness is profitable for all things, since it holds promise for the present life and *also* for the *life* to come. (1 Tim. 4:1–8, New American Standard Bible [NASB])

The NASB (1995) translation is perhaps one of the best available for this text, together with the New Revised Standard Version (NRSV, 1989). On the other hand, the KJV creates some confusion by its use of 17th-century English and the word "meats":

> Forbidding to marry, and commanding to abstain from meats, which God hath created to be received with thanksgiving of them which believe and know the truth. For every creature of God is good, and nothing to be refused, if it be received with thanksgiving: For it is sanctified by the word of God and prayer. (1 Tim. 4:3–5)

Another Bible translation, Young's Literal Translation (YLT), from 1862, again uses the old English "meats," which simply means food:

> And the Spirit expressly speaketh, that in latter times shall certain fall away from the faith, giving heed to seducing spirits and teachings of demons, in hypocrisy speaking lies, being seared in their own conscience, forbidding to marry—to abstain from meats that God created to be received with thanksgiving by those believing and acknowledging the truth because every creature of God [is] good, and nothing [is] to be rejected, with thanksgiving being received, for it is sanctified through the word of God and intercession. These things placing before the brethren, thou shalt be a good ministrant of Jesus Christ, being nourished by the words of the faith, and of the good teaching,

which thou didst follow after, and the profane and old women's fables reject thou, and exercise thyself unto piety, for the bodily exercise is unto little profit, and the piety is to all things profitable, a promise having of the life that now is, and of that which is coming. (1 Tim. 4:1–8)

The problem with the KJV, like the YLT, is that "meat" in 17th-century English simply meant food and not animal flesh. What is supposed to be received with thanksgiving is likely *food*, and creation, in general. While many tend to read vegetarianism into this passage, this is never explicitly mentioned and is simply the bias of the reader. In this sense, many interpreters seem to *have confused legalism with asceticism* and have conflated the two; ascetics are almost invariably legalistic to some degree, yet not all legalists are ascetics (see Figure 1). They are two distinct phenomena that need to be understood separately *even* when asceticism is a subset of legalism. The New International Version (NIV) translation, for example, adds the word "certain" to "foods," which is not found in the original Greek and is simply the opinion of the translator. This can be seen in *The Strongest NIV Exhaustive Concordance* (Goodrick & Kohlenberger, 1999, p. 190), where it states that "certain" in this verse is "*NIG, or Not In Greek.*" This choice of adding "certain" slants the reading of the text and makes it appear that Paul is talking about specific foods that are being forbidden, whereas this is not specifically talked about in these verses.

At the same time, some modern interpreters seem to carelessly use the term "asceticism"; this term ends up being a particularly vague and broad concept without any definite meaning. For these exegetes, *any* form of dietary restriction seems to be described as "ascetic." Even following a healthy diet with abundant food, excellent taste, and ample variety would likely be considered a type of "asceticism" by them. But this form of understanding *betrays* what is being talked about in this context. What is being

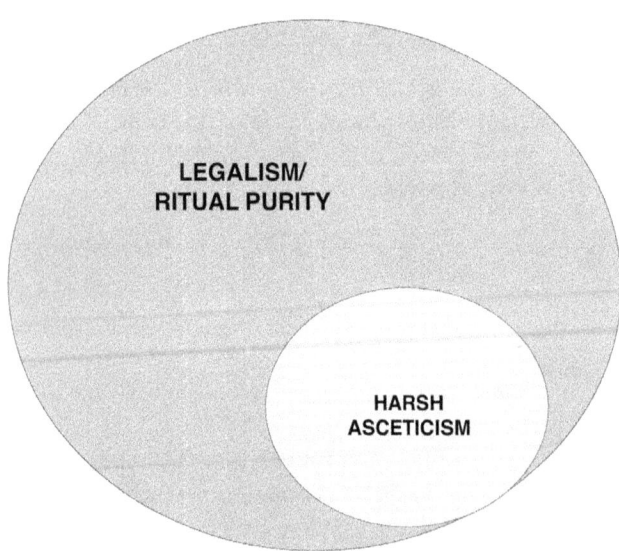

FIGURE 1: Asceticism as a Subset of Legalism/Ritual Purity

discussed here appears to go far beyond *even* the temperance, moderation, and self-control promoted, for example, by Buddhism, or originally by Plato in ancient Greece, and which are often mistaken for severe asceticism.[5] What Paul has in mind is not a moderate "asceticism," in the sense of a certain level of temperance, but a *harsh form* of asceticism (see also Dell'Osso et al., 2016, pp. 1651–1660); it is not simply a kind of normal modern-day dietary regimen. Paul extolled self-control as a fruit of the Spirit (2 Tim. 1:7, 3:3; Tit. 1:8; Gal. 5:22–23), and his own life was particularly difficult: He had been imprisoned, stoned, shipwrecked, whipped, exposed to the cold, attacked, and persecuted; he had gone without food for days; he was used to fasting; and he had been raised in the strict discipline of the Pharisees (2 Cor. 11:21–33; Phil. 3:5–6). Paul even talked metaphorically of disciplining (the Greek says "I pummel my body and make it a slave") his body like an athlete: "So I do not run aimlessly; I do not box as one beating the air. But I discipline my body and keep it under control, lest after preaching to others I myself should be disqualified" (1 Cor. 9:26–27, English Standard Version [ESV]). If Paul called something "harsh," it must have been *particularly* so. This is very different from the idea most contemporaries have of "asceticism," which appears to be a distortion of the concept.

Others have instead correctly understood that these verses are talking about asceticism—many commentaries underline this, so it is not a mystery—but then retroactively read veganism/vegetarianism into them. Their reasoning goes something like this: "Veganism is ascetic therefore every time the Bible talks about asceticism it is talking about veganism." Or they simply *assume* that since some Gnostic/dualistic groups refrained from eating meat, particularly red, that this is automatically what Paul is criticizing; some of the confusion may also in part be due to the fact that the concept of "abstinence" has often been associated with refraining from meat in certain Christian traditions. This is wrong on two accounts. First, Gnosticism, and proto-Gnosticism, was particularly varied and often contradictory in its positions and even in its dietary requirements; some Gnostic groups—like the Nicolaitans (Rev. 2:14–15)—even encouraged their followers to eat meat sacrificed to idols because they had been freed from the constraints of the body and were beyond normal morality. Second, as I mentioned earlier, asceticism is often a subset of legalism and alloyed with it, so it is normal that the two would appear together, or seem correlated, but they *must* at the same time be distinguished. They are simply *not* the same thing. In this sense, not eating meat, or animal foods more generally, was likely somewhat *incidental* within an overall framework of harsh asceticism; it is normally a marker for a much deeper severe asceticism present in these Gnostic/dualistic groups.

These exegetes seem to begin with a series of prejudices against veganism, or what they believe these verses are talking about, and then read them back into the text. This strong form of *circular reasoning* works as shown in Figure 2.

And yet there is no reason to believe that veganism *is intrinsically* a harsh form of asceticism in any way—while no doubt it can be made to be if one were to semistarve oneself on tiny amounts of tasteless plant foods. Either way, veganism's modern version is for the most part anything *but* harsh and is normally a positive message that promotes

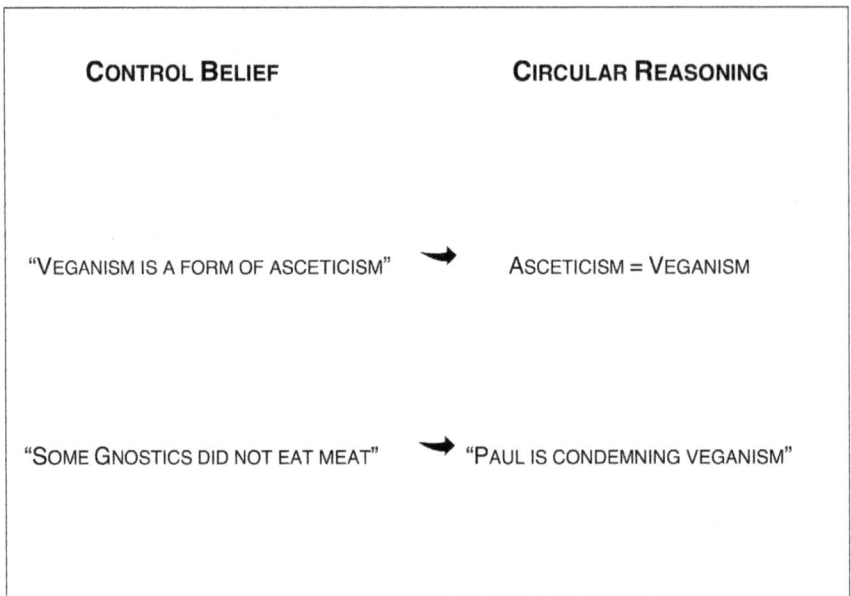

FIGURE 2: Circular Reasoning: Asceticism and Veganism

compassion, environmental responsibility, abundance, enjoyment of life, and healthy living.[6] Far from condemning their asceticism, Augustine even criticized certain vegans of his day for being gluttonous and overeating (Grumett & Muers, 2010, p. 92)! There is, in reality, a wide spectrum of diets that would technically fall under the category of "vegan" or "vegetarian," ranging from the most ascetic possible to the most indulgent, and everything in-between.

Moreover, seeing veganism as synonymous with asceticism is based on modern erroneous ideas on diet and lifestyle. In the ancient world of the Roman Empire, the main staples were cereals and bread, and not meat or animal products—which were consumed sparingly among the common people. In fact, "The diet of most Greeks and Romans was basically vegetarian and consisted of cereals, fruit, vegetables and legumes, and wine diluted with water" (Grandjean, 1997, p. 874S). Likewise, Jesus called himself the "bread of life," as bread was the food that gave sustenance, and instructed that people pray "give us today our daily bread" (Matt. 6:11). Meat was essentially a *luxury item* that was eaten rarely by the poor and the working classes, which made up the bulk of the population. While the aristocrats and royalty ate meat and animal foods much more abundantly, the rest of the population subsisted primarily on a vegetarian diet. Actually, most of humanity throughout *recorded* history has subsisted on primarily vegan/vegetarian eating patterns, without which large populations would not have been possible (McDougall, 2012). Apart from certain tribes and groups living on the edges of the human ecumene, during most of the history of human civilization meat has generally been eaten rarely, if at all (Brock & Gordon, 1959; Crawford, 1987; Morse & Beh, 1937; Shaper & Jones, 2012; Willcox et al., 2007).[7] Similarly, the basic diet of the majority of people living in the Roman Empire consisted of starches, oil, legumes (the Mediterranean triad also included grapes), and locally grown produce (Carr, 2017; Kessler & Temin, 2007; Longo et al., 2008). Most of the poor population in Rome lived off the so-called "Corn Dole," which consisted of huge amounts of wheat that the Roman authorities gave for free to the large urban population to keep them under control (Bauckham, 1993, pp. 362–363, 2010b, p. 96). The idea that Paul would be condemning the average diet of the working classes for not being "rich" enough—or for being "ascetic"—appears absurd. Moreover, according to the biblical record, all of God-fearing humanity from Adam to Noah subsisted on a *completely* vegan diet (Gen. 1:29, 9:2–4). We have to be careful not to read modern Western dietary patterns, where people eat huge amounts of meat and animal products, into the Bible. Even 200 years ago, the current dietary patterns of modern-day Western countries would have been seen as incredibly extravagant by all but the kings, queens, and aristocrats of the earth (Burkitt, 1973; McDougall, 2011).

So what is Paul condemning here? From the context, it is clearly underlined; Paul is condemning *apechesthai brōmatōn* (ἀπέχεσθαι βρωμάτων), literally "abstaining from foods/food." While *broma* is used many times in the New Testament, the expression *apechesthai brōmatōn* appears *only* here in the entire New Testament. *Apéchō* (ἀπέχω), the verb *apechesthai* comes from, can mean to "abstain," but its root signifies to keep "distant from," "stand away from," or "hold off" (Bible Hub, 2020a; StudyLight, 2018). *Bromaton*, likewise, is a genitive plural of *broma* (βρῶμα), which simply means "food" or "that which is eaten" (Bible Hub, 2020b). Even though it is plural, it can also be rendered a *collective noun* as "food," as the NASB, ESV, Revised Standard Version (RSV), NRSV, and NIV *specifically* do in 1 Corinthians 6:13a: "You say, 'Food for the stomach and the stomach for food.'" Furthermore, *broma* is fairly generic and does not specifically signify animal flesh in any way, which in ancient Greek is *kreas* (κρέας), and which is a word that Paul could have used if that had been his intention (Bible Hub, 2020d).

From the context, the phrase *apechesthai brōmatōn* appears to depict a *very negative attitude toward food,* and this is what Paul is condemning. Furthermore, the emphasis here is probably more on the very limited *quantity of food* (major caloric restriction),[8] and in particular the *inner attitude* of self-mortification it was based on, rather than on the specific types of food eaten. It is in this that a lot of exegetes seem to go astray. Paul is not condemning legalism *but a dualistic asceticism*—telling someone not to eat a *certain* food could be legalistic but it wouldn't qualify automatically as ascetic. He highlights this in verse 8 when talking about "bodily exercise" (*sōmatikē gymnasia*, σωματικὴ γυμνασία) translated as "bodily discipline" by the NASB, but which is referring to the self-mortification (Sorokin, 1954/2002, p. 276) he was attacking—in this context it is not about going to the gym, or doing sport, as some have assumed. The very word "asceticism" comes from the Greek *askeō*, which technically has the meaning of "to exercise" or "to train." Paul certainly does attack legalism in other passages of Scripture,[9] but it does not seem to be his intention here. It is true that some proto-Gnostic groups indeed had various dietary restrictions—they were often pescatarian—depending on the sect; at the same time, the strand of proto-Gnostic thought that Paul is attacking here is an ascetic one, not just a simple form of ritual purity, *hence also* the mention of not permitting marriage, which fits perfectly with their severe asceticism but much less so with a simple legalism or moderate temperance.

As mentioned before, asceticism in Paul's day could be *extremely harsh* and in dietary terms could mean eating the *bare minimum* for survival, eating one meal every three days, or essentially living off bread and water (Bemporad, 1996, p. 219). Among the monks living in the desert of Egypt in the fourth century, we have several examples of the kind of asceticism that was present, or pursued, in the ancient world. In the work *Historia Monachorum in Aegypto*, we are told that Abba Or—Father Or—would often eat *only once* a week and contented himself with pickled vegetables (*The Lives of the Desert Fathers*, 1980, p. 63). Furthermore, a monk called John stood under a rock for 3 years in uninterrupted prayer, without ever lying down to sleep, his only food being the communion that the priest would bring him every week. After years of standing still, his feet split and putrefaction began; at this point he moved again and started to roam the desert, eating wild plants along with communion (*The Lives of the Desert Fathers*, 1980, pp. 93–94). The monk Pityrion, on the other hand, would eat "twice a week, taking on Sundays and Thursdays a little soup made with corn meal" (*The Lives of the Desert Fathers*, 1980, p. 99). Finally, among the monks in Nitria, many "ate neither bread nor fruit but only endives," and "some of them never slept at night, but either sitting or standing persevered in prayer until morning" (*The Lives of the Desert Fathers*, 1980, p. 107). A Father in Nitria also told his disciples not to drink water, and like other communities, they sought to obtain sufficient hydration from vegetables and foods alone (*The Lives of the Desert Fathers*, 1980, p. 107). As can be seen, the ascetic practices, whether exaggerated or real, were very severe and on a totally different scale from what is commonly imagined.

In contemporary Western society, we have few examples of this kind of asceticism, as opposed to the fakirs and ascetics in India and the Far East, and perhaps the closest example would be forms of semianorexia, semistarvation, or full-blown anorexia nervosa (Dickens, 2000, pp. 67–76; Griffin & Berry, 2003, pp. 43–51). In the Middle Ages, these tendencies developed into what has been described as "holy anorexia" (Bell, 1985; Corrington, 1986); many "saints" from this period practically starved themselves—some to death—as a way of attaining holiness.[10] In a similar way, the very ascetically oriented groups in the ancient world also practiced harsh and exaggerated forms of fasting. These practices resulted in forms of *severe* deprivation. Some scholars have even historically linked forms of semistarvation and extreme asceticism in the West *directly* to the influence of Gnosticism and its dichotomy between spirit and body (Bemporad, 1996, pp. 217–220; see also Miller & Pumariega, 2001, p. 95). In general, the ascetic proto-Gnostic groups believed that treating the body and its desires harshly was a means to purity and salvation: A similar group led by the famous dualist Marcion was created shortly after 1 Timothy was written in the first century. According to Church tradition, Marcion had had debates with Polycarp, who was a direct disciple of the Apostle John. Marcion believed that the physical world was evil and the God of the Old Testament was malevolent: Humanity was trapped in the material world but could one day hope to escape and reach a pure spiritual realm (see also Von Harnack et al., 1901, pp. 266–281). Following this profoundly dualistic worldview, Marcion commanded his followers not to marry and practiced harsh forms of asceticism; we are told, for example, that "his habits were exceedingly ascetic; for he considered it the chief object of life to mortify the body. It was a rule with his sect to eat and drink merely enough to sustain existence. They fasted often" (Child, 1855, p. 390). Marcion was chastised *even* by Tertullian—one of the most austere and rigoristic Church fathers and a strong advocate of both fasting and temperance—for his excessive severity toward the body, his rejection of marriage, and denigrating the Creator through his rigid dualism (*Adv. Marc.* cc. 1, 2, 24, 29; *De Jejun.* c. 15; see also De Wet, 2019, pp. 3–4; Jonas, 1958/2001, pp. 139–145). Likewise, in describing the asceticism of the dualistic Manicheans of his time, the eastern Church father Chrysostom (347–407 AD), who had lived as a particularly disciplined monk in his youth, underlines how their practices go far beyond the self-control of the Christian monks and resemble starvation. Chrysostom also highlights how while the Christian monks took their food with thanksgiving, the Manicheans showed contempt for their Creator through their despising of food and the body (see also Barnstone & Meyer, 2009, pp. 606–607):

> Therefore they [the Christian monks] say, "Glory be to You, o Lord, glory be to You, o King, that you have given food to delight us." For we ought to give thanks not only for the greater things, but also for the lesser things. And they also give thanks for the lesser things bringing the heresy of the Manicheans in disrepute, and many of those who profess our current life to be evil. For it is not that you should hold them [i.e., the Christian monks] in suspicion, by their high-discipline and contempt for the stomach, as abhorring the food, like the aforementioned heretics, who almost starve themselves to death. (*Matthaeum homilia* 55.8, translated in De Wet, 2019, p. 3)

Furthermore, Chrysostom saw the Manicheans as "rigorous ascetics, basically starving themselves, because of their hate of foodstuffs, the body and matter more generally" (De Wet, 2019, p. 3).

Sorokin (1954/2002) describes some of the main features of this harsh form of asceticism and its mortification of the body through history:

> This accounts, then, for the fantastically varied practices of mortification of the body by many an ascetic of the East and West, of the past and the present . . .
>
> Here we meet, first, hundreds of forms of fasting as a suppression of the *bodily need for food*—complete fasting for days and weeks; lifelong relative fasting in the form of eating only a little bread and drinking a little water; eating only raw herbs, or inedible garbage; or eating with only two teeth; or fasting unto death.
>
> Second, there is the violent suppression of the *sex impulse* in all its forms, beginning with castration and mutilation of the sex-organs, and ending with weakening of the sex impulse through fasting, strenuous physical work, destruction of all its conditioned and unconditioned stimuli; fleeing from such stimuli and environment; imposing upon the body all sorts of cooling pains like prolonged immersion in cold water or snow. . . .
>
> Third is the violent denial to the body of anything which gives *sensual pleasure* and imposition upon the body of all kinds of pains and hardships. These practices include exposure of the body to cold and hot temperatures or climatic conditions; keeping it free from the comfort of cleanliness and subject to the hardships of dust, dirt, being

besmeared, and physically defiled by all kinds of pollution; wearing either nothing or dirty and lousy rags, or horsehair undergarments.... Fourth is the denial to the body of its *need of sleeping in comfortable conditions*. Most of the followers of this method of subjugation of the body regularly practiced sleeplessness for many days and nights; or reduced the period of sleep to an unbelievable minimum. (pp. 274–275)

Similarly, Waddell, in her *The Desert Fathers*, tells us of an ascetic monk who describes his life of voluntary deprivation:

Since the time that I became a monk I have never given myself my fill of bread, nor of water, nor of sleep, and tormenting myself with appetite for these things whereby we are fed, I was not suffered to feel the stings of lust. (Waddell, 1957, p. 80)

This same harsh form of asceticism also makes up the background of the letter to the Colossians. This letter is clearer in many respects—and helps us to understand better 1 Timothy 4—as it shows that this form of mortification of the body was *distinct from* ritual purity and legalism, while possibly being a subset of it. After attacking legalism/ritual purity in 2:16, Paul goes on to denounce harsh forms of religious asceticism (these may have constituted two separate groups). Here I include both the NASB and the ESV:

Let no one keep defrauding you of your prize by delighting in self-abasement and the worship of the angels, taking his stand on *visions* he has seen, inflated without cause by his fleshly mind. (Col. 2:18, NASB)

Let no one disqualify you, insisting on asceticism and worship of angels, going on in detail about visions, puffed up without reason by his sensuous mind. (Col. 2:18, ESV)

If you have died with Christ to the elementary principles of the world, why, as if you were living in the world, do you submit yourself to decrees, such as, "Do not handle, do not taste, do not touch!" (which all *refer to* things destined to perish with use)—in accordance with the commandments and teachings of men? These are matters which have, to be sure, the appearance of wisdom in self-made religion and self-abasement and severe treatment of the body, *but are* of no value against fleshly indulgence. (Col. 2:20–23, NASB)

If with Christ you died to the elemental spirits of the world, why, as if you were still alive in the world, do you submit to regulations—"Do not handle, Do not taste, Do not touch" (referring to things that all perish as they are used)—according to human precepts and teachings? These have indeed an appearance of wisdom in promoting self-made religion and asceticism and severity to the body, but they are of no value in stopping the indulgence of the flesh. (Col. 2:20–23, ESV)

Paul talks of "self-abasement," translated as "false humility" in the NIV and *more precisely* as "asceticism" in the ESV, *twice* and once of "the severe treatment of the body"—rendered "harsh" in the NIV. The error here is similar to that of 1 Timothy 4 and is a *severe asceticism and food restriction*, which believed that through the mortification of the physical body and the senses a higher form of holiness and spirituality could be attained.[11]

In Colossians Chapter 3, Paul underlines true Christian holiness, which is not obtained through self-mortification of the physical body but "by putting to death" (i.e., mortifying)

```
┌─────────────────────────────────────────────────────────────┐
│                                                             │
│      HARSH ASCETICISM              TRUE INNER GODLINESS     │
│                                                             │
│                                                             │
│        COLOSSIANS 2:18-23  ⇒⇒⇒⇒  COLOSSIANS 3:5-6           │
│     "HARSH TREATMENT OF THE BODY"  VS  MORTIFICATION OF THE │
│                                         "FLESH"/SIN         │
│                                                             │
│                                                             │
│         1 TIMOTHY 4:8A  ⇒⇒⇒⇒  1 TIMOTHY 4:8B                │
│        "BODILY EXERCISE"     VS    TRUE "PIETY"/GODLINESS   │
│                                                             │
└─────────────────────────────────────────────────────────────┘
```

FIGURE 3: Pattern in 1 Timothy 4:8 and Colossians 2:18–3:5–6

evil desires, and ungodly behavior. Paul actually *plays* on this contrast in Chapter 3 and mocks the false form of ascetic holiness; for Paul and Jesus, true holiness is holiness of the heart, which expresses itself through love and genuine goodness not by semistarving oneself: "Put to death, therefore, whatever belongs to your earthly nature: sexual immorality, impurity, lust, evil desires and greed, which is idolatry. Because of these, the wrath of God is coming" (Col. 3:5–6, NIV). In 1 Timothy 4, Paul does essentially the same thing he did in Colossians; in 1 Timothy 4:7–8 he contrasts *sōmatikē gymnasia* (σωματικὴ γυμνασία), "bodily exercise," with true godliness ("piety") and tells Timothy to "exercise" this: "And exercise thyself unto piety, for the bodily exercise is unto little profit, and the piety is to all things profitable, a promise having of the life that now is, and of that which is coming" (KJV). This is in line with his initial words at the start of the letter in which he underlines love as the foundation of his message and which he contrasts with the "myths" (1 Tim 1:4; see also 2 Tim. 4:4) of the proto-Gnostics: "The aim of our charge is love that issues from a pure heart and a good conscience and a sincere faith" (1 Tim. 1:5). Surprisingly, many commentators seem to ignore Paul's comment on "bodily exercise," which is *fundamental* in understanding what he meant by *apechesthai brōmatōn* or "abstaining from food/foods." We can see how the pattern in 1 Timothy 4 mimics what Paul does in Colossians, as shown in Figure 3.

THE GOODNESS OF CREATION

After having condemned harsh forms of asceticism, Paul goes on to counter the teaching of the proto-Gnostics in regard to creation in 1 Timothy 4:4. Once again, the older translations, while excellent, like the KJV and even the YLT, obscure the sense of Paul's words by using archaic English expressions. The KJV, for example, tells us that "every creature of God is good," which some have erroneously understood as talking about animals being "good" to eat.[12] "Every creature" from "ktisma" (κτίσμα), simply refers to creation or that which is created and is not talking in particular about individual animals. The idea that Paul is talking of "every creature" in the sense of actual animals and meat would not even make sense *biblically*, as God did *not* create animals as food in the first two chapters of Genesis (Gen. 1:29). This only occurred later as a reluctant *concession* to human hard-heartedness, and perhaps necessity, after the Flood (see also Schwartz, 2001, pp. 2–6).[13] Conversely, the verses are correctly rendered in the NASB: "For everything created by God is good"; Mounce's (2011) Reverse-Interlinear translation is even clearer with its literalism: "Since all of God's creation is good." At this point, it appears Paul is referring to Genesis 1 and God's pronouncement of creation as "good" six times and finally "very good" at the end of the chapter and is refuting the proto-Gnostics' dualistic view of creation, which saw the lower material realm as evil and the spiritual realm above as pure. This is also underlined in Colossians 1:16–20, where Paul highlights repeatedly that "all things," whether "in heaven" or "on earth" (i.e., whether material or spiritual), were *both* created by Christ and redeemed by him, in contrast with the dualism of the proto-Gnostics (see also Eph. 1:10). *Every part* of God's original world is called "good" as the 7 days of creation progress. The fact that God calls his creation "good" seven times in total, with the final utterance being "very good," indicates its completeness:

PROTO-GNOSTIC ACCOUNT	BIBLICAL ACCOUNT
1. ORIGINAL CREATION (DUALISM): GOOD AND EVIL	1. ORIGINAL CREATION: TOTALLY GOOD
2. MATERIAL WORLD AND MATTER ARE EVIL	2. MATERIAL WORLD AND MATTER ARE GOOD
3. MARRIAGE AND PROCREATION ARE EVIL	3. MARRIAGE AND PROCREATION ARE GOOD
4. FOOD IS NOT A BLESSING	4. FOOD IS A BLESSING
5. MORTIFICATION OF THE BODY	5. CARE FOR THE BODY
6. DENY ALL SENSORY PLEASURES AND REJECT CREATION	6. ENJOYMENT OF GOD AND CREATION

FIGURE 4: Comparison Between the Proto-Gnostic and Biblical Account of Creation

seven in Scripture is always the number of *divine perfection* and fullness. The word for "good" in Hebrew is ṭôwb בוט (translated as *kalos*, καλός, in ancient Greek and used by the Septuagint in Genesis 1 and by Paul in 1 Timothy 4.4), which is feminine and can also mean beautiful, excellent, right (ethically), or pleasant (BibleHub, 2020c). Scripture is communicating that there is complete harmony and beauty in God's perfect world. Furthermore, Paul in this passage is upholding the goodness of Genesis 1 and 2 against the false accounts ("myths") of creation of the proto-Gnostics: In this sense, the apostle is contrasting various aspects of the proto-Gnostic account of creation with the biblical one (1 Tim. 1:3–7); we see this with the underlining of the goodness of God's creation (Gen. 1:4, 10, 12, 18, 21, 25, 31), the goodness of food (Gen. 1:29–31), and the goodness of marriage and procreation (Gen. 1:28, 2:18–25). Paul's quoting of Genesis 1 and 2 can be seen as a *point-by-point* rebuttal of the dualistic proto-Gnostic creation story, which he calls "worldly fables fit for only old women" (NASB) in 1 Tim 4:7 (see Figure 4).

It is important to reread the sevenfold pronouncement of "good" in Chapter 1 of Genesis and notice how veganism and nonviolence, far from being demonic, are *in fact* foundational to the *final* pronouncement by God that all of creation is "very good":

1. "God saw that the light was good; and God separated the light from the darkness" (1:4).
2. "God called the dry land earth, and the gathering of the waters He called seas; and God saw that it was good" (1:10).
3. "The earth brought forth vegetation, plants yielding seed after their kind, and trees bearing fruit with seed in them, after their kind; and God saw that it was good" (1:12).
4. "God placed them in the expanse of the heavens to give light on the earth, and to govern the day and the night, and to separate the light from the darkness; and God saw that it was good" (1:17–18).
5. "God created the great sea monsters and every living creature that moves, with which the waters swarmed after their kind, and every winged bird after its kind; and God saw that it was good" (1:21).
6. "God made the beasts of the earth after their kind, and the cattle after their kind, and everything that creeps on the ground after its kind; and God saw that it was good" (1:25).
7. "God blessed them; and God said to them, 'Be fruitful and multiply, and fill the earth, and subdue it; and rule over the fish of the sea and over the birds of the sky and over every living thing that moves on the earth.' Then God said, 'Behold, I have given you every plant yielding seed that is on the surface of all the earth, and every tree which has fruit yielding seed; it shall be food for you; and to every beast of the earth and to every bird of the sky and to every thing that moves on the earth which has life, *I have given* every green plant for food'; and it was so. God saw all that He had made, and behold, it was very good. And there was evening and there was morning, the sixth day" (1:28–31, NASB).

The verses from 1 Timothy 4:4 we have been discussing would, therefore, appear to be best understood as highlighting how *God's creation*, which was so beautifully described in Genesis 1, should be received with thanksgiving by those who believe and know the truth, as it is God's gift to us and was pronounced good by his word.

JEWISH TRADITION AND FOOD

In this context, it is interesting to analyze how Jewish tradition has understood the blessing of food before meals. This may be closer to Paul's worldview compared to the Greco-Roman culture within which Christianity initially grew, and the other cultures it has been influenced by. In Jewish tradition, meat and fish, together with animal foods, come last in the list of foods to be blessed and do not receive a *specific* blessing over them but only a general one. They are not even mentioned by name and come last; in many ways, their blessing appears *concessionary* (Linzey & Cohn-Sherbock, 1997, pp. 56–58): This helps to show the limited place meat and fish have, at least *symbolically*, in Jewish tradition and what were considered the important "foods." On the contrary, plant-based foods of various kinds come first, and each category receives a specific blessing. If bread is eaten, this is blessed first and the blessing over it covers all foods except wine/grape juice. On Sabbaths and festivals, wine/grape juice is the first to be blessed. The order of blessing, *bracha*, when there is no bread is: (a) wine/grape juice, (b) baked grains, (c) tree fruits, (d) vegetables, and (e) all of the other foods, including meat and fish (Schwartz, 2001, pp. 10–11). It is especially important to read the texts of the various blessings to understand how Jewish tradition in the final blessing, the *Shehakol*—which simply means "by whose word all things come to be"—does not even directly bless, or mention, animal foods but merely blesses God generally as Creator, and for his Word:

> A) *Hamotzi*: The Blessing on Bread
> בָּרוּךְ אַתָּה יְ-יָ אֱ-לֹהֵינוּ מֶלֶךְ הָעוֹלָם הַמּוֹצִיא לֶחֶם מִן הָאָרֶץ:
> BA-RUCH A-TAH A-DO-NOI
> ELO-HAI-NU ME-LECH HA-O-LAM
> HA-MO-TZI LE-CHEM MIN HA-A-RETZ.
> Blessed are You, L-rd our G-d, King of the
> Universe, Who brings forth bread from the earth.
> B) *Mezonot*: The Blessing on the Five Grains
> בָּרוּךְ אַתָּה יְ-יָ אֱ-לֹהֵינוּ מֶלֶךְ הָעוֹלָם בּוֹרֵא מִינֵי מְזוֹנוֹת
> BA-RUCH A-TAH A-DO-NOI
> ELO-HAI-NU ME-LECH HA-O-LAM
> BO-RAI MI-NAI ME-ZO-NOT.
> Blessed are You, L-rd our G-d, King of the
> Universe, Who creates various kinds of sustenance.
> C) *Hagafen*: The Blessing on Wine and Grape Juice
> בָּרוּךְ אַתָּה יְ-יָ אֱ-לֹהֵינוּ מֶלֶךְ הָעוֹלָם בּוֹרֵא פְּרִי הַגָּפֶן
> BA-RUCH A-TAH A-DO-NOI
> ELO-HAI-NU ME-LECH HA-O-LAM
> BO-RAI PRI HA-GA-FEN.
> Blessed are You, L-rd our G-d, King of the
> Universe, Who creates the fruit of the vine.

D) *Ha'etz*: The Blessing on Fruits
בָּרוּךְ אַתָּה יְ-יָ אֱ-לֹהֵינוּ מֶלֶךְ הָעוֹלָם בּוֹרֵא פְּרִי הָעֵץ
BA-RUCH A-TAH A-DO-NOI
ELO-HAI-NU ME-LECH HA-O-LAM
BO-RAI PRI HA-AITZ.
Blessed are You, L-rd our G-d, King of the Universe, Who creates the fruit of the tree.

E) *Ha'adamah*: The Blessing on Vegetables
בָּרוּךְ אַתָּה יְ-יָ אֱ-לֹהֵינוּ מֶלֶךְ הָעוֹלָם בּוֹרֵא פְּרִי הָאֲדָמָה
BA-RUCH A-TAH A-DO-NOI
ELO-HAI-NU ME-LECH HA-O-LAM
BO-RAI PRI HA-A-DA-MAH.
Blessed are You, L-rd our G-d, King of the Universe, Who creates the fruit of the earth.

F) *Shehakol*: The Blessing on All Other Foods, including Meat and Fish
בָּרוּךְ אַתָּה יְ-יָ אֱ-לֹהֵינוּ מֶלֶךְ הָעוֹלָם שֶׁהַכֹּל נִהְיָה בִּדְבָרוֹ
BA-RUCH A-TAH A-DO-NOI
ELO-HAI-NU ME-LECH HA-O-LAM
SHE-HA-KOL NI-H'YAH BI-D'VA-RO.
Blessed are You, L-rd our G-d, King of the Universe, by Whose word all things came to be. (Chabad, 2018)

A DENIAL OF THE INCARNATION

Finally, it is also important to note that 1 Timothy 4 comes immediately after the end of 1 Timothy 3. Chapter *divisions* are not part of the Bible, and while often useful for reference purposes, here they end up obfuscating the passage. The verse directly before our chapter, 1 Timothy 3:16, underlines the *incarnation*, and the resurrection, as foundational to the gospel: "He appeared in the flesh, was vindicated by the Spirit, was seen by angels, was preached among the nations, was believed on in the world, was taken up in glory." This is in line with the Apostle John's condemnation of those who denied the incarnation:

> Dear friends, do not believe every spirit, but test the spirits to see whether they are from God, because many false prophets have gone out into the world. This is how you can recognize the Spirit of God: Every spirit that acknowledges that Jesus Christ has come in the flesh is from God, but every spirit that does not acknowledge Jesus is not from God. This is the spirit of the antichrist, which you have heard is coming and even now is already in the world. (1 Jn. 4:1–3, NIV)

In this sense, Paul in 1 Timothy 4:1–8 is simply continuing what he underlined in 1 Timothy 3:16: The faith that is "departed from" is the faith in the *incarnation, death, and resurrection* of Christ that he just highlighted, and which the proto-Gnostics strongly denied (2 John 7; see also Col. 1:22). In fact, one of the foundational hermeneutical principles of the early Church was the continuity between the Old and New Testament, and the God of creation and that of redemption: Christ is both the Creator-God and the

Savior-God; he is the Word that became flesh and dwelt among us (Col. 1:15–20; John 1:1–4, 14; Kasper, 1974/1977, p. 201).

It would appear, therefore, that *instead* of applying the apostolic and scriptural test for orthodoxy, namely the *incarnation* of Christ and belief in Jesus's death and resurrection, as John, Peter, and Paul underlined in their letters,[14] and for orthopraxy, that is, a life of true inner holiness and love (1 John 3:1–19; Gal. 5:6; 1 Cor. 13:13), many Christians and churches have created a *false dietary test* for orthodoxy. Belief in the incarnation of God in Christ and in the crucifixion and resurrection as the foundation of the gospel, and a life of authentic holiness, have been replaced by a legalistic and unbiblical dietary imposition that makes meat-eating the *hallmark* of a true Christian, a doctrine nowhere to be found in Scripture, and which denies Jesus's teaching (Mark 7:1–23; Matt. 15:20; Rom. 14:17; 1 Cor. 10:31).

CONCLUSIONS

In summary, in this article I have argued that 1 Timothy 4:1–8 is reiterating the teachings of the Hebrew Bible and of traditional Judaism about the goodness of God's creation, food, marriage, and the body. It does this within the framework of Genesis 1 and 2 and is also based on the incarnation and resurrection of Christ in the *body*, which definitively vindicated the goodness of creation, and of God. Furthermore, in these verses, Paul is condemning a *particularly harsh* form of asceticism regarding food and the body. Paul's condemnation of this form of dualistic asceticism in 1 Timothy 4 follows closely the same pattern used in Colossians 2 and 3: It juxtaposes severe bodily mortification and false humility with true inner holiness and love. This is also one of the reasons why Paul at the end of the letter talks about "God, who richly provides us with everything for our enjoyment" (1 Tim. 6:17), in contrast to the proto-Gnostics and their depreciation of the physical world. Moreover, Paul is not inventing some novel doctrine that Christians have to eat meat or animal foods in order to please God, but is underlining that *food*, in general, and creation—having been pronounced good—are to be received with thanksgiving.

Unfortunately, in the exegesis of 1 Timothy 4:1–8, the text has often been severed from its immediate context, the other Scriptures of the New Testament, the overarching biblical story that began in Genesis, a historical understanding of diet, and traditional concepts found within Judaism. In this distorted interpretation, Paul ends up condemning and contradicting the very Genesis account that he was strenuously defending. Paradoxically, in this view, Paul is cut off from the Hebrew Scriptures and is *himself* cast as a sort of Gnostic who believes that God's original perfection was demonic.

Jesus's mission was—and is—to restore the perfect world of Genesis 1 and 2 (Matt. 18:11; Luke 19:10). Moreover, death, killing, and predation are the result of sin in the Bible story (Linzey, 1998, pp. 32–39), and meat-eating is a reluctant concession made by God in Genesis 9 only after the Flood. Jesus himself considered Genesis 1 and 2 to be God's ideal world (Matt. 19:8), and we are told that one day God intends to restore it (Isa. 11:6–9; Rom. 8:19–23; Rev. 21–22). All this makes up the Bible story that has at its center the cosmic redemption—of humans, animals, and creation—purchased by Jesus's sacrifice on the cross: This is also the framework for the gospel message of which Paul was both a preacher and apostle (Col. 1:20; Eph. 1:10). Conversely, many interpretations of 1 Timothy 4:1–8 create a fracture in the Bible narrative and end up pitting the New Testament against the Old.

No doubt various factors have brought about what is a deeply distorted interpretation of 1 Timothy 4:1–8, including a general Church tradition and the development of Christianity in the West which, while deeply interesting, go beyond the scope of this article (see also Grumett & Muers, 2010, pp. 89–106). This interpretation has also been used more recently by forces within society that are seeking to make a case against the growing vegan movement. And yet the whole argument simply falls apart under greater scrutiny and creates stilted and legalistic doctrines that are contradicted by the rest of Scripture. This interpretation also misrepresents God and his character. God cares for the smallest sparrow (Luke 12:6), and he is merciful to both humans and animals: "The LORD is good to all; he has compassion on all he has made" (Pss. 36:6, 145:9). Furthermore, meat-eating is made into a *false* test for Christian orthodoxy and orthopraxy: a doctrine not found in Scripture, which upholds Jesus's incarnation, death, and resurrection, and authentic Christian holiness based on love, as the basis for both.

Contrary to what is often promoted, following a vegan diet is a choice that is perfectly in line with the Bible if a Christian is led by God to make it.[15] Paul talked about Christians abstaining from certain foods for the Lord (Rom. 14:1–5) and even affirmed that he would never eat meat again if necessary (1 Cor. 8:13). While it may not have always been possible for all believers throughout history, veganism still represents God's original blueprint for humanity, and new reasons for being vegan have arisen *strongly* in the late 20th and early 21st centuries. These range from human health, animal cruelty, and the environment to the use of resources, climate change, and world hunger, with many of these becoming more compelling by the day (Eshel & Martin, 2006; Poore & Nemecek, 2018; Regan, 2004; Springmann, et al., 2016).[16] But above all, veganism can be seen as a sign of hope for the restoration of God's creation, and a disruption of the history of death and violence of the world (1 Cor. 15:54–56). In this sense, it can help to create a horizon of expectation for the coming Kingdom of God, and the ultimate victory of Christ (Rev. 19–22; Moltmann, 1967, pp. 325–329).

It is sad and dumbfounding that God's ideal and future hope has been maligned to the point of being called "demonic" or "evil"; no doubt even this is part of the pain and mockery that Christ has to bear in his journey through history, and it is part of the cross that Christian vegans and vegetarians have had to faithfully carry with him. But, together with the Apostle Paul, we eagerly look forward to the coming resurrection of the body and the restoration of God's *good* creation beyond all death, violence, and suffering.

Notes

1. Tertullian laments, for example, that Marcion has ignored Paul's two letters to Timothy and his letter to Titus (*Adv. Marc.* 5.21). He appears to consider them part of the Christian canon

and does not dispute their authorship (Novenson, 2015, pp. 471–483). Furthermore, Tertullian condemns a certain presbyter for having compiled a spurious document called the "Acts of Paul," and he warns that such a practice was forbidden even if the writer had done it out of love for Paul:

> But if certain Acts of Paul, which are falsely so named, claim the example of Thecla for allowing women to teach and to baptize, let men know that in Asia the presbyter who compiled that document, thinking to add of his own to Paul's reputation, was found out, and though he professed he had done it for love of Paul, was deposed from his position. (*De bapt.* 17.5)

Tertullian also seems to have believed that the letters of the apostles were authentic and in *De Praescriptione* he underlines this with force:

> Go through the apostolic churches, where the very thrones of the apostles at this very day preside over their own districts, where their own genuine letters [authenticae litterae] are read, which speak their words and bring the presence of each before our minds. If Achaia is nearest to you, you have Corinth. If you are not far from Macedonia, you have Philippi. If you can travel into Asia, you have Ephesus. Or if you are near to Italy, you have Rome, where we too have an authority close at hand. (*Praesc.* 36.1–2)

In a similar way, Irenaeus denounced pseudonymous works that claimed to have been written by the apostles themselves. Irenaeus in his work *Against Heresies* (3.3.3; see also 2.14.7; Payton, 2017) also appears convinced of the Pauline authorship of 1 Timothy: "The blessed apostles, then, having founded and built up the Church, committed into the hands of Linus the office of the episcopate. Of this Linus, Paul makes mention in the Epistles to Timothy." Polycarp (69–155 AD), on the other hand, appears to allude to the Pastoral Epistles in his works and seems to consider them to be works of Paul, such as in his *Letter to the Philippians* (Berding, 1999).

2. A fairly early writing of 1 Timothy (second half of the first century) makes my case against an early form of proto-Gnosticism more credible, but my arguments do not depend on it. Later, and more developed, forms of Gnosticism—or different religious movements that followed a similar worldview like Manicheism—in the late second century all the way to the fifth, may have at times become milder in their asceticism and more organized than the early forms encountered by Paul. This is typical of new religious movements that often tend to mellow over time and seek the acceptance of the surrounding culture after the death of their charismatic founder; this is frequently followed by periods of reform and an attempt to return to the original teachings of the group (see also Morioka, 1979).

3. Their teachings seem to have little to no resemblance to traditional forms of Judaism and are often the complete opposite of the way these Scriptures were interpreted, with the addition of elaborate elements. One only needs to read a small amount of Gnostic literature to comprehend how foreign it is to Judaism, and the Hebrew Scriptures more generally. In particular, the early chapters of Genesis were often subjected to particularly elaborate and far-fetched interpretations by Gnostic groups; this has been confirmed by the discovery of the Nag Hammadi texts in the mid–20th century (Meyer, 2007, pp. 119–128, 199–221).

4. Colossians 2 seems to describe first a Jewish (probably Judeo-Gnostic) form of legalism and then to focus on a specific ascetic, primarily proto-Gnostic, variant of it. The letter to Titus, on the other hand, contains elements that recall the situation described in Colossians—and even in certain aspects in 1 Timothy—but seems to underline primarily a legalistic Jewish (together with circumcision) teaching that was not ascetic in nature. In this sense, there appears to be two main groups addressed in these three letters (Colossians, 1 Timothy, Titus): one is a Jewish or

perhaps Judeo-Gnostic group that insists on circumcision and other legal observances but that does not have strong ascetic elements, and the other is a dualistic proto-Gnostic group based upon severe mortification of the body.

5. While the Buddha seems to have initially practiced a severe form of asceticism, he eventually considered this unfruitful and chose a middle path of moderation and avoidance of extremes. Buddhism is in reality opposed to harsh forms of asceticism. Likewise, the philosopher Plato, while advocating for a certain temperance in food and drink, believed that a healthy body was important for a healthy mind and for citizens and never promoted this kind of harsh asceticism (Lopez, 2018; Plato, 2000, pp. 54–56).

6. In fact, Seventh-Day Adventist vegetarians and vegans are among some of the longest living people in the world. Vegan Seventh-Day Adventists, in particular, also tend to have low cancer, diabetes, and heart disease rates (Fraser, 2009, pp. 1607S–1612S; Fraser & Shavlik, 2001, pp. 1645–1652; Le & Sabaté, 2014; Tantamango-Bartley et al., 2013, pp. 286–294; Tonstad et al., 2013, pp. 292–299).

7. Plant-based diets were typical in Africa (Brock & Gordon 1959, p. 228; Shaper & Jones, 2012, pp. 1221–1222). Various populations in China also followed a plant-based diet where meat was eaten very rarely (Morse & Beh, 1937, pp. 966–968); the situation was similar in Okinawa, Japan (Willcox et al., 2007, p. 443). Likewise, Irish workers subsisted almost entirely on potatoes at the beginning of the 19th century (Crawford, 1987, p. 113).

8. Ascetics would follow very low-calorie diets. From the information we have, many seem to have been eating less than 1,000 calories per day. John Cassian describes an "exceptional" feast among ascetics in the desert in which around 1,000 calories were eaten, meaning that the daily calorie intake was probably lower. This very low-calorie intake was also effective in suppressing sexual desire, which disappears below a certain calorie intake (1,700–1,400 calories) and was one of the goals of the ascetics (Abbott, 2001, p. 101; Rousselle, 1983/1988, p. 166, pp. 174–178; see also Corrington, 1986). This is even more striking when we realize that the average man or woman needs roughly 2,000–2,500 calories per day for a moderately active lifestyle. In the famous Minnesota Starvation Trial (1944–1945), it was likewise found that a drastic reduction in calories and 25% loss of body weight over the course of 6 months brought about an almost complete elimination of sexual desire (Kalm & Semba, 2005, p. 1349). Proto-Gnostic asceticism most likely promoted similar very low-calorie intakes with the express goal of mortifying the body and annulling all sexual desire.

9. Rom. 14; Tit. 1:15; Col. 2:16.

10. Catherine of Siena, for example, suffered from a severe form of anorexia nervosa and spent years eating hardly anything (Rampling, 1985, pp. 89–94).

11. For an overview of severe food restriction, see Bemporad (1997).

12. This interpretation may have been influenced by the Aristotelian and Thomist traditions (Linzey & Cohn-Sherbock, 1997, pp. 6–8).

13. Gen. 9:2–4: The chapters leading up to this describe humanity's descent into violence and evil, and the consequent judgment which follows. The language used to describe God's giving of animals to the post-diluvian generation appears to be concessional and based on the low spiritual and moral condition humanity had sunken to. Richard Bauckham (2010a, pp. 23–26; 2010b, pp. 134–136) describes it as a sort of "holding operation" until humanity regained a greater spiritual condition. It may also have been based on a lack of plant food available at the time.

14. Paul highlights the gospel in 1 Corinthians 15:1–4 (RSV):

> Now I would remind you, brethren, in what terms I preached to you the gospel, which you received, in which you stand, by which you are saved, if you hold it fast—unless you believed in

vain. For I delivered to you as of first importance what I also received, that Christ died for our sins in accordance with the scriptures, that he was buried, that he was raised on the third day in accordance with the scriptures.

15. I understand that veganism encompasses more than just food and diet and seeks to eliminate the use and exploitation of animals for food, entertainment, clothing, and other purposes as far as practicable and possible. My focus here, though, is primarily on the dietary aspect of veganism (Vegan Society, 2019).

16. Plant-based diets also help to tackle the issues of antibiotic resistance, pandemics, and poor conditions for workers in factory farms and slaughterhouses (FAIRR, 2016).

References

Abbott, E. (2001). *A history of celibacy*. Cambridge, England: The Lutterworth Press.
Barker, K. (Ed.). (1995). *The NIV study Bible: 10th anniversary edition*. Grand Rapids, MI: Zondervan.
Barnstone, W., & Meyer, M. (Eds.). (2009) *The Gnostic Bible*. Boulder, CO: Shambhala.
Bauckham, R. (1988). Pseudo-apostolic letters. *Journal of Biblical Literature, 107*(3), 469–494. https://doi.org/10.2307/3267581
Bauckham, R. (1993). *The climax of prophecy*. Edinburgh, Scotland: T&T Clark Ltd.
Bauckham, R. (2010a). *Bible and ecology: Rediscovering the community of creation*. Longman and Todd Ltd.
Bauckham, R. (2010b). *The Bible in politics: How to read the Bible politically* (2nd ed.). London, England: SPCK.
Bell, R. M. (1985). *Holy anorexia*. Chicago, IL: University of Chicago Press.
Bemporad, J. R. (1996). Self-starvation through the ages: Reflections on the pre-history of anorexia nervosa. *International Journal of Eating Disorders, 19*(3), 217–237.
Bemporad, J. R. (1997). Cultural and historical aspects of eating disorders. *Theoretical Medicine, 18*(4), 401–420. https://doi.org/10.1023/A:1005721808534
Berding, K. (1999). Polycarp of Smyrna's view of the authorship of 1 and 2 Timothy. *Vigiliae Christianae, 53*(4), 349–360. https://doi.org/10.2307/1584486
Bible Hub. (2020a). *568 Apechó*. http://biblehub.com/greek/568.htm
Bible Hub. (2020b). *1033 Broma*. http://biblehub.com/str/greek/1033.htm
Bible Hub. (2020c). *2896 Towb*. http://biblehub.com/hebrew/2896.htm
Bible Hub. (2020d). *2907 Kreas*. http://biblehub.com/str/greek/2907.htm
Brock, J. F., & Gordon, H. (1959). Ischaemic heart disease in African populations. *Postgraduate Medical Journal, 35*(402), 223–232. https://doi.org/10.1136/pgmj.35.402.223
Brown, R. E., Fitzmyer, J. A., & Murphy, R. E. (1992). *The new Jerome Bible handbook*. London, England: Geoffrey Chapman.
Burkitt, D. P. (1973). Some diseases characteristic of modern Western civilization. *British Medical Journal, 1*(5848), 274–278. https://doi.org/10.1136/bmj.1.5848.274
Carr, K. E. (2017, September 1). *Roman food—rich and poor: Quatr.us study guides*. https://quatr.us/romans/roman-food-rich-poor.htm
Chabad. (2018, March 13). *Texts of blessings before eating*. https://www.chabad.org/library/article_cdo/aid/90551/jewish/Texts-of-Blessings-Before-Eating.htm
Child, L. M. (1855). *Progress of religious ideas, through successive ages* (4th ed., Vol. 2). New York, NY: James Miller.
Corrington, G. (1986). Anorexia, asceticism, and autonomy: Self-control as liberation and transcendence. *Journal of Feminist Studies in Religion, 2*(2), 51–61. https://www.jstor.org/stable/25002041

Crawford, E. M. (1987). Death rates from diabetes mellitus in Ireland 1833–1983: A historical commentary. *Ulster Medical Journal, 56*(2), 109–115.

Dell'Osso, L., Abelli, M., Carpita, B., Pini, S., Castellini, G., Carmassi, C., & Ricca, V. (2016). Historical evolution of the concept of anorexia nervosa and relationships with orthorexia nervosa, autism, and obsessive-compulsive spectrum. *Neuropsychiatric Disease and Treatment, 12*, 1651–1660. https://doi.org/10.2147/NDT.S108912

De Wet, C. L. (2019). John Chrysostom on Manichaeism. *HTS Theological Studies, 75*(1), 1–6. https://dx.doi.org/10.4102/hts.v75i1.5515

Dickens, S. H. (2000). Anorexia nervosa: Some connections with the religious attitude. *British Journal Of Medical Psychology, 73*, 67–76. https://doi.org/10.1348/000711200160309

Eshel, G., & Martin, P. A. (2006). Diet, energy, and global warming. *Earth Interactions, 10*, 1–17. https://doi.org/10.1175/EI167.1

FAIRR. (2016). *Factory farming: Assessing investment risks.* http://www.fairr.org/wp-content/uploads/FAIRR_Report_Factory_Farming_Assessing_Investment_Risks.pdf

Fraser, G. E. (2009). Vegetarian diets: What do we know of their effects on common chronic diseases? *American Journal of Clinical Nutrition, 89*(5), 1607S-1612S. https://doi.org/10.3945/ajcn.2009.26736K

Fraser, G. E., & Shavlik, D. J. (2001). Ten years of life: Is it a matter of choice? *Archives of Internal Medicine, 161*(13), 1645–1652. https://doi.org/10.1001/archinte.161.13.1645

Goodrick, E. W., & Kohlenberger J. R., III (1999). *The strongest NIV exhaustive concordance* (2nd ed.). Grand Rapids, MI: Zondervan.

Grandjean, A. C. (1997). Diets of elite athletes: Has the discipline of sports nutrition made an impact? *The Journal of Nutrition, 127*(5), 874S-877S. https://doi.org/10.1093/jn/127.5.874S

Griffin, J., & Berry, E. M. (2003). Modern day holy anorexia? Religious language in advertising and anorexia nervosa in the West. *European Journal of Clinical Nutrition, 57*, 43–51. https://doi.org/10.1038/sj.ejcn.1601511

Grumett, D., & Muers, R. (2010). *Theology on the menu: Asceticism, meat and Christian diet.* London, England: Routledge.

Guthrie, D. (1990). *The pastoral epistles: An introduction and commentary* (2nd ed.). Grand Rapids, MI: Eerdmanns. (Original work published 1957.)

Jonas, H. (2001). *The Gnostic religion: The message of the alien God and the beginnings of Christianity.* Boston, MA: Beacon Press. (Original work published 1958.)

Kalm, L. M., & Semba, R. D. (2005). They starved so that others be better fed: Remembering Ancel Keys and the Minnesota Experiment. *The Journal of Nutrition, 135*(6), 1347–1352. https://doi.org/10.1093/jn/135.6.1347

Kasper, W. (1977). *Jesus the Christ* (V. Green, Trans.; 2nd ed.). London, England: Burns and Oates Limited. (Original work published 1974.)

Kessler, D., & Temin, P. (2007). The organization of the grain trade in the early Roman empire. *Economic History Review, 60*(2), 313–332.

Klinker-De Klerck, M. (2008). The pastoral epistles: Authentic Pauline writings. *European Journal of Theology, 17*(2), 101–108.

Kroeger, R. C., & Kroeger, C. C. (1998). *I suffer not a woman: Rethinking 1 Timothy 2:11–15 in light of ancient evidence.* Ada, MI: Baker Books.

Le, L. T., & Sabaté, J. (2014). Beyond meatless, the health effects of vegan diets: Findings from the Adventist cohorts. *Nutrients, 6*(6), 2131–2147. https://doi.org/10.3390/nu6062131

Linzey, A. (1998). *Animal gospel: Christian faith as though animals mattered.* London, England: Hodder & Stoughton.

Linzey, A., & Cohn-Sherbock, D. (1997). *After Noah.* London, England: Mowbray.

Longo, U. G., Spiezia, F., Maffulli, N., & Denaro, V. (2008). The best athletes in ancient Rome were vegetarian! *Journal of Sports Science & Medicine, 7*(4), 565. https://doi.org/10.1093/jn/127.5.874S

Lopez, D. S. (2018, April 6). *Eightfold path: Buddhism*. https://www.britannica.com/topic/Eightfold-Path

McDougall, J. (2011, May). *The McDougall newsletter: The Egyptian mummy diet paradox*. https://www.drmcdougall.com/misc/2011nl/may/egyptian.htm

McDougall, J. (2012). *The starch solution*. Emmaus, PA: Rodale.

Metzger, B. M. (1972). Literary forgeries and canonical pseudepigrapha. *Journal of Biblical Literature, 91*(1), 3–24. https://doi.org/10.2307/3262916

Meyer, M. (Ed.). (2007). *The Nag Hammadi scriptures: The international edition*. San Francisco, CA: HarperOne.

Miller, M. N., & Pumariega, A. J. (2001). Culture and eating disorders: A historical and cross-cultural review. *Psychiatry, 64*(2), 93–110. https://doi.org/10.1521/psyc.64.2.93.18621

Moltmann, J. (1967). *Theology of hope* (J. W. Leitch, Trans.; 5th ed.). London, England: SCM Press. (Original work published 1965)

Moore, E., & Turner, J. (2000). Gnosticism. In L. Gerson (Ed.), *The Cambridge History of Philosophy in Late Antiquity* (pp. 174–196). Cambridge, England: Cambridge University Press.

Morioka, K. (1979). The institutionalization of a new religious movement. *Japanese Journal of Religious Studies, 6*(1/2), 239–280. www.jstor.org/stable/30233200

Morse, W. R., & Beh, Y. T. (1937). Blood pressure amongst aboriginal ethnic groups of Szechwan province, West China. *Lancet, 229*(5929), 966–968.

Mounce, W. D. (2011). *Mounce reverse-interlinear New Testament. 1 Timothy 4*. https://www.biblegateway.com/passage/?search=1+timothy+4&version=MOUNCE

Novenson, M. (2015). The Pauline epistles in Tertullian's Bible. *Scottish Journal of Theology, 68*(4), 471–483. https://doi.org/10.1017/S0036930615000253

Olson, R. (1999). *The story of Christian theology: Twenty centuries of tradition and reform*. Downers Grove, IL: InterVarsity Press.

Payton, J. R., Jr. (2017). Irenaeus, pseudonymity, and the pastoral letters. In A. Bastit & J. Verheyden (Eds.), *Irénée de Lyon et les débuts de la Bible chrétienne: Actes de la Journée du 1.VII.2014 à Lyon.* (pp. 273–282). Turnhout, Belgium: Brepols Publishers. https://doi.org/10.1484/M.IPM-EB.5.113500

Pearlman, M. (1935). *Through the Bible book by book, Part IV: Epistles and Revelation*. Springfield, MO: Gospel Publishing House.

Plato. (2000). *The Republic* (T. Griffith, Trans. & G. R. F. Ferrari, Ed.). Cambridge, England: Cambridge University Press.

Poore, J., & Nemecek, T. (2018). Reducing food's environmental impacts through producers and consumers. *Science, 360*(6392), 987–992. https://doi.org/10.1126/science.aaq0216

Rampling, D. (1985). Ascetic ideals and anorexia nervosa. *Journal of Psychiatric Research, 19*(2–3), 89–94. https://doi.org/10.1016/0022-3956(85)90003-2

Regan, T. (2004). *Empty cages: Facing the challenge of animal rights*. Lanham, MD: Rowman & Littlefield Publishers.

Richards, E. R. (2004). *Paul and first-century letter writing: Secretaries, composition and collection*. Downers Grove, IL: InterVarsity Press.

Rousselle, A. (1988). *Porneia: On desire and the body in antiquity* (F. Pheasant, Trans.; 2nd ed.). Eugene, OR: Wipf & Stock. (Original work published 1983.)

Schwartz, R. H. (2001). *Judaism and vegetarianism* (Rev. ed.). Brooklyn, NY: Lantern Books.

Shaper, A. G., & Jones, K. W. (2012). Serum-cholesterol, diet, and coronary heart-disease in Africans and Asians in Uganda. *International Journal of Epidemiology, 41*(5), 1221–1222. https://doi.org/10.1093/ije/dys137

Sorokin, P. A. (2002). *The ways and power of love: Types, factors, and techniques of moral transformation* (3rd ed.). West Conshohocken, PA: Templeton Foundation Press. (Original work published 1954.)

Springmann, M., Godfray, H. C. J., Rayner, M., & Scarborough, P. (2016). Analysis and valuation of the health and climate change cobenefits of dietary change. *PNAS, 113*(15), 4146–4151. https://doi.org/10.1073/pnas.1523119113

StudyLight. (2018, April 10). *Entry for Strong's 568.* https://www.studylight.org/lexicons/greek/568.html

Tantamango-Bartley, Y., Jaceldo-Siegl, K., Fan, J., & Fraser, G. (2013). Vegetarian diets and the incidence of cancer in a low-risk population. *Cancer epidemiology, biomarkers & prevention, 22*(2), 286–294. https://doi.org/10.1158/1055-9965.EPI-12-1060

The lives of the desert fathers: The historia monachorum in Aegypto (1980). (N. Russell, Trans.). Collegeville, MN: Cistercian Publications.

Tiessen, T. L. (2007). Gnosticism as heresy: The response of Irenaeus. *Didaskalia, 18*(1), 31–48.

Tonstad, S. K., Stewart, K. O., Batech, M., Herring, R. P., & Fraser, G. E. (2013). Vegetarian diets and incidence of diabetes in the Adventist Health Study-2. *Nutrition, Metabolism and Cardiovascular Diseases, 23*(4), 292–299. https://doi.org/10.1016/j.numecd.2011.07.004

Vegan Society. (2019). *Definition of veganism.* https://www.vegansociety.com/go-vegan/definition-veganism

Von Harnack, A., Cheyne, T. K., & Bruce, A. B. (Eds.). (1901). *History of dogma* (N. Buchanan, Trans.; 3rd ed., Vol. 1). New York, NY: Little, Brown, and Company.

Waddell, H. (1957). *The desert fathers: Translations from the Latin with an introduction.* Ann Arbor, MI: University of Michigan Press.

Willcox, B. J., Willcox, D. C., Todoriki, H., Fujiyoshi, A., Yano, K., He, Q., Curb, J. D., & Suzuki, M. (2007). Caloric restriction, the traditional Okinawan diet, and healthy aging. *Annals of the New York Academy of Sciences, 1114,* 434–455. https://doi.org/10.1196/annals.1396.037

On Imitating the Regimen of Immortality or Facing the Diet of Mortal Reality: A Brief History of Abstinence from Flesh-Eating in Christianity

CARL FRAYNE
The University of Chicago, Chicago, Illinois

Abstinence from meat has been a subject of much controversy and friction from the dawn of Christian history. Relatively widespread in the early Church, it was praised when it formed part of a temporary ascetic fasting regimen, but condemned if it amounted to a permanent rejection of animal flesh, as it would be associated with heretical ideas found in various dissident groups, gnostic sects, and pagan philosophical schools. Nevertheless, several patristic authors put forth a number of compelling arguments in defense of a meatless diet, all of which would be revisited by future generations of Christian thinkers. Laying the emphasis upon the ethical incentives for abstaining from animal flesh, as well as upon enduring ambivalent attitudes toward vegetarian dietary practices, this article offers a brief overview of abstinence from meat throughout Christian history.

Key words: history of vegetarianism, Christian ethics, abstinence from meat, asceticism, askesis, fasting, Edenic diet, heresy

And God said, "See, I have given you every herb *that* yields seed which *is* on the face of all the earth, and every tree whose fruit yields seed; to you it shall be for food. Also, to every beast of the earth, to every bird of the air, and to everything that creeps on the earth, in which *there is* life, *I have given* every green herb for food"; and it was so. Then God saw everything that he had made, and indeed *it was* very good.
—Genesis 1:29–31 (emphasis added)

Now the Spirit speaketh expressly, that in the latter times some shall depart from the faith, giving heed to seducing spirits, and doctrines of devils; speaking lies in hypocrisy; having their conscience seared with a hot iron; . . . commanding to abstain from meats, which God hath created to be received with thanksgiving of them which believe and know the truth. For every creature of God is good, and nothing to be refused, if it be received with thanksgiving.
—1 Timothy 4:1–4

On Imitating the Regimen of Immortality or Facing the Diet of Mortal Reality—Carl Tobias Frayne

The earliest records of vegetarian dietary practices in the Western world date back to classical antiquity. In ancient Greece, vegetarianism, or rather "abstinence from beings with a soul" (*apoche empsuchon*), was promoted by various philosophical schools, most notably the Pythagoreans. In fact, until modern times, it was not uncommon to talk about the "Pythagorean diet" to refer to vegetarianism.[1] Many Neoplatonists were also vegetarian, such as the third-century BC philosopher Porphyry of Tyre (1832), who wrote a seminal essay "On Abstinence from Animal Food" (*De Abstinentia ab Esu Animalium*) stating that "to deliver animals to be slaughtered and cooked, and thus be filled with murder, not for the sake of nutriment and satisfying the wants of nature, but making pleasure and gluttony the end of such conduct, is transcendently iniquitous and dire" (p. 113). However, following the gradual Christianization of the Roman Empire, occurrences of vegetarian dietary practices declined, to the point of practically disappearing from the map of medieval Christendom. It was not until the Renaissance that they resurfaced and then became increasingly more prevalent from the 19th century to the present day. Did the Church encourage or supress vegetarianism? What was the attitude of Christians toward abstinence from meat? Were there any influential vegetarians among the followers of Christ? In hopes of uncovering some of the complexity of the Church's relation to vegetarianism, this article will examine vegetarian practices and arguments for abstinence from meat in Christianity as well as the sects that see themselves as continuous with Christian history and mythology.

Tracing the history of vegetarianism is no easy task. On some level, it is bound to be an anachronistic investigation, as the term "vegetarian" made its first appearance in England only in the mid-19th century.[2] One could turn to the phrase "abstinence from meat" as a way of negatively defining vegetarianism, but may then run up against the historical equivocality of the term "meat." From the Old English *mete*, meat used to refer to any article of food and came to be used in today's narrower sense of "animal flesh used as food" only in the 14th century.[3] To further dissect our lexicon, let us also bear in mind that the term "animal" began to be widely used as "any living being" only in the 17th century (which may also make the phrase "animal flesh" ambiguous). In the vast majority of cases prior to modern times, the concept of a vegetarian diet amounted to abstinence from the flesh of specific animals, in particular mammals and birds. For the sake of clarity and simplicity, I shall nonetheless continue to use the terms "animal" and "meat" as well as "vegetarian" and its cognates throughout this article; these are to be understood in their modern sense, unless otherwise specified.

As far as I know, no brief yet comprehensive history of vegetarian dietary practices in Christianity has been written.[4] I shall endeavor to give an overview of this issue by looking at the Church's attitude toward vegetarianism throughout its history along with some of the arguments that have shaped Christian discourse on abstinence from meat. In order to narrow the wide scope of this study, I shall focus mostly upon Western Christianity, especially for the medieval and modern periods. I shall endeavor to show that although vegetarianism as a long-term lifestyle or a sustained diet has never been a conventional Christian practice, let alone an official Church doctrine, instances of temporary abstinence from animal flesh can nevertheless be found in various strands and branches of the Christian tradition and its many ramifications.

This article is divided into three main parts that simply follow the chronological order of Christian history. First, I shall look at vegetarian practices in the early Church and show that diet was a subject of great concern and controversy for early Christians. I shall stress ancient writers' ambivalent attitude toward vegetarianism and the fear of heresy. Second, I shall turn to the medieval period, during which ascetic dietary practices were sustained in monastic circles. Additionally, I shall argue that many saints showed great care for animals, but that it was heretical sects that despised animals which ended up abstaining from eating them. Finally, in surveying the modern era, I shall emphasize the fact that vegetarianism developed for the most part in Protestant traditions that put forth arguments that strongly echoed those of their predecessors from late antiquity.

THE EARLY CHURCH

Biblical Basis for Meat Eating

The question of diet constituted a central aspect of the construction of Christian identity from its earliest stages, as early Christians ceased to follow Jewish dietary restrictions. In the New Testament, the eating of animal flesh was presented as a direct command of the Holy Spirit. According to the Acts of the Apostles, St. Peter recounted:

> I was in the city of Joppa praying, and in a trance I saw a vision. I saw something like a large sheet being let down from heaven by its four corners, and it came down to where I was. I looked into it and saw four-footed animals of the earth, wild beasts, reptiles and birds. Then I heard a voice telling me, *"Get up, Peter. Kill and eat."* I replied, "Surely not, Lord! Nothing impure or unclean has ever entered my mouth." The voice spoke from heaven a second time, *"Do not call anything impure that God has made clean."* This happened three times, and then it was all pulled up to heaven again. (Acts 10:13–16; emphasis added)[5]

The message is clear: Followers of Christ were no longer required to abide by Jewish dietary laws; they could eat anything—no food was impure. Christians ought to be omnivorous, for "everything God created is good, and *nothing is to be rejected* if it is received with thanksgiving" (1 Tim. 4:4; emphasis added). This led many patristic authors, such as the Church Father Irenaeus of Lyon (1979, p. 354), to view vegetarianism as a form of repudiation of and ingratitude for God's creation, not unlike abstinence from marriage and sexual intercourse. Hence, complete and long-term vegetarianism was considered to be sinful: It is "out of pride," wrote the third-century Christian philosopher Hippolytus of Rome (1986), that vegetarians abstain from the flesh of animals.

It was thought the attitude the Christian should adopt toward the moral value of food was one of indifference (*adaiaphora*):[6]

> *Eat anything sold in the meat market without raising questions of conscience*, for, "The earth is the Lord's, and everything in it." If an unbeliever invites you to a meal and you want to go, *eat whatever is put before you without raising questions of conscience.* (1 Cor. 10:25–7; emphasis added)

One can discern some ambivalence in the Pauline epistles' teachings on abstinence from meat. Although they denounce vegetarianism as a diet for "weak" people, they also urge followers of Christ not to judge, but to tolerate, vegetarians:

> Accept the one whose faith is weak, without quarreling over disputable matters. One person's faith allows them to eat anything, but *another, whose faith is weak, eats only vegetables*. The one who eats everything must not treat with contempt the one who does not, and the one who does not eat everything must not judge the one who does, for God has accepted them.... *Whoever eats meat does so to the Lord, for they give thanks to God; and whoever abstains does so to the Lord and gives thanks to God.*... I am convinced, being fully persuaded in the Lord Jesus, that nothing is unclean in itself. But if anyone regards something as unclean, then for that person it is unclean. If your brother or sister is distressed because of what you eat, you are no longer acting in love. *Do not by your eating destroy someone for whom Christ died*. (Rom. 14:1–15; emphasis added)[7]

A few lines below, abstinence from meat is described as being morally uplifting: "Let us therefore make every effort to do what leads to peace and to mutual edification. ... *It is better not to eat meat* or drink wine or to do anything else that will cause your brother or sister to fall" (Rom. 14:19–21; emphasis added).

Thus, the teachings on abstinence from meat found in the Pauline epistles are somewhat equivocal. As we shall see, the call for respect for the dietary choices of one's neighbor has resonated rather faintly in Christian history when considered in its entirety. Those who professed ethical vegetarianism were more often the subjects of persecution than toleration. From its earliest years, the Church looked askance at vegetarians and commonly viewed them as a threat to be eradicated. Significantly, however, some Christian individuals heeded St. Paul's recommendation to refrain from the consumption of animal flesh as a way to foster spiritual flourishing.

Total Abstinence as Heresy

At the end of the second century, total and long-term abstinence from meat was generally considered to be a heretical practice closely associated with deviant groups and individuals, such as the second-century Christian bishop Marcion and the theologian Tatian, or more generally those known as "Encratites."[8] Several religious groups, such as the Jewish-Christian Ebionites, the quasignostic Priscillianists, and other heretical Christian sects (e.g., Montanism[9]), made their followers adopt a strict vegetarian diet.[10] For example, in a second-century noncanonical gospel known as the Gospel of the Ebonies, Jesus and John the Baptist are portrayed as vegetarians. According to this gospel (Epiphanius, 1908, pp. 16–18), Jesus rejects the Passover meal saying: "I have no desire to eat the flesh of this Paschal lamb with you."

Another gnostic sect whose adherents endorsed strict forms of vegetarianism was Manicheanism, which originated in the third century. St. Augustine, once a keen supporter of the sect, became an adamant detractor. Manicheans were radical dualists who believed in a cosmic struggle between a good, spiritual world of light and an evil, material world of darkness. The Manicheans' goal was to remove themselves from the world of matter in order to become pure spirit. In his *Codex Manichaicus Coloniensis*, Mani, the founder of the cult, wrote: "All defilement is from the body." Copulation was seen as evil, as it basically ensured the propagation of matter. The consumption of meat—or dead flesh, the result of copulation—was thus considered to be an impediment to spiritual liberation.[11] As Colin Spencer (1993) explained: "Matter is evil, all flesh derives from the realm of darkness and the partaking of flesh will weigh the spirit down, so that it can no longer fly to God. Eat meat and you will trap the spirit in more flesh" (p. 144). Not all Manicheans, however, were required to abide by the stringent rules of the sect. They were divided into two main groups: the Elect and the Hearers. Only the former had to follow the rigorous Manichean way of life, which included a strict vegetarian diet. The latter, on the other hand, were allowed to eat fish. Augustine, who was a Hearer for a decade, wrote about the Elect group in his treatise *De Haeresibus*:

> *They do not eat meat* ... on the grounds that the divine substance has fled from the dead or slain bodies, and what little remains there is of such quality and quantity that it does not merit being purified in the stomach of the Elect. *They do not even eat eggs*, claiming that they too die when they are broken and it is not fitting to feed on any dead body; only that portion of flesh can live which is picked up by flour to prevent its death. Moreover, *they do not use milk for food* although it is drawn or milked from the live body of an animal. (46; emphasis added)[12]

After converting to the Christian faith, Augustine repudiated his former Manichean beliefs and vehemently lambasted the Manichean practices that he came to view as contrary to the spirit of Christianity; this included dietary practices. In his *Contra Faustum* (1887), a polemical work against the Manichean bishop Faustus of Mileve, Augustine wrote: "Christians, not heretics, but Catholics, in order to subdue the body, that the soul may be more humbled in prayer, abstain not only from animal food, but also from some vegetable productions, without, however, believing them to be unclean" (XXX, 5).

In defense of the claim that no food is unclean, Augustine referred to the First Epistle to Timothy several times. The passage is worth citing in full as its influence upon Christian thought on vegetarianism cannot be overemphasized:

> The Spirit clearly says that in later times some will abandon the faith and follow *deceiving spirits and things taught by demons*. Such teachings come through hypocritical liars, whose consciences have been seared as with a hot iron. They forbid people to marry and order them *to abstain from certain foods, which God created to be received with thanksgiving* by those who believe and who know the truth. (1 Tim. 4:1–3; emphasis added)

This is what led Augustine to repeatedly speak out against dietary restrictions of all kinds and to write that abstinence from meat is "clearly against faith and holy doctrine."[13]

In short, in the early Church, abstinence from flesh eating was often seen as a dangerous form of deviance from Christian doctrines, closely linked to blasphemous ideas found in gnostic sects and pagan philosophical schools. Strict and long-term vegetarians were among those who "abandon the faith and follow deceiving spirits and things taught by demons" (1 Tim. 4:1–3). Ungrateful and prideful, they were portrayed as unfaithful to the goodness of God's creation.

Temporary Vegetarianism as Ascetic Practice

Following St. Paul's advice in his Epistle to the Romans, various early Christian writers spoke in favor of abstinence from meat as a form of temperance (*sophrosyne*) best suited to the life of faith. Some of the Apostles and disciples of Christ have been depicted as vegetarians. One of the earliest examples of this can be found in the *Clementine Homilies* (1886) a second-century text purportedly based upon the teachings of St. Peter. It argued that "the unnatural eating of meats is as polluting as the heathen worship of devils, with its sacrifices and its impure fears, through participation in it a man becomes a fellow eater with devils" (Homily XII). In a similar fashion, in the second and third century, Church Father Clement of Alexandria (1960) said that "the apostle Matthew partook of seeds, nuts and vegetables, without flesh" (2.1,16).[14] Clement also referred to meals shared between Christians as *agapes*, or "love feasts," which "should not include the smell of roasting meat" (Leyerle, 1995, p. 153). Furthermore, he offered one of the earliest ascetic readings of John the Baptist's diet.[15] He wrote that he ate locusts and wild honey (*akrides kai meli agrion*) and that his diet was "without flesh" (*anei kreon*; Clement, 1960, 2.11).[16]

Early accounts of John the Baptist being vegetarian can also be found in various non-canonical texts from as early as the second century. Two textual sources that I mentioned above in passing, namely the *Gospel of the Ebionites* and perhaps Tatian's *Diatessaron*, deny that John ate locusts.[17] For the fourth-century patristic author Epiphanius (1902, 30.13.4–5; *Haeres*, XXX 13), the aforementioned gospel claims that John ate only wild honey, which tasted like "manna" and like "cakes in olive oil." According to several commentators, Tatian's *Diatessaron* purportedly stated that his food consisted of "milk and mountain honey."[18] Other interpreters sought to prove that John's locusts were in fact vegetables, such as Athanasius of Alexandria, the third-century patristic author, and Desert Father Isidore of Pelusium from the fourth and fifth centuries.[19] These interpretations of John the Baptist's diet are significant because, as the fourth- and fifth-century Doctor of the Church and Bible translator Jerome observed, lay Christians and monks had sought to imitate his dietary practices (*Adversus Jovinianum*, 2.15). Indeed, his diet came to be seen as forming part of the training (*paideia*) for aspirant ascetics. Clement (1960, 2.11) described it as "sweet and with spiritual significance," and Isidore (*Epistulae*, 1.132) wrote that it "demonstrated exceeding suffering, not in poverty only, but also in ruggedness, by embittering every yearning of the body."

Several other early authors regarded meat abstinence as a fruitful askesis. The prolific second- and third-century writer Tertullian of Carthage (1980) argued that man's original sin was that of gluttony. Consequently, he claimed that fasting was to be seen as the compensation for Original Sin. He also noted that man's prelapsarian diet in Eden was vegan, just as that of other animals.[20] As stated explicitly in Genesis:

Then God said, "*I give you every seed-bearing plant on the face of the whole earth and every tree that has fruit with seed in it. They will be yours for food.* And to all the beasts of the earth and all the birds in the sky and all the creatures that move along the ground—everything that has the breath of life in it—I give every green plant for food." And it was so. (1:21–30; emphasis added)

It was only after the Flood that God gave humans "*everything*," just as they were first given "green plants."[21] Interestingly, Tertullian (1980, 3–4) interpreted this dietary relaxation as implying a stricter form of abstinence. As we shall see, his reading would influence future ascetic practices.

Fasting, which consisted mainly in sustaining a frugal meatless diet, was an integral part of the ascetic, modest, and humble life that early Christians sought to lead. The fourth-century Doctor of the Church Basil of Caesarea (1970) contended that it was "the law of fasting and abstinence (*enkrateia*)" that was first commanded to Adam and Eve in Eden; namely the command not to eat from the tree of knowledge of good and evil (Tertullian, 1980, I.3).[22] Hence, fasting, in his view, was "the image of the way of life in paradise" (Tertullian, 1980, I.3). Indeed, following Tertullian, he stressed that before the Flood in paradise "there was . . . not yet meat eating" (Tertullian, 1980, I.5). Although Basil contended that the humans' omnivorous diet was a "consolation for the loss of paradise" in a postdiluvian age, he also urged Christians to repudiate unnecessary foods and to live in imitation of the humans' original home wherein Adam and Eve lived on a strict vegetarian diet.[23] Moreover, he praised fasting for being conducive to physical and spiritual health for *all* Christians. Fasting, he argued, promoted the health of the body and assisted in the formation of the "harmonious repose" necessary for prayer (Basil, 1970, I.2.9). Basil allegedly recited the following prayer: "The earth is the Lord's and the fullness thereof. O God, enlarge within us the sense of fellowship with all living things, our brothers the animals to whom Thou gavest the earth as their home in common with us."[24]

Jerome followed Basil in arguing that humankind's original diet was vegan, that refraining from eating from the tree of knowledge was akin to fasting, and that fasting promoted physical and spiritual strength (*Epistulae*, 22.10). He supposedly wrote:

> *The eating of meat was unknown up to the big flood*, but since the flood they have the strings and stinking juices of animal meat into our mouths, just as they threw in front of the grumbling sensual people in the desert. Jesus Christ, who appeared when the time had been fulfilled, has again joined the end with the beginning, so that *it is no longer allowed for us to eat animal meat.*[25]

However, Jerome departed from Basil in making fasting a perfectionist askesis for a religious elite only (*Adversus Jovinianum*, 393). Yet, it is significant that for both theologians, strict vegetarianism was the Edenic and angelic diet, which we should strive to emulate in this fallen earthly existence.

From late antiquity until the Middle Ages, Christians were required to fast at various times throughout the year. Lent, the 40-day period prior to Easter, constituted the longest fasting period. In addition, Christians fasted about 30 days during Advent as well as on Wednesdays and Fridays. Finally, fasts were also common during vigils, prior to important festivals, and during the Ember days marking the changing of the "seasons."[26] This could potentially amount to up to approximately 150 fasting days per year. That said, it must be borne in mind that fasting practices varied greatly between traditions and across time and place. For example, the French historian Bruno Laurioux (2002, pp. 107–109) calculated that there were 96 fast days (*jours maigres*) in the diocese of Cambrai in northern France in the year 1413. Monks in the medieval era, on the other hand, were required to follow a stricter regimen. According to Spencer (1993, p. 177), some monks would fast for two thirds of the year.

It is interesting to note that fasting during Lent originally consisted of a strict vegetarian or vegan diet. It is only in the eighth century that dietary restrictions were reduced to abstinence from meat alone, albeit fish was tolerated.[27] Jerome (*Epistulae*, CVII, 10), for instance, allowed the consumption of fish provided that it remained occasional. As a result, fish gradually became the Lenten food par excellence. This raised the concern that it may have undermined the ascetic nature of the fast. For instance, in a fifth-century treatise on the contemplative life, the priest Julianus Pomerius (*De vita contemplativa*, II) expressed his worry vis-à-vis the overindulgence of fish, which he considered to be in opposition to the spirit of Lent.

That abstinence from meat was not the result of regard for animal well-being, but an ascetic practice tout court, is made clear by the fact that the Church sought to make sure that its members did not have a permanent aversion to meat and actually enjoyed it; for abstinence could not otherwise have fulfilled its mortifying and penitentiary purpose. If religious devotees abstained from meat for any other reason than asceticism, they were likely to incur severe punishments. As the council of Ancyra that took place in 314 clearly stated:

> It is decreed that among the clergy, presbyters and deacons who abstain from flesh shall taste of it, and afterwards, if they shall so please, may abstain. *But if they disdain it, and will not even eat herbs served with flesh, but disobey the canon, let them be removed from their order* (Canon 14).

In the same vein, in 447, the second council of Toledo declared: "If anyone believes he must abstain from the flesh of birds and beasts which is given us for nourishment; and does so not in a spirit of bodily mortification but out of disgust, *let him be anathema*."[28] Thus, those who sought to sustain a long-term vegetarian diet would have exposed themselves to no less than one of the gravest sentences for the Christian believer: excommunication.

In sum, early Christian attitudes toward abstinence from meat were ambivalent. Teresa Shaw (2008) provided a concise summary of the state of vegetarianism in the early Church:

> A vegetarian diet is praised, though usually as part of a limited fasting regimen, for its spiritual and health benefits and as an "imitation" of the diet of paradise or angelic regimen. . . . Otherwise, it is a suspect practice associated with the worst long-standing heretical tendencies. (p. 86)[29]

To put it in a nutshell, temporary ascetic abstinence was praised and encouraged, and long-term vegetarianism was shunned and condemned.

MEDIEVAL CHRISTIANITY

Saintly Compassionate Meat Eaters and Heretical Ascetic Vegetarians

One can find a significant number of instances of concern for and kindness toward animals in the medieval Church. In fact, many devout Christians were canonized as a result of their pious attitude toward their fellow creatures. This is what led Stephen H. Webb (2001) to write that "one of the criteria for sainthood seems to be the compassionate treatment of animals"(p. 29). This may not be far from the truth since, according to Andrew Linzey (1989), more than two thirds of the medieval saints demonstrated "a practical concern for, and befriending of, animals." Even earlier, in the fourth century, St. John Chrysostom wrote:

> The Saints are exceedingly loving and gentle to mankind, and even to brute beasts ... Surely we ought to show [animals] great kindness and gentleness for many reasons, but, above all, because they are of the same origin as ourselves. (As cited in Walters & Portmess, 2001, p. 123)[30]

Myths and legends about saints' special and intimate relationship with animals in the Middle Ages abound. A couple of examples of such stories, which most of us would now consider quaint, will suffice. In the seventh century St. Giles, who lived as a hermit in a French forest, was said to have befriended a deer. One day, King Flavius went out hunting and shot an arrow at the deer. St. Giles interposed himself and had his chest pierced by the king's arrow. He then declined medical treatment worrying about nothing but protecting his deer friend (Roberts, 2004, p. 186).

Legend has it, the famous 11th-century theologian St. Anselm had just been made archbishop of Canterbury when he saw a group of men hunting a hare with their dogs. Anselm felt compassion for the innocent creature; he intervened and prevented the dogs from harming it. The dogs then starting licking the hare in a friendly manner. The men, however, eventually caught the hare, which caused St. Anselm to weep bitterly (Roberts, 2004, p. 205).

It is not only in myths and legends that saints showed great concern for animal welfare. In the 13th century the English bishop St. Richard of Wyche expressed great sympathy toward animals led to slaughter: "Poor innocent little creatures, if you were reasoning beings and could speak, you would curse us. For we are the cause of your death, and what have you done to deserve it?" (as cited in Butler, 1956, p. 24).[31] Yet the most eminent example that comes to mind is of course St. Francis of Assisi, whose celebrated 13th-century *Canticle of the Creatures* reminds us of the psalmic exhortation to "Let everything that has breath praise the LORD" (Psalm 150:6). He is believed to have said: "All things of creation are children of the Father and thus brothers of man.... God wants us to help animals, if they need help. Every creature in distress has the same right to be protected" (as cited in Murti, 2003, p. 100).[32]

Finally, some saints believed that animals were spiritual and moral creatures. St. Anthony of Padua, one of St. Francis's best-known followers, delivered a sermon in which he claimed fishes adored God and praised God better than unbelievers: "Blessed be eternal God, for the fishes of the sea honor him more than men without faith, and animals without reason listen to his word with greater attention than sinful heretics" (as cited in Peters, 1980, p. 181). Another Franciscan, the 15th-century missionary Bernadino of Siena Some, claimed that animals were not only moral creatures but that they could also be more virtuous than some humans. He declared:

> Look at the pigs who have so much compassion for each other that when one of them squeals, the others will run to help him. . . . And your children who steal the baby swallows. What do other swallows do? They all gather together to try to help the fledglings. . . . Man is more evil than the birds." (As cited in Fox, 1989, p. 3)

Despite instances of regard for the welfare of animals and benevolent attitudes toward them, there is little evidence that Christians denounced animal slaughter or embraced ethical vegetarianism. Notwithstanding his apparent kinship with animals, it is unlikely that St. Francis was vegetarian, since neither Bonaventure nor Celano, his early biographers, made mention of his following a special diet. Celano (1983) portrayed St. Francis as displaying "great tenderness towards lower and irrational creatures" (p. 228) and Bonaventure (1978) told us that he called "creatures, no matter how small, by the name of brother or sister" (p. 153). However, this did not seem to have prevented these "brothers" and "sisters" to occasionally end up on his plate. The same applied to his followers; for no passage in the Rule of Saint Francis suggested that Franciscans were encouraged, let alone required, to abstain from meat. In fact, in compliance with orthodox Church doctrine and the traditional Catholic view, it specified that "according to the Holy Gospel [the brothers] can eat whatever food is set before them" (*Rule of St. Francis of Assisi*, III).[33]

Besides the saints, the medieval Catholic view of "the animal" was by and large a resource to be exploited. The 13th-century theologian and Doctor of the Church Thomas Aquinas (himself also a saint) was by all accounts one of the most influential Catholic thinkers. He represented a much commoner view of animals in the Middle Ages than that of the aforementioned saints. That God intended for animals to be used as means to human ends, such as food, was clear in St. Thomas's mind:

> *All animals are for man*. Whereof, it is not unlawful if men use . . . animals for the good of man. . . . This cannot be done unless [animals] are deprived of life . . . this is in keeping with the commandment of God Himself. (*Aquinas*, 1922, II.I. q. 159, art. 2; emphasis added)

St. Thomas went even further and argued that humans could treat animals in whatever way they saw fit. In his view, one could not commit a sin against an animal because humans had complete dominion over all of creation: "It matters not how man behaves to animals because God has subjected all things to man's power" (*Aquinas*, 1922, II.I. q. 102, art. 6). Unsurprisingly, St. Thomas was not a vegetarian. As a matter of fact, he asserted that chicken was of aquatic origin and hence could be eaten on fast days along with fish.

The main religious groups that adopted a vegetarian diet in the medieval period were considered to be heretics. In Western Christendom, Catharism,[34] which developed from the 11th century in northern Italy and flourished in southern France until the 13th century, was a prominent example of one of these groups.³⁵ Though it would be an anachronistic stretch to call them Manicheans of the Middle Ages, the similarities between the two groups were significant. Not unlike the Manichean distinction between the Elect and the Hearers, the Cathars were divided into *perfecti* and *credentes*. The former were required to follow much stricter rules, including dietary ones. Whilst the perfecti abstained from all animal products except fish, the credentes were allowed to consume animal flesh. As in early gnostic sects, Cathar abstinence from meat was purely ascetic in nature. It resulted not from a concern for animal welfare but from a repulsion with the material world and with sex as the affirmation and propagation of matter. Cathars despised all flesh, be it dead flesh meant for human consumption or the creation of new living beings.³⁶ In the 12th century, the German Benedictine Abbot Eckbert of Schönau listed a number of Cathar doctrines that were condemned by the Church:

> The second heresy: avoiding meat. *Those who have become full members of their sect avoid all meat . . .* they say that meat must be avoided because all flesh is born of coition, and therefore they think it unclean.
>
> The third heresy: the creation of flesh. That is the reason they give in public. Privately they have an even worse one, that *all flesh is made by the devil*, and must therefore not be eaten even in the direst necessity. (As cited in Moore, 1975, p. 22; emphasis added)

Anselm referred to a Cathar community that was discovered between 1043 and 1048 by a French bishop who wrote to him seeking advice as to how to deal with followers of Manichean's teachings who "abhor marriage, shun the eating of meat, and believe it profane to kill animals" (as cited in Moore, 1975, p. 22). Though Anselm's reply was that one should show understanding vis-à-vis those matters, the sentence was oftentimes much more severe. In 1052, a group of Cathars was brought before the Roman Emperor and German King Henry III, and the following occurred:

> Among other wicked Manichean doctrine (which had by now become a term of abuse for any heresy) they condemned all eating of animals, and with the agreement of everybody present, [the emperor] ordered them to be hanged, to prevent the disease of their heresy from spreading widely and infecting more people. (Spencer, 1993, p. 163)

With the rise of the Inquisition in the 12th century, the Cathars were totally annihilated by the early 14th century.

In summation, the relationship between Christians and animals in the medieval period thus developed in a way that may seem counterintuitive, even contradictory, to many of us today. Orthodox Christians seemed to have displayed much greater concern for the well-being of animals than the heretical Cathars who loathed them. The irony is that the former continued dining on them with no apparent qualms of conscience, whereas the latter (or at least some of them) abstained from almost all animal foods. To put it briefly and bluntly, it seems that in the medieval period, animals were more likely to be butchered by a compassionate Catholic than a disdainful heretic.³⁷

Monastic Abstinence

The only place in which Christian vegetarianism survived in the Middle Ages was in monasteries and nunneries. Vegetarianism was present in Christian monasticism from its earliest development. Pioneering the eremitic life, the third-century Desert Father St. Antony the Great was a strict vegetarian. According to the patristic writer Athanasius of Alexandria (1976), his source of sustenance consisted of little more than "bread and salt" (p. 72). What is more, he made explicit that his vegetarian diet was far from being unique or uncommon among Christian devotees; he wrote that "of meat and wine it is needless to speak, for nothing of this sort was to be found among the other monks either" (Roberts, 2004, p. 81). This suggests that other Desert Fathers and Mothers followed a vegetarian diet. Their ascetic way of life was to be a source of inspiration for future monastic orders.

The most influential extant monastic rule to have been written down is that of the fifth-century abbot St. Benedict of Nursia. The Rule of St. Benedict commanded monks to "abstain altogether from eating the flesh of four-footed animals" with the exception of "the very weak" (Chapter 39). Some monastic orders followed an even stricter vegetarian diet. This was the case for the Culdeans, an Irish and Scottish fifth-century monastic order whose food consisted of "cooked vegetables, seasoned only with salt. Never did they eat flesh or fish, nor did they permit cheese and butter, except on Sundays and feast days" (as cited in Boas, 1997, p. 115).[38] This last statement showed that meat was a divine gift that was to be treasured, not the flesh of an animal that was to be cherished. Moreover, as in the Rule of St. Benedict, the "infirm or those bowed down by age, or wearied by a long journey, were given the *pleasure* to [consume animal flesh]" (as cited in Boas, 1997, p. 115; emphasis added). It may be inferred from these rules that eating meat was considered to sustain and promote physical health.

It is therefore clear that, for the majority of medieval monks, the goal was never to spare animal lives or to alleviate nonhuman suffering, but rather to find a balance between the observance of an omnivorous diet and cultivating self-discipline, or, as St. Paul put it, "Striking a blow to [our] body and make it [our] slave" (1 Cor. 9:27). In other words, just as early Christian authorities argued, monks should have sought to enjoy all foods as gifts of God whose permanent rejection would be a mark of pride, yet from which they also ought to abstain in order to discipline their body. As the 12th-century founder of the Cistercian order, Bernard of Clairvaux (1870), stated in one of his sermons:

> *I am wary of this qualm towards meats.* . . . If you observe here a rule prescribed by sober persons, by spiritual doctors, we shall approve the virtue which leads you to tame the flesh and enchain the passions. But if, heir of the insanity of the Manicheans, you impose boundaries to God's magnanimity, if you reject with ingratitude that which He has created, that which He gave us to serve as food, even if, by an audacious censure, you declare it vile, and if you abstain from it as a bad thing; far from praising you abstinence, *I shall loathe your mischief and blasphemy, and I shall call you yourself vile*. . . . *Woe to you who reject meats created by God*, deeming them sullied and unworthy to enter your body . . . this is why the body of Jesus Christ, the Church, reject you as impure and vile beings. (Sermon LXVI; emphasis added)

This passage strongly echoed some of Bernard's predecessors from the ancient world. Indeed, it could have easily been written 10 centuries earlier. It is worth noting that Bernard of Clairvaux was a vegetarian himself. Like many monastic orders, Cistercians followed the Rule of St. Benedict, but they sustained an even stricter diet. As their *Constitution* (C. 28), read: "In accordance with tradition the brothers abstain from meat at all times, except in case of necessity"; for this will "arouse spiritual desire in the heart of a monk and let him share in Christ's pity for the hungry" (as cited in Preece, 2008, p. 129). Once more, pity appeared to be toward humans only. There does not seem to be any spiritual desire to value animals' lives for their own sake. Abstinence from flesh was about acquiring virtue for humans, not cultivating mercy for animals.

In conclusion, with the exception of monks and nuns as well as holy men and women, long-term vegetarianism seems to have been almost nonexistent in medieval Catholic Europe. Although it must be borne in mind that meat would have been relatively scarce for the medieval peasant and consumed only on feast days and other special occasions, these quasivegetarian diets were the result of social circumstance rather than ethical choice. Hence, when it comes to instances of vegetarianism in the Middle Ages, one must turn to heretical sects, such as the Cathars. Yet the Cathars were by no means the only heretical vegetarians in those days. In fact, several other heretical sects abstained from meat, such as the Bogomils.[39] As the Irish historian Robert I. Moore (1985, p. 158) argued, "[Vegetarianism] was preached not only by Cathars but by other religions which opposed Catholic orthodoxy in this period." As we shall now see, Catholics in the modern period kept on shunning vegetarianism.

THE MODERN CHRISTIAN ERA

Catholicism: Enduring Suspicion

Observance of fasting practices among Catholics has decreased significantly since medieval times. This is illustrated by the gradual relaxation of Lenten dietary restrictions. In 1707 Fénelon, the then archbishop of Cambrai, lamented the fact that the faithful no longer followed fasting practices as rigorously as they used to: "This discipline which was so austere and practiced with such fervour during Antiquity is but the shadow of what it once was" (Fénelon, 1713, p. 60). Fasting norms became gradually looser to the point of being almost obsolete. In 1949, Catholics were required to abstain from meat only two days per year—on Ash Wednesday and Good Friday. Although it is still customary in traditionally Catholic countries to eat fish on Fridays, this practice is but a mere remnant of the stringent dietary regulations of former times, during which one could be imprisoned, or even condemned to death, for breaking dietary laws.[40] With the exception of some monastic orders, Lenten observance of abstinence from meat and other fasting practices are moribund, not to say extinct, in the Western Catholic Church.

Suspicion toward complete and long-term abstinence from animal flesh remained prevalent in Catholic countries after the Renaissance. In 1702, the French theologian

Lebrun listed vegetarianism as a superstitious practice in his *Critical History of Superstitious Practices*. Some rare Catholics lamented the pain inflicted upon animals and declared wanting to adopt a vegetarian diet. For example, in 1735, the Marquis of St. Aubin, Gilbert-Charles Legendre, wrote that he was sometimes "filled with remorse of humanity before the torments that we inflict upon beasts" (p. 272). Notwithstanding, he quickly qualified his statement and argued that vegetarianism was a vicious practice contrary to the divine word. The adoption of a vegetarian diet was, more often than not, considered to be an antireligious act in various Catholic countries.[41] Although the Church has expressed greater concern toward the environment in recent decades and now urges its members to respect, protect, and care for animals along with the rest of creation, these exhortations do not seem to ever translate into a concrete change in diet.[42] It seems that the Catholic Church has remained wary of vegetarianism to this day.

We can nonetheless identify a small number of Christian groups promoting vegetarianism that branched out from Catholicism. For example, the early 20th-century Liberal Catholic Church supported and recommended vegetarianism. In fact, most of the members of its clergy are vegetarian.[43] In a 1972 French conference on vegetarianism and Christianity, Monsignor Lhote, a member of the Liberal Catholic Church, described abstinence from animal flesh not only as an ascetic practice, but rather as a condition for the perfect life to which Christ called upon humankind: "On the path to perfection, we do not consider abstinence from meat as penitence ... but we consider this abstinence as a technical necessity for the purification of feelings, of emotions, and of desires."[44] The Universal Catholic Church (*Église Catholique Universelle*) emerged in France in 1980 as a result of a schism with the Liberal Catholic Church. Its founder, Monsignor Maurice Chardine, was an affiliate of the *Alliance Végétarienne*, the first vegetarian society in France.[45] A staunch proponent of a meatless diet, he declared:

> *Vegetarianism is recommended for us, for all members of the clergy and of the faithful*, it is taught in the homilies. ... On 19 May [1998], in the Cathedral square in Rouen, there were young people who represented an organisation for the defence of battery hens. I told them: "Become vegetarian and teach vegetarianism, and the problem will be solved." (Emphasis added)[46]

However, it is important to bear in mind that these traditions no longer officially form part of the Roman Catholic Church. With few adherents, the influence they have upon modern Western Christendom is very limited, not to say negligible. When it comes to the wider Catholic Church, where there are cases of vegetarian advocacy, suspicion still prevails above all else. As Larue (2015) argued, "In the Catholic World, nothing seems to be able to reconcile the vegetarian ethic with faith: by fidelity to the Scriptures, the Church guarantees [Christians'] inalienable right to kill animals" (p. 128). That said, with the rise of the modern animal rights movement, the past few decades have brought significant changes in Catholic attitudes toward animals. Pope John Paul II even declared that animals were "as near to God as men are."[47] After nearly two millennia of mistrust of ethical abstinence from meat, these are encouraging signs for Catholic vegetarians.

Part III: Historical Controversies: Meat Eating

Protestant Traditions: Recovering the Edenic Diet

Initially, Protestant views of abstinence from meat were very much aligned with traditional Catholic ones. In his 1554 *Commentary on Genesis*, Calvin (1996) claimed that humans could rightfully consume meat and condemned vegetarianism:

> And why is this done, but that the faithful may boldly assert their right to that which, they know, has proceeded from God as its Author? For it is an insupportable tyranny, when God, the Creator of all things, has laid open to us the earth and the air, in order that we may thence take food as from his storehouse, for these to be shut up from us by mortal man, who is not able to create even a snail or a fly. I do not speak of external prohibition; but I assert, that *atrocious injury is done to God, when we give such license to men as to allow them to pronounce that unlawful which God designs to be lawful*, and to bind consciences which the word of God sets free, with their fictitious laws. (p. 287; emphasis added)

Nevertheless, Protestants who chose to adopt a vegetarian diet were not chastised as severely as Catholics, and the liberalism of Protestant traditions allowed vegetarianism to thrive. As a result, vegetarians came to be much more prevalent in predominantly Protestant countries, such as the United Kingdom, the United States, or Germany, than in Catholic countries, such as France, Spain, or Portugal.[48] Those would-be vegetarians who would once have been vilified, shunned, or lambasted by the Catholic Church for their dietary choices emancipated themselves from established institutions that were not in accord with their worldview. As we shall see, the reformed sects that emerged from these schisms played a decisive role in launching the modern vegetarian movement.

It is in Victorian England that Christian vegetarianism flourished most energetically. Let me first note, however, that the Church of England did not really embrace vegetarianism in those days. As a matter of fact, instances of vegetarian dietary practices were scarce in the Victorian Anglican Church. As the English historian James Gregory (2008) remarked: "The vegetarian movement was long frustrated *by the rarity of sympathetic Anglican clerics: so rare, one such cleric joked, that he felt he should be exhibited in a glass case*" (p. 138; emphasis added).[49] As in ancient and medieval times, one has to look outside dominant traditions to find proponents of vegetarianism. Indeed, a significantly large number of English vegetarians in the Victorian times belonged to minority *reformed churches*.[50] One of the reformed churches that included many vegetarian members was the Bible Christian Church, which officially came to be in the year 1800. Its founder, the former Anglican clergyman William Cowherd, was a fervent advocate of the "vegetable diet."[51] His followers went on to found the Vegetarian Society in 1847, the first association of its kind in the Western world.[52] The first membership list of the Vegetarian Society (1848) included 265 members, and approximately half were Cowderites (later to be known as Bible Christians).[53] Seeking to ground their dietary choice in their reading of the Bible, they believed that Jesus and his early followers were vegetarian (Brotherton, 1829, p. xiii).

It took 11 weeks for the 40 devout English Bible Christians to reach the New World, and only 18 remained vegetarian after their perilous voyage.[54] The historian

Adam Sprintzen (2003) stated that "the group was the first to adopt meatless dietetics at the center of its members' lives while also advocating for this lifestyle in American society at large" (p. 10). As a matter of fact, a few decades later, in 1850, Bible Christians founded the American Vegetarian Society, which came to be formed during the American Vegetarian Convention. Its organizer, William Metcalfe, was a strong proponent of a biblically based vegetarianism.[55] Ordained as a Bible Christian minister in 1811, Metcalfe also believed that Jesus was a vegetarian. He claimed that the belief that Jesus ate fish during the feeding of the 5,000 was based upon a misinterpretation of the Bible and that the word for fish in the Gospels actually referred to some non-animal food.[56] Moreover, Metcalfe praised the vegetarian diet for being spiritually edifying and health giving, unlike meat eating, which "has unquestionably a baneful affect [sic] upon the physical existence and the intellectual, the moral and religious powers of man" (Shprintzen, 2003, p. 15). People in the United States were generally wary of Metcalfe, and relatively few chose to abstain from meat permanently. His son and biographer, Joseph Metcalfe (1849), lamented the morally corrosive impact of meat eating to which people remained oblivious because of ingrained cultural conventions: "There is a desolation wrought in the soul by the sin of flesh-eating more fearful than any outward ghastliness, but which cannot be understood, because of the long and unlimited prevalence of the custom" (Maintenance Committee, 1922, p. 39). Despite people's reluctance to become vegetarian, Metcalfe and his followers persevered in preaching the virtues of a meatless diet.

The Seventh-Day Adventist Church is another American Christian tradition that was influential in the worldwide spread of vegetarianism from the mid–19th century onward.[57] Ellen G. White, a former Methodist, claimed to have visions from God instructing her to tell people to cease eating meat. Although she herself followed that rule only later in life, she zealously preached vegetarianism as the divinely ordained diet for humans:

> God gave our first parents the food. He designed what the race should eat. It was contrary to His plan to have the life of any creature taken. There was to be no death in Eden. The fruit of the trees in the garden, was the food man's wants required. (As cited in Iacobbo & Iacobbo, 2004, p. 99)

Furthermore, laying an even greater emphasis on the importance of health than the Bible Christian, White claimed that it was a "sacred duty to attend to our health" (Knight, 2004, p. 69). Unsurprisingly, she believed a meatless diet ensured optimal physical and spiritual health.

In the 20th century, various other Christian denominations and quasi-Christian sects continued to emerge. One of these was the Order of the Cross founded in 1904 by the Scottish former Congregational Minister John Todd Ferrier. Ferrier (1980) rejected Paul's teachings claiming that he did not know Christ and that his writings had led Christians astray: "[Paul] had not come under the influence of the life of [Christ], and had no vision of its glorious purity and sweetness, had he done so, he could never have said what he did concerning the eating of flesh" (p. 44). Among the aims and ideals of the foundation statement of the order, Ferrier (1980) invited his followers "to protest against, and to work for the abolition of . . . the slaughter of animals for food, fashion and sport . . . [and] to advocate the universal adoption of a bloodless diet" (Order of the Cross, n.d., p. 44).[58] The first sentence of today's online description of the tradition states: "The members of The Order of the Cross are dedicated to living a life of compassion and follow a pacifist and vegetarian or vegan way of life" (Order of the Cross, n.d.).

Nevertheless, it must be borne in mind that these religious groups are all marginal minorities and that mainstream denominations remained by and large aligned with the traditional Catholic position. For instance, Karl Barth (1961), undoubtedly one of the most influential Protestant theologians of the 20th century, addressed the question of meat eating in his magnum opus *Church Dogmatics*. Though he began saying that the Edenic diet was a plant-based one, he ultimately argued that the vegetarianism in this life represented a "wanton anticipation of the new aeon for which we hope" (Barth, 1961, p. 3:4). He believed we are to be omnivores in this postdiluvian world.

In recent decades several quasi-Christian sects promoting various forms of vegetarianism for optimal health have flourished. Hallelujah Acres, founded in 1976 by the Christian medical doctor George H. Malkmus, and Universal Life, founded in 1984 by the self-proclaimed Prophetess Gabriele, are examples of Christian communities that seek to follow a biblically based vegetarian diet.[59] These groups lay special emphasis upon the health benefits of the Edenic diet.[60] "The healthy vegetarian physical form," remarked Calvert (2008), "is evidence of the 'rightness' and 'naturalness' of the diet ordained by God for humankind" (p. 128). Meat abstinence is no longer simply a form of penance, as it was predominantly in the Middle Ages; it has become an element of one's personal well-being.

Finally, in a world faced with global ecological crises caused in part by the greenhouse gases produced to a significant degree by the meat industry, some Christians now promote vegetarianism as the most environmentally sustainable diet. In 1999, the theologian Stephen H. Webb founded the Christian Vegetarian Association (n.d.), whose mission statement declared that: "A vegetarian diet can be a powerful and faith-strengthening witness to Christ's love, compassion, and peace" and "represent[s] good, responsible Christian stewardship for all God's Creation."[61] In a 2013 homily, Pope Francis told the faithful that "the vocation of being a 'protector' . . . means respecting each of God's creatures and respecting the environment in which we live."[62] However, following the saint whom he honored by taking the name, animal protection does not seem to preclude meat consumption for the pope, who is not a vegetarian.[63] In his so-called "ecology encyclical," Pope Francis (2015) made several references to animals, all alongside plant life with the exception of one paragraph commenting on animal experimentation in which he reminded the faithful that "the *Catechism* firmly states that . . . '*it is contrary to human dignity to cause animals to suffer or die needlessly*'" (p. 130; emphasis added).[64] He failed, however, to mention the mass-produced meat originating from factory farms, wherein animals are being slaughtered in atrocious conditions, and which millions of Catholics consume on a daily basis.

CONCLUSION

This article is far from being a comprehensive study of the relationship between vegetarianism and Christianity. In addition to the limitation of my study to Western Christianity, examples from the medieval and modern periods were primarily drawn from the English-speaking world, as well as the regions that are now France and Italy. Moreover, there are many themes that I have not explored, such as the connection between vegetarianism and marriage and sexual abstinence[65] or the place of women in the early and medieval churches.[66] I hope, however, to have shown that abstinence from animal flesh is no trivial matter, but that it has been a subject of much controversy and friction from the dawn of Christian history and remains in question to this day. As such, it is a remarkable and all too often neglected topic of inquiry, upon which historians, theologians, as well as all people of faith ought to reflect.

In summary, vegetarian dietary practices were relatively widespread in the early Church. They were certainly accepted, even encouraged to a certain point. Praised when it formed part of temporary ascetic fasting regimen, abstinence from meat was condemned if it were a permanent rejection of animal flesh; for it would often be associated with heretical ideas found in various dissident groups, gnostic sects, and pagan philosophical schools. Nevertheless, various patristic authors put forth several arguments in defense of vegetarianism, all of which will be revisited by future generations of Christians. The two most influential of these is that vegetarianism is the divinely ordained diet, as Adam and Eve were strict vegetarians in Eden, and that abstinence from meat is best suited to the life of faith insofar as it promotes physical and spiritual flourishing.

The medieval era maintained ambivalent relations to animals. Although care for nonhuman creatures was associated with pious behavior, abstinence from flesh remained predominantly an ascetic practice for both heretical sects like the Cathars and Catholic monks like the Cistercians. The fact that the weak and the sick were given meat as a health food clearly shows that monastic abstinence from meat was first and foremost a form of self-mortification.

In modern times, just as in ancient and medieval times, it was dissident groups that embraced vegetarianism. After the Renaissance, the majority of Christian vegetarians were Protestant reformers who broke away from established churches. The modern vegetarianism movement was strongly influenced by reformed traditions such as the Bible Christian Church. These churches revived arguments that had been overlooked during the medieval period, in particular the claim that vegetarianism is the divinely ordained diet that ensures spiritual flourishing. In addition, they seem to be more aware of animal welfare and lay greater emphasis upon physical health than most early and medieval Christian authors.

AFTERWORD

This examination of abstinence from flesh eating has also shed light upon the enduring and pervasive anthropocentric currents within the Christian tradition. Theological reflections throughout Christian history have by and large been centered upon the human creature, more often than not at the detriment of the animal creature. Abstinence from flesh appears to be always about human life, almost never about animal life, and hardly ever about the ethical relations between these lives. What is more, very few Christians have denounced the slaughtering of animals as a morally reprehensible act. In fact, the connection between the food one eats and the killing of other sentient beings is seldom drawn. For most Christians, a meatless diet is not so much cruelty free as deprived of bodily pleasure. Indeed, vegetarianism is generally more about ascetic self-regard than benevolent other-regard—it is more about self-love than neighbour-love. The refusal to partake of flesh is ethical only insofar as it orients human life, but not in the sense of caring for the beings who are slaughtered and eaten. In other words, abstinence from meat is first and foremost a mere diet and all too rarely viewed as an ethical choice that values and seeks to preserve the lives of animals.

The rightful Christian worldview is not anthropocentric, but theocentric: God is the locus of all value. All of creation is to be valued for God's sake. One cannot but lament the fact that so few individuals in two millennia of Christian history endorsed abstinence from flesh, not because of a concern for their own salvation, but so as to refuse to kill God's creatures. Some holy men and women do nevertheless remind us that rather than mere self-discipline and abnegation, we should seek peaceable communion with our fellow creatures. This vision of hope for a harmonious coexistence between humans and other animals is to be found in the Book of Isaiah, which anticipates the kingdom to come, wherein the Edenic relationship between all creatures shall be restored:

> The wolf also shall dwell with the lamb,
> and the leopard shall lie down with the kid;
> and the calf and the young lion and the fatling together;
> and a little child shall lead them.
> And the cow and the bear shall feed;
> their young ones shall lie down together:
> and the lion shall eat straw like the ox.
> And the sucking child shall play on the hole of the asp,
> and the weaned child shall put his hand on the cockatrice' den.
> They shall not hurt nor destroy in all my holy mountain:
> for the earth shall be full of the knowledge of the LORD,
> as the waters cover the sea. (Isa. 11:6–9)

Notes

1. For example, see Cocchi (1757).

2. The earliest known uses of the term "vegetarian" can be traced back to Alcott House Academy, a small school near London. The first printed occurrence of the term dates back to 1847, which is the year in which the English Vegetarian Society was founded (the first of its kind in the world). Prior to this, there were several instances of the phrase "vegetable diet." See Davis (n.d.).

3. According to the *Online Etymology Dictionary*, in Middle English, vegetables were sometimes called *grene-mete* (15th century).

4. Spencer's *The Heretic's Feast* (1993) is the most comprehensive history of vegetarianism that talks extensively about Christianity available to date.

5. All biblical passages are taken from the *New International Version* (NIV), except the first two quotations that are from the *Revised King James Version* (RKJV).

6. This Stoic term was used by Clement of Alexandria (1960): "the natural use of food is *adiaphora*" (2.1.9–10).

7. Note that the Pauline epistles do not promote respect for those who abstain from meat in a consistent manner and sometimes deem vegetarianism heretical. Cf. 1 Timothy 4 and Corinthians 8.

8. From *ankrateia*, "power over oneself."

9. The best remembered Montanist convert is Tertullian (1980). See a later discussion in this article on his commentary on Genesis.

10. Examples of later vegetarian heretical sects include the Paulicians and the Massalians. See Spencer (1993, pp. 152–153) for further discussion.

11. For a more detailed discussion about the Manichean diet and the beliefs in which it was grounded, see Spencer (1993, 135–136).

12. Cf. Moore (1975).

13. Augustine wrote this as part of a response to a question posed by a pious man named Januarii in the year 400: "You have written that several of your brothers abstain from eating meat, as an impure thing. This is clearly against faith and holy doctrine" (*Ad inquisitions Januarii*, XX).

14. Note that Clement himself never fully embraced vegetarianism; he favored a balanced and temperate omnivorous diet. Ultimately, he believed that to completely denigrate meat amounted to opposing God's creation. See *Stromata*, III.6.51. Interestingly, Clement came close to quoting Musiunius Rufus and Plutarch when he recommended a diet of "onions, olives, some vegetables, milk, cheese, fruits in season, and boiled food of all sorts without sauce." However, unlike the aforementioned authors, he added, "If roasted or boiled meat is required, let a portion be given" (Clement, 1960, II.I.15). Cf. Musonius Rufus, *Discourse*, 18A; Plutarch, *Quaestiones convivales*, 4, 664a.

15. For a detailed and thorough investigation of John's diet, see Kelhoffer (2005).

16. Cf. Matthew 3:4. See also Kelhoffer (2005, p. 154).

17. Tatian's (1984, p. 23) statement is uncertain because only secondary sources written several centuries later are extant.

18. For example, the ninth-century bishop of Hadatha Isho'dad of Merv wrote that "[John's] food was locusts and wild honey, but the *Disatessaron* says his food was honey and milk of the mountains." For further discussion, see Gibson (1911–1916, pp. 23–24).

19. Athanasius wrote that "Solomon teaches us that some kind of plat is translated as 'locust': 'The almond tree will blossom, and the locust will become thick'" (Anathanius, *Fragmenta in Matthoeum*, 8A). Isidore wrote that "the locusts on which John fed are not creatures like dung-beetles, as some ignorantly suppose. . . . Rather, they are twigs of herbs or plants" (Isidore, Epistulae, 1.132). For further discussion, see Kelhoffer (2005, pp. 171–174).

20. See Genesis 1:29.

21. Genesis 9:2–4: "Everything that lives and moves about will be food for you. Just as I gave you the green plants, I now give you everything." This revision was part of the Noahic covenant.

22. Cf. Basil (1970).

23. See Basil (1970). The attribution of these homilies to Basil is a moot point. In other writings, however, Basil put forth the traditional argument in favor of meat eating, namely that one

should gratefully receive the food that God has mercifully offered. Like Clement and others, Basil never clearly said to adopt a strict and permanent vegetarian diet. It is likely that this was due to their fear of being associated with the beliefs held by heretical sects. See his Letters and Rules for examples.

24. Note that prayer is traditionally ascribed to Basil, but there does not seem to be any historical evidence to support this.

25. Emphasis added. It is doubtful that this quotation is actually from Jerome's writing. Various authors attributed it to Jerome, yet none provided an original source. For example, see Murti (2003, p. 95).

26. The Ember Days are four sets of three days (Wednesdays, Fridays, and Saturdays) within the same week devoted to fasting, meditation, and prayer. It is also known as the Quarter Tense, derived from the Latin *quattuor anni tempora* (four seasons of the year) or the *jejunia quattuor temporum* (fast of the four seasons). The Ember Weeks occur: (1) between the third and fourth Sundays of Advent, (2) between the first and second Sundays of Lent, (3) between Pentecost and Trinity Sunday, and (4) the week beginning on the Saturday after Holy Cross Day.

27. Various Orthodox traditions still consume only vegan foods during Lent today. For further discussion on Christian fasting practices, see Larue (2015, p. 115).

28. Emphasis added. Cf. the council of Braga, the council of Gangra (340), and the second council of Orléans (533).

29. Preece (2008, pp. 125–130) challenged the traditional view according to which vegetarianism in antiquity was solely an ascetic practice devoid of concern for animals. He grounded his argument mainly in passages from the teachings of the fourth-century Church Father John Chrysostom who praised monks' vegetarian diet as follows: "no stream of blood are among them; no butchering and cutting up of flesh; no dainty cookery; no heaviness of head. Nor are there horrible smells of flesh meats among them or disagreeable fumes from the kitchen" (Preece, 2008, p. 130). This, however, seems to be an exception to the much more widespread view of abstinence as askesis.

30. No original source provided.

31. For further examples of Christian saints who embraced vegetarianism, see Roberts (2004).

32. No original source provided. Though this quote may be a historically fictitious modern invention, it may nonetheless be said to accurately describe the Franciscan attitude toward animals.

33. This concerned the divine office and fasting and how the brothers ought to travel through the world.

34. The word "Cathar" comes from the Greek katharos, "pure."

35. Prior to Catharism, the Bogomil movement, which originated in the first Bulgarian Empire in the 10th century, was another gnostic and dualist heretical medieval sect whose members were strict vegetarians. Interestingly, some Bogomils also sought to reinterpret John the Baptist's diet as vegetarian. See Spencer (1993, pp. 154–162) for further discussion.

36. Like the Pythagoreans, Cathars believed that souls continued to be reborn in human or animal form until they were fully freed from the material realm.

37. There are, however, some rare yet notable exceptions to this trend. In the 10th century, St. Paul of Latros, for example, ate only wild vegetables in order to make sure that he inflicted as little harm as possible upon God's creation. See Roberts (2004, p. 81).

38. See Preece (2008, p. 129).

39. See Spencer (1993, pp. 154–162) for a detailed discussion of the Bogomil sect and its dietary beliefs and practices.

40. For example, Voltaire (1770, "Requête à tous les magistrats du Royaume," pp. 342–343) told us that someone was condemned to death in 1629 for having eaten horsemeat during a day

of abstinence. Interestingly, in 653, the eighth council of Toledo decided that the sentence for breaking dietary laws during Lent would be to remain vegetarian for an entire year.

41. *Vegetarian Messenger*, October 1907, p. 293.

42. See, for example, John Paul II's 1992 *Catechism of the Catholic Church*.

43. Despite its name, the Liberal Catholic Church is not a member of the Roman Catholic Church. It has its roots in the Old Catholic Church, which separated from the Roman Catholic Church in the 19th century.

44. *Conférence Végétarisme et Christianisme*, April 12, 1972.

45. The Alliance Végétarienne was founded in 1994. It changed its name in 2007 and is now called the *Association Végétarienne de France*. It remains to this day the largest vegetarian organization in France.

46. Mgr. Maurice Chardine, *Letter to André Méry*, May 25, 1998.

47. Pope John Paul II made this statement to a public audience in 1990.

48. This trend is still true today. It is estimated that approximately 1 to 2% of the population in France is vegetarian and 3 to 4% in Spain in contrast to 7 to 9% in the United Kingdom and 8 to 10% in Germany. Note, however, that Italy seems to be an exception to the rule with around a 10th of its population being vegetarian. See, for example, http://www.euroveg.eu/lang/en/info/howmany.php. According to Linzey (1989), there are now more practicing vegetarians in the United Kingdom and the United States than there are practicing Roman Catholics. See Iacobbo & Iacobbo (2004, p. x).

49. In recent years, however, the Anglican Church has counted among its members Reverend Andrew Linzey, who pioneered the modern animal rights movement and who previously held the world's first post in Christian theology and animal welfare at the University of Oxford. He is by all accounts one of the most outspoken and influential contemporary voices for Christian animal ethics and vegetarianism in the Western world.

50. Gregory (2008, p. 137) identified 435 religious affiliates in a database of 1,470 vegetarians between the years 1837 and 1901.

51. Cowherd officially promoted vegetarianism from 1809 onward. For further discussion, see Antrobus (1997) and the Maintenance Committee (1922, pp. 20–24).

52. See Davis (2011). Joseph Brotherton succeeded Cowherd in leading the Bible Christian Church and was one of the founding fathers of the Vegetarian Society. Brotherton's wife, Martha, published the first "vegetable diet" cookery book in 1832. Note that the British and Foreign Society for the Promotion of Humanity and Abstinence from Animal Food was founded four years earlier (i.e., in 1843); it is considered to be a forerunner of the Vegetarian Society.

53. By 1850, the society counted 478 members. See Calvert (2013, p. 17).

54. The Bible Christians reached the United States on June 14, 1817. See Shprintzen (2003, p. 12).

55. The American Vegetarian Convention took place in New York on May 15, 1850. See Metcalfe (1840, p. 16).

56. See Metcalfe (1840). Note that this reinterpretation bears some resemblance to readings of John the Baptist's diet of "locusts and wild honey" as being in fact vegetarian.

57. Approximately 35% of Adventists are vegetarian, according to a 2002 worldwide survey of local church leaders. See Lockhart (2006, pp. 22–27). Note that Adventists are also expected to follow the kosher laws from Leviticus 11.

58. Ferrier also defined one of the aims and ideals of the order as "abstaining from hurting the creatures, eschewing bloodshed and flesh eating, and living upon the pure foods so abundantly provided by nature." Influenced by the theosophists, the members of the Order of the Cross hold

various beliefs that are absent from dominant Christian traditions, the most notable of which being perhaps the belief in reincarnation.

59. See Calvert (2008) for further discussion vis-à-vis recent vegetarian practices grounded in Christian beliefs.

60. As noted above, some early Christian writers, such as Basil of Caesarea and Jerome, also thought of vegetarianism being of benefit to human health. However, this aspect of the vegetarian diet was not their primary concern. Rather, abstinence from meat was first and foremost meant to be an askesis central to fasting practices.

61. The Christian Vegetarian Association is international and non-denominational.

62. Pope Francis, Homily, Solemnity of Saint Joseph, March 19, 2013.

63. There is an online petition that seeks to urge Pope Francis to adopt a vegetarian diet. On June 1, 2015, it had only 238 signatures. https://www.credomobilize.com/petitions/urge-pope-francis-to-declare-himself-a-vegetarian-1

64. Cf. *Catechism of the Catholic Church*, 2418.

65. For further discussion see, for example, Shaw (2008).

66. For further discussion see, for example, Spencer (1993, pp. 132–134, 157).

References

Alcott, W. (1849). Society of Bible Christians. *Library of Health, 121*, 260–262.
Antrobus, D. (1997). *A guiltless feast: The Salford Bible Christian Church and the rise of vegetarianism*. Salford, England: Salford City Council.
Aquinas, T. (1922). *Summa Theologica*. London, England: Burns, Oates and Washbourne.
Athanasius. (1976). *The life of St. Antony the Great*. Willis, CA: Eastern Orthodox Books.
Augustine. (1887). Contra faustum. In P. Schaff (Ed.), *Nicene and post-Nicene fathers*. Buffalo, NY: Christian Literature Publishing Co.
Barth, K. (1961). *Church dogmatics*. Edinburgh, Scotland: T & T Clark.
Basil. (1970). Homiliae de hominis structura. In A. Smets and M. ban Esbroeck (Eds.), *Basile de Césarée: Sur l'origine de l'homme*. Paris, France: Cerf.
Bernard of Clairvaux. (1870). *Œuvres*. Bar-le-Duc, France: Guérin.
Boas, G. (1997). *Primitivism and related ideas in the Middle Ages*. Baltimore, MD: Johns Hopkins University Press.
Bonaventure. (1978). *Life of St. Francis* (E. Cousins, Trans.). Malwah, NJ: Paulist Press.
Brotherton, M. (1829). *Vegetable cookery*. London, England: Effingham Wilson.
Butler, A. (1956). *Lives of saints*. London, England: Burns & Oates.
Calvert, S. J. (2008). Ours is the food that Eden knew. In R. Muers and D. Grumett (Eds.), *Eating and believing*. London, England: T & T Clark.
Calvert, S. J. (2013). Vegetarianism in Britain and America. In A. Linzey (Ed.), *The global guide to animal protection*. Chicago: University of Illinois Press.
Calvin, J. (1966). *Commentary on Genesis* (J. King, Trans.). Grand Rapids, MI: Baker Books.
Celano. (1983). First life of St. Francis (Vita Beati Francisci). In M. A. Habig (Ed.), *St. Francis of Assisi*. Chicago, IL: Franciscan Herald Press.
Christian Vegetarian Association. (n.d.). *Our mission*. Retrieved from http://www.all-creatures.org/cva/mission.htm
Clementine Homilies. (1886). In A. Roberts, J. Donaldson, and A. C. Coxe (Eds.), *Ante-Nicene fathers* (T. Smith, Trans.). Buffalo, NY: Christian Literature Publishing Co.
Clément d'Alexandrie. (1960). *Le pédagogue* [Paedagogus]. H. I. Marrou et al. (Eds.), Paris, France: Cerf.

Cocchi, D. A. C. (1757). *Del vitto pitagorico per uso della medicina*, Venice, Italy: Simone Occhi.
Davis, J. (Comp.). (n.d.) *Extracts from some journals 1842–48—the earliest known uses of the word "vegetarian."* Retrieved from http://www.ivu.org/history/vegetarian.html
Davis, J. (2011). *History of the vegetarian society.* Retrieved from https://www.vegsoc.org/history.
Epiphanius. (1902). Panarion. In P. Amidon (Ed.), *The Panarion of St. Epiphanius*. Oxford, England: Oxford University Press.
Epiphanius. (1908). Haeres. In B. Pick (Ed.), *Paralipomena: Remains of gospels and sayings of Christ*. Chicago, IL: Open Court Publishing Co.
Fénelon, F. de S. (1713). Mandement pour le carême de l'année 1707. *Recueil des mandements*. Paris, France: Babuty.
Ferrier, J. T. (1980). *The master: His life and teachings*. London, England: Order of the Cross.
Fox, M. W. (1989). *St. Francis of Assisi, animals and nature*. Washington, DC: Center for Respect of Life and Environment.
Gibson, M. D. (1911–1916). *The commentaries of Isho'dad of Merv*. Cambridge, England: Cambridge University Press.
Gregory, J. (2008). A Lutheranism of the table. In R. Muers and D. Grumett (Eds.), *Eating and believing*. London, England: T & T Clark.
Hippolytus. (1986). Refutatio omnium haeresium, 8.16. In M. Marcovich (Ed.), *Patristische text und studien (p. 25)*. Berlin, Germany: De Gruyter.
Iacobbo, K., & Iacobbo, M. (2004). *Vegetarian America*. Westport, CO: Praeger.
Irenaeus. (1979). Adversus Haereses, I. 28. In A. Rousseau and L. Doutreleau (Eds.), *Sources chrétiennes*. Paris, France: Cerf.
Kelhoffer, J. A. (2005). *The diet of John the Baptist*. Tübingen, Germany: Mohr Siebeck.
Knight, G. R. (2004). *A brief history of Seventh-Day Adventists*. Hagerstown, MD: Review and Herald.
Larue, R. (2015). *Le végétarisme et ses ennemis*. Paris, France: Presses Universitaires de France.
Laurioux, B. (2002). *Manger au Moyen Âge*. Paris, France: Hachette.
Legendre, G. C. (1735). *Traité de l'opinion ou mémoires pour servir à l'histoire de l'esprit humain*. Paris, France: Briasson.
Leyerle, B. (1995). Clement of Alexandria on the importance of table etiquette. *Journal of Early Christian Studies, 3* (2), 123–141.
Linzey, A. (1989, August). Christianity and the Rights of Animals. *Animals' Voice*.
Lockhart, K. (2006). The myth of vegetarianism. *Spectrum, 34*.
Maintenance Committee. (Comp.). (1922). *History of the Philadelphia Bible-Christian Church*. Philadelphia, PA: J.B. Lippincott Company.
Metcalfe, W. (1840). *Bible testimony, on abstinence from the flesh of animals as food*. Philadelphia, PA: J. Metcalfe & Co. Printers.
Moore, R. I. (1975). *The birth of popular heresy*. London, England: Edward Arnold.
Moore, R. I. (1985). *Origins of European dissent*. London, England: Basil Blackwell.
Murti, V. (2003). *They shall not hurt or destroy*. Cleveland, OH: Vegetarian Advocates Press.
Order of the Cross. (n.d.) Retrieved from http://orderofthecross.org/about-us/foundation-statement/
Peters, E. (1980). *Heresy and authority in medieval Europe*. Philadelphia: University of Pennsylvania Press.
Pope Francis. (2015). *Laudato Si [encyclical letter]*. Retrieved from http://w2.vatican.va/content/francesco/en/encyclicals/documents/papa-francesco_20150524_enciclica-laudato-si.html
Porphyry. (1832). Abstinence from animal food. In *Select works of Porphyry* (T. Taylor, Trans.). London, England: Thomas Rodd.

Preece, R. (2008). *Sins of the flesh*. Vancouver, BC: UBC Press.Roberts, H. H. (2004). *Vegetarian Christian saint: Mystics, ascetics, and monks*. Anjeli Press.

Shaw, T. M. (2008). Vegetarianism, heresy, and asceticism in late ancient Christianity. In R. Muers and D. Grumett (Eds.), *Eating and believing*. London, England: T & T Clark.

Shprintzen, A. D. (2003). *The vegetarian crusade*. Chapel Hill: The University of North Carolina Press.

Spencer, C. (1993). *The heretic's feast*. London, England: Four Estate Limited.

Tatian. (1984). Oratio ad greco. In T. Zahn (Ed.), *Das evangelium des Matthäus*. Wuppertal, Germany: R Brockhaus.

Tertullian. (1980). De ieiunio adversus psychicos. In A. Reifferscheid and G. Wissowa (Eds.), *Tertulliani opera omnia*. Vienna, Austria: Tempsky.

Voltaire. (1770). *Oeuvres completes*. Paris, France: Garniers.

Walters, K. S., & Portmess, L. (2001). *Religious vegetarianism from Hesiod to the Dalai Lama*. Albany: State University of New York Press.

Webb, S. H. (2001). *Good eating*. Grand Rapids, MI: Brazos.

Morality and Meat in the Middle Ages and Beyond

CHRISTENE D'ANCA
University of California, Santa Barbara

Abstract: Food is intimately associated with the body, and what a person chooses to consume can easily be used to craft one's identity. Food brings people together, in much the same way as culinary preferences can divide. As veganism is gaining traction around the world, this article examines its origins in religious practices, philosophy, literature, and economic trade within the Middle Ages, elucidating how contemporary decisions to abstain from animal consumption mirror medieval ones and further how similar obstacles to this lifestyle exist today.

Key Words: veganism, animal relations, medieval studies, vegan philosophy, medieval literature, Cathars, Pearl Poet, meat industry

Robert Ian Moore (2007) draws the distinction between the two types of persecution in a society—that which is usually directed only toward those individuals who do not adhere to social norms and a more widespread manifestation of persecution that envelopes an entire class of people, no longer operating case by case. This latter, more pervasive form of persecution, involves the development of sweeping categories of people oppressed for a variety of overlapping beliefs. Moore (2007) suggests this was the exact process undergone in Europe between the 10th and 13th centuries, leading to the creation of networks of oppression that systematically emerged each time the status quo was challenged. As persecution increased, and in some ways became organized, it led to social divisions grounded in meat consumption, the viewpoints concerning its practice, and the social implications it carried. During this period, a war was waged against dissenting views on the consumption of meat (Pegg, 2001, 2008; Sumption, 1999), and those who did not share the ideologies of the majority were vehemently punished and exterminated from society. In the medieval period, the Cathars became heretics according to the church due to their religious beliefs and outcasts from society due to their nonconformist cultural practices (Newman, 2009), which were inextricably tied into their abstinence from meat.

Food is intimately associated with the body, and what a person chooses to consume can be used to craft one's identity. Food brings people together, in much the same way as culinary preferences can divide. Meat consumption has remained the normal means of sustenance, and it is those groups who perpetually refrain from different aspects of meat eating that are marked as existing outside normal cultural parameters. For example, even though Kosher laws prohibit the mixing of certain foods and the eating of pork for those practicing the Jewish religion (Regenstein & Regenstein, 2003), Hindus abstain from consuming cows, and Christians refrain from eating meat during certain holy days (Grant, 1980; Staples, 2017), none of these dietary taboos are concerned with animal welfare as much as with the consequences suffered by the humans consuming them. Moreover, the different prohibitions do not extend beyond a short list. Thus, such religious restrictions still allow practitioners to, at least in part, integrate into mainstream society. Historically, however, not all religious doctrines followed the same pattern, and participants were ostracized more for their beliefs on meat consumption than any other aspect of their religion.

While the refusal to consume animal flesh can certainly be traced to ancient doctrines (Adams, 1990; Ricard, 2016; Steiner, 2005), a more accessible entry point for modern discourse has its roots in the Middle Ages, with the Cathars, who participated in far more ascetic behaviors than their conventional Christian contemporaries. Further, the philosophies of those others who have historically refused to eat meat, and the receptions they received, extend well beyond religion and the church into social and economic considerations over the centuries. As veganism is gaining traction around the world, this article examines its origins in religious practices, philosophy, literature, and economic trade within the Middle Ages, elucidating how contemporary decisions to abstain from animal consumption mirror medieval ones and further how similar obstacles to this lifestyle exist today.

THE HERETICAL DIET

In 1018, Adhemar of Chabannes (1829, p. 138) made mention of "Manichees" in writings from Aquitaine. Consequently, this launched the Manichees into their role of ubiquitous heretics. The Cathars (Migne, 1853) were quickly equated with the beliefs of Manichaeism found in the writings of St. Augustine. These connections led others, such as Wazo of Liège, to consider contemporaneous Cathars as having stemmed from fourth-century predecessors (Pertz, 1839). However, a more plausible understanding of their presence has them migrating from the Balkans and occupying territories such as the Languedoc, Northern Italy, and the Low Countries (Peters, 1980). This presumed migration coincided with an influx of heretical charges in those same areas during the first part of the 11th century that would later explode into fully developed pockets of Catharism by the middle of the 12th (Lansing, 1998; Moore, 1984). In other words, the ideology may have migrated from the east into Western Europe during the 11th century. But the ways in which Cathar disciplines and doctrines progressed (Lambert, 1998) in Western Europe during this period[1] point toward the development of a new system that created an altogether different set of Cathar beliefs with which the Christian church had to contend (Moore, 2007).

Unlike other well-established Christian heretics throughout Europe, Cathars contested the very core of Christian dogma as they insisted on the existence of not one, but two, gods, of which the second was inherently evil and connected to the entirety of the physical world (Moore, 1984). Their acceptance of dual deities marked the foundation for their entire system of belief, which was the factor that led others to draw the parallel between them and their Manichean forbearers, regardless of whether the connection actually existed. In the Middle Ages, views such as Catharism that deviated from the mainstream came under scrutiny, especially in regard to women, and those found guilty were often condemned to death (Lambert, 1998; Omont, 1916; Roquebert, 1970; Ward, 2002). A prominent practice among Cathars, and one that was often used as a means to discern their loyalties, was their unorthodox diet that avoided meat and other animal products, such as milk, cheese, or eggs (Hoffman, 2000; Sullivan, 2000). Interestingly, the eating of fish was allowed. Apparently Cathars would not eat any creature that could give birth to another being with a soul, but they believed souls could only inhabit terrestrial bodies, and thus not reincarnate in fish, allowing eating fish to be permissible (Théry, 2010). Yet, despite their refusal to consume any animal capable of procreation, they did not make the same connection between the flesh of animals and sexual reproduction found in traditional Christian teachings. For example, Saint Jerome criticized conspicuous consumption of meat, save for those wishing to procreate, such as "quae ligatae maritis" [those tied in marriage] or pregnant women, "quarum uteri portant fetus" [whose uteruses carry a fetus] (Hilberg, 1892, p. 55:96).[2] In other words, Cathars did not equate the eating of meat with sexual appetite, and their predominant preoccupation with the flesh regarded eating and sexual activity as separate restricted acts, the importance of which will be discussed below.

Michel Foucault (1984) comments on the historical perception of the preoccupation with food as the gateway to sin. He believed this was a result of the ways in which people identify themselves—if food was tied into religious beliefs, and religion was no longer a predominant means of self-identification, then a new guiding principle would need to be instated in order to dichotomize the in crowd and the othered group. He concluded that sexual activity and sexual identity were considered the new sins of the flesh that had overtaken food consumption. However, while dietary choices have occasionally at various points in history subsided as being points of contention among people, they have recently reemerged as contentious. The conflicts over dietary choices operate with the same force as their medieval predecessors and quite often encounter friction for similar reasons.

In the early 1990s, Canadian country music singer K. D. Lang divulged her sexual orientation toward other women and her dietary preferences for vegetarianism. Despite the rampant homophobic sentiments circulating in the latter part of the 20th century, it was her dietary revelation that sparked the most controversy (Bourette, 2008; Herek, 2004). While her newly forged public identity as a lesbian was initially met with derision and a loss in album sales, her vegetarianism was met with violent outrage. It culminated with a telling act of vandalism against the "welcome" sign in her hometown of Consort, Alberta, that had previously boasted housing the international superstar. Across its surface, someone sprayed "eat meat, dyke" (Mathews, 1992). More recently, with the advent of social media, visiting any number of provegan or vegetarian Facebook pages, such as LiveKindly, will elucidate the scorn that vegans and vegetarians face. Innumerable comments far surpass the vitriol encountered on the signage outside Consort. These comments evince a deeper relationship people have with seemingly unconventional beliefs, not just about food, but animals and their role in our society. In a historically parallel fashion, even as the Cathars' heretical reputation stretched well beyond their chosen dietary considerations (Arnold, 2001; Sumption, 1999), this facet of their lifestyles was maintained as a predominant cause for their disinheritance from the larger church. This begs the question as to why such a seemingly inconsequential aspect of their belief system would garner such attention and moreover endure for more than 800 years of scrutiny.

Cathars inhabited a curious position along the spectrum of ideologies about flesh eating. Unlike their Christian contemporaries who were concerned with taming desires and used abstinence as a form of virtuous punishment (which ironically gave way to an almost ecstatic pride for their tenacity), Cathars were far more concerned with the eradication of fleshly encounters (Arbesmann, 1966; Bazell, 1997). Not unlike Pythagoras, they believed humans and animals shared equal souls and through the process of reincarnation they became interchangeable. The physical qualities of a body, whether human or animal, rendered it a mere shell to house a soul that could belong to anyone, and thus killing an animal was regarded as being on par with killing a human (Goodich, 1998). However, the ways in which they practiced this belief perhaps provide more questions about their ideologies than answers. Pierre Maury's 1307 personal narrative (Weis, 2000) of a supper with a fellow Cathar, Bernard, along with a superior member of the Cathar faith[3] offers an informative perspective (Sullivan, 2000; Lambert, 1998). After procuring a separate pot and lid from an innkeeper, the men cleansed the pot of any animal residue and set it to boil with fish while watching it closely to prevent any meat or gravy from other pots coming into contact with theirs. As Maury and his companion were about to sit down

> the Perfect advised us to buy eggs for two pennies and put them in front of us on the table, to ensure that our diet would not betray us as a heretical party. We bought the eggs. Then, after Bernard had prepared a dish of fish and fish broth for the Perfect, he lifted the [remaining] fish out of the pot, and he and I broke the eggs into it. Then Bernard and I ate the eggs as well as the fish, but the Perfect did not eat eggs, but only fish and broth. (Weis, 2000, p. 168)

The Cathars in question were most likely attempting to impersonate mainstream fasting Christians who would still consume eggs as part of their diet and relied on fish as a substitute for meat. Nevertheless, their concern with being discovered and the precaution taken with the purchase of the eggs (Müldner & Richards, 2005) was justified considering the consequences they would suffer had they been revealed as heretics—certain death, specifically by being burned alive. Note the dichotomy between the ways in which the Perfect was protected from impurity and the far laxer restrictions placed upon Maury and Bernard. Even though theoretically Cathars had alternate motives for refraining from eating animal products, the crux of their compassion still resided solely within their reverence for the soul, and not, like their ancient forbearers, for the animals themselves (Adamson, 2004), as illustrated in the above passage. Yet even a consideration for the soul, if not the animal's body itself, demonstrated more respect for animals than other religious groups held. The Cathars' abilities to reason beyond the capacity practiced by the church fathers—who, as shall be established, operated within the confines of their religious limitations—consequently cast the Cathars into the role of Christian antagonizers.

Modern social anthropology draws the distinction between groups with which one chooses to associate (Tajfel, 1970; Tajfel et al., 1971) and those that are outside a particular sphere of acceptable interaction. To apply these concepts directly to meat eating, modern philosopher Cathryn Bailey (2007) has analyzed the ways in which her own decision to abstain from meat has crafted her identity and bonded her with others who have made the same life choices. She also admits that it has placed her into certain othered groups that have negative connotations. In other words, she is compassionate, health oriented, and focused on animal and human liberation but also thrust into the role of an upper-class White female, seemingly detached from the plight of her less fortunate counterparts who are unable to make the same choices. Her refusal to eat meat has simultaneously provided a place for her in one group while serving as her exclusion from another. While these concepts, much less the terminology associated with them, did not exist in the Middle Ages, such behaviors can be traced to the earliest known humans and can, with caution, be applied to medieval religious orders. Even though the initial recognition of abstinence from meat has traditionally been a trait associated with a multitude of Christian denominations, it also served as a dividing force. Only those who avoided meat for the proper reasons were welcomed into the fold of Christianity, whereas others were often violently punished (Spencer, 1993). These delineations between belief systems have their origins in biblical proclamations; for example, in Romans 14:2–3 in the King James Bible it states:

> for one beleeveth that he may eat all things: another who is weake, eateth herbes. Let not him that eateth, despise him that eateth not: and let not him which eateth noth, iudge him that eateth. For God hath received him.

Despite the commandment to not disparage one another in light of dietary choices and the multiple statements made by disciples, such as St. Paul, against using food as a means of discrimination, that is precisely the role that it served. Further, those who delighted in the flesh but resisted its temptation found themselves morally superior to those, such as the Cathars, who took no pleasure from meat eating and found not doing so a source of comfort. The Cathars became regarded on par with Jews and other heretics who did not view their religiously mandated dietary resistance to meat and animal by-products as a choice to be commended. Instead, these practices simply comprised an entire lifestyle that they wholeheartedly embraced, but which was looked down upon by others (Fabre-Vassas, 1997). In other words, since the lack of meat eating produced no suffering for the Cathars, their abstinence from it was not considered virtuous. Therefore, Cathars became the "weak" who resided on "herbes," as in Romans 14:2, and bore the burden of their categorization, henceforth positioned to receive derision from mainstream Christians and to be condemned to heresy. Through this practice, Cathars inadvertently rendered vegetarianism as a defining aspect of an "outgroup" among people for centuries to come.

Moreover, even as the commandment in Romans 14 extols refraining from judgment against those who partake in eating flesh, it does not account for the ways in which meat eaters may interpret their position alongside their contemporaneous counterparts who do not eat meat. This is similar to the way those who do not eat meat in modern times are assumed to be more judgmental and suffer derision for their choices as meat eaters attempt to ameliorate their anticipated moral inferiority. Recently Minson and Monin (2012) studied the reaction of meat eaters to vegetarians, who responded negatively to the idea of being judged on a moral basis. The meat eaters would shut down conversations with the vegetarians in response to their anticipated outcome, rather than based on any actual interaction, demonstrating that their reaction was more self-preservatory than grounded in actual observed encounters. The findings of their study can be extrapolated to apply not only to the reaction against vegetarians historically but also to trace resentment against many minority groups and their respective beliefs. Christian charity, one of the defining characteristics for most people who practice the religion, is focused on compassion. However, by refusing to eat the flesh of animals for reasons other than virtuous fasting, Cathars openly demonstrated compassion on a greater level than mainstream Christians. Thus, since acquiescing to the existence of persons who could be thought of as more compassionate than Christians themselves was unthinkable, there was only one option remaining. As Renan Larue (2015) asserts, "la condamnation du végétarisme moral" [the condemnation of moral vegetarianism] became "une constante remarquable de la longue histoire du christianisme" [a notable constant in the long history of Christianity] (p. 101). It was precisely this point that brought the Cathars' dietary choices into the foreground and brought the focus upon them almost to the exclusion of other Cathar beliefs. Meat eating became the defining element in their condemnation as well as the means by which they could be identified.

According to Deborah Root (1988), testing one's faith using dietary preferences had long been established in the Middle Ages, going as far back as the seventh century. It was used on converted Jews who were force-fed pork in order to broadcast their newfound Christian loyalty, it was used on Moors during the Spanish Inquisition (Root, 1988), and with the Cathars it went a step further. Not only were Cathars ordered to eat meat in order to prove their innocence from heresy, but they were often times asked to kill animals such as chickens, which would most often lead to their discovery and ensuing punishment (Gui & Douais, 1886; Steven of Bourbon, 1877). Since Christians did not have any relationship with abstinence from any particular food per se, but rather with the idea of fasting in general, they were able to place those with specific food restrictions into an othered category. This facilitated a dichotomization between themselves and those perceived to be heretics. By distancing themselves from those who were considered different, they were able to eschew the moral condemnations implied by the Cathars' behavior while simultaneously condemning Cathars for their views. This distancing enabled Christians to claim the moral high ground that would otherwise have been denied to them in light of their lack of compassion toward the animals they chose to regularly consume.

ANIMAL FRIENDS AND FEASTS OF FLESH:
A PROBLEMATIC PARADOX

Concurrent with the advent of Catharism throughout Western Europe and the perpetuation of ascetic eating habits among religious followers of various denominations, another preoccupation with animals was occurring in the form of concern for their well-being and a general curiosity about their existence. This newfound interest resided among those in religious orders as well as laymen who were privy to the lives of animals. Some, such as Richard de Wyche or Anselm of Canterbury, who were noteworthy bishops and ascetically conscious religious men, felt remorse for the slaughter of animals and refused to eat animal flesh well beyond what their religious disciplines demanded (Roberts, 2004). Others, such as Walter Map and John of Salisbury purportedly deplored certain court activities, such as hunting, considering the injustice done to the animals as much as the inhumanity demonstrated by the humans who participated (Preece, 2017). According to Saint Bonaventure (1988), Saint Francis was "filled with even more piety, calling creatures, no matter how small, by the name of brother or sister, because he knew they had the same source as himself" (p. 28). Throughout every town he visited, he mingled with the animals and instilled in them the same devotion for their Creator as any human possessed, if not arguably more, implying both animal intelligence and perhaps indirectly the presence of an animal soul. Nevertheless, some of these men, such as Walter Map and John of Salisbury, quite notably, did not abstain from eating meat, and their decision points directly toward the paradox surrounding those who asserted their love and pity for animals, condemned others who were perceived as abusing animals, but did little to change their own behaviors to support their proclamations. Their affection and admiration for animals was most curious, even unique for the time, but apparently did not go as far as the dinner table.

Even among the nonreligious, animals found centralized positions in society through their emergence within texts. Bestiaries became increasingly popular in the 12th and 13th centuries, fueling the general curiosity about animal behaviors and providing a quasiencyclopedic documentation of their different kinds (Baxter, 1998; George & Yapp, 1991; Hassig, 1995, 1999). Their provenance and habits were accompanied by luxurious artwork within lengthy illuminated manuscripts, underscoring the desire for a general collection of information about animals while engendering a state of awe in readers. However, the bestiary was not the only genre to undergo a revival from the times of antiquity; fables benefitted as well, and numerous writers in the same period, such as Marie de France, appropriated *Aesop's Fables*. While she reconceptualized them to fit the demands of courtly life for her intended audience, the animals remained ever-present to deliver their didactic messages (Bruckner, 2011; Jambeck, 1992; Mann, 2009). She used animals in her *Lais* as well, in tales such as *Bisclavret*, *Yonec*, and *Le Rossignol*. Moreover, whereas some animals had always figured into the olden *chansons de geste*, or national origin stories, such as horses in *La Chanson de Roland* or dragons in *Beowulf*, with the growing popularity of romance, innumerable possibilities appeared for animals, real or mythical, to further feed the popular demand for animalistic narratives and encounters (Eckert, 2013; McCracken, 2017; Salter, 2001).

The fixation on animals and the line between human and animal became further blurred as animals began occupying roles previously reserved solely for humans. For example, criminal trials began in which an animal's physical and spiritual innocence would be defended in courts of law, and entire towns would participate (Evans, 1906; Salisbury, 2011; Sykes, 2011). Nevertheless, despite the broadening concern *with* animals, there appeared to be little concern *for* animals, and the majority of people continued consuming their flesh. In fact, the greater the interest in an animal, the more likely it would be sought out as a novelty for consumption, a form of entertainment or for other uses. Those who wished to preserve animals for their sui generis nature remained in the minority, as part of the social outgroup.

Three recent texts have explored the ways vegans are viewed in modern society. Veganism as a social movement has been steadily growing in recent years. However, the studies concluded that people who abstain from meat eating for moral or ethical reasons are still more often than not perceived as outcasts and persecuted to various extents—from subtle or inadvertent slights to outright derision—demonstrating little has changed in 800 years, save for the potential of being dealt the death penalty (Bertuzzi, 2017; Griffin, 2017; Turner, 2017). Thus, meat eating has remained the primary means of sustenance, as well as one of the most prevalent activities in social events, even being used as a tool for networking and asserting dominance in society.

MEAT, THE OMNIPRESENT SOCIAL "COVENANT"

Monastic members rejoiced over abstaining from the much-coveted consumption of meat as a means of adhering to their respective orders and, accordingly, for fitting into a social system. For laypersons, it was hunting and attendance at the ensuing feast that became the appropriate activities to signal participation within a group (Pluskowski, 2006). Literary examples pave the way in examining the means through which preparing and sharing food functioned on a cultural level. The anonymously written 14th-century tale, *Sir Gawain and the Green Knight*, provides perhaps one of the most overt examples of medieval social networking made possible through the procurement and consumption of meat, while simultaneously marginalizing those outside the system. Despite the characters' French provenance, the poem was adapted for an English audience and was entrenched in the Anglo-Saxon culture in which the "feast hall was at the heart of early English society" (Brown, 1998, p. 1).

As the tale begins during Christmastide, Arthur and his knights are found in the banquet hall, enjoying "the dearest of treats: / the freshest of foods in the finest of ways" (Andrew et al., 1993, p. 215) as a way of bonding. This scene is analogous with the later sequence of "meat and merriness, mirth, and deep joy" (Andrew et al., p. 255) encountered by Gawain during his expedition that leads to the creation of a different bond. However, such feasts were also a means of maintaining the social order that would necessarily place the host in a superior position (Woolgar, 2011), outlining the court structure and the hierarchy of the land (Roach, 2011). Additionally, Arthur's round table can be considered the descendant of the tradition created during the Last Supper, further solidifying the top-down structure displayed during the feast (Bellis, 2011).

Notably, feasting was also associated with excess, and it remained the duty of the host to refrain from gluttony in order to set an example (Byrne, 2011; Farrier, 1995), as Arthur does while he would "not eat until all had been served" (Andrew et al., p. 213) nor "eat / of his food not the first bite before he had heard / some adventurous story" (p. 215), underscoring his ability to delay his reward. Nevertheless, while he temporarily abstains, he does not completely forsake the frivolity of the banquet, leaving the door open for further reproof of the practice. The procurement of food for the main meal is not directly addressed as it will be in subsequent parts of the poem. However, the hunt is implied, and the audience witnesses the aftermath as Arthur demonstrates his largesse, a noteworthy medieval quality, through sharing his boon. After all, then as much as now, "carnivalesque blood sport thus leads to communal sharing of resources," and Christmas, as much as other celebratory holidays throughout the year such as Martinmas, unify those present while also distancing those who do not participate (Walsh, 2000, p. 246).

During the banquet, the merriment comes to an abrupt halt as an interlocutor, the Green Knight, enters and disrupts the festivities with his challenge to anyone willing and able to deal him a blow, with the understanding that he would return the favor. Gawain accepts and proceeds to lop off the Green Knight's head. The Green knight picks up his fallen head, reattaches it, and issues the time and place of Gawain's repayment as the somber consequence of Gawain's failure reverberates throughout the hall. In this instance, much as in other medieval texts where knights were fitted with a specific color (Tiller, 2007; Tremlett, 1967; Wheeler, 1994), green symbolizes the vegetative cycle, earthliness, purity, and most tellingly poses a challenge to the status quo of courtly life that centers around feasting and festivity. By introducing a different natural order that is intricately tied to nature itself, and to which the knights of Arthur's court must adhere, virtue and morality are redefined. In other words, the dichotomy between those observing social norms and those with seemingly heretical or dissenting views is inverted, as it is no longer clear on which side the characters stand. Moreover, the differing relationships between humanity and nature are briefly brought to the fore to be examined throughout the story within the multiple hunting episodes that combine the imagery of animals and humans, bringing into question the ethics and morality of hunting and meat eating.

The initial pact Gawain enters into with the Green Knight stipulates that a year from the day of the banquet the Green Knight would serve Gawain the same as Gawain gave him. Thus, Gawain would travel to the knight's dwelling and receive a blow to the neck in the same fashion as he originally delivered to the knight before realizing his folly in underestimating the Green Knight's potency. The episode offers the first taste of Gawain's hubris in initially assuming his superiority as a courtly knight over the natural order. Nevertheless, the chivalric code demands that Gawain fulfill his promise, and so he embarks on his journey toward certain death, since unlike the Green Knight, Gawain would not be able to reattach his severed head after the ordeal. Along the way, he encounters a nobleman in whose castle he sojourns for the subsequent Christmas season and with whom he enters a second "covenant" (Andrew et al., p. 259) that echoes his earlier one with the Green Knight. The host states that each day that Gawain remains a guest the host shall go on a hunt while Gawain remains comfortably at home, and at the end of the day, he tells Gawain that "what you gain you will give, bad or good, in exchange," while "what we gain we will give, whether great or else poor" (Andrew et al., p. 259). Even though it is not immediately apparent what Gawain could possibly gain within the confines of the castle that he could feasibly exchange with the host, hunting becomes the uniting activity between the two men. Additionally, just as Arthur shared his meat with his knights as a conveyance of power, the host negotiates with the same currency.

The following morning, shortly after the host leaves for the hunt, Gawain is presented with his first opportunity for gain in the castle. The host's wife comes to his bedside and attempts to seduce him. He politely refuses and only consents to a single courtly kiss, which he then returns to the host upon his return, rightfully relinquishing all of his gains while partaking in the meat brought back from the hunt. Notably, the first animal "hunted down" (Andrew et al., p. 261) and "cut up according to custom with skill" (p. 269) is a doe, a female deer, that in Christian allegory has been associated with purity and devotion (Shuffleton, 2008a, 2008b). While the "high lord prohibited hunting male deer" (Andrew et al., p. 261), the animal chosen for the first kill alludes to the slippery slope toward irrefutable sin on which Sir Gawain has embarked. Each of the following narrative sequences in the poem transpose the brutal images of the hunt with the equally visceral images in Gawain's chamber, where he is cornered and chased in the same fashion as the animals in the woods. His flesh belongs to his female visitor no more or less than the animals' flesh belongs to the hunters, but both him and the animals must succumb to the game according to the presiding social order. Afterall, as Camille (1998) asserts, courtly love games were predatory in nature. Even as Gawain continues to refuse the host's wife's advances, he is unable to avoid the encounters and acquiesces to her a little more each time.

Further, even as he does not participate in the hunt and does not fully partake in the wife's temptations, he nevertheless consumes portions of each, which ultimately leads to his moral breach and undoing. With every nightly feast and ensuing morning kiss, he spirals further into hubris and is derailed from his initial virtuous campaign to repay his debt to the Green Knight. After tasting various forms of flesh, his worldly desires overcome him and on his last day, he accepts a token from the wife that he believes will render him invincible to the Green Knight's blow, thus denying the Green Knight a fair exchange. Additionally, as he later partakes in the last banquet comprised of the host's daily hunt, he does not relinquish the token, effectively reneging on his oath to give all that he receives throughout the day. In short, he feels as entitled to his life, which he believes the token will safeguard, as much as to the meat he eats, while neither rightfully belong to him, as he will soon realize.

Sir Gawain and the Green Knight is the fourth and last poem in a series composed by the same anonymous author, with the other three being *Pearl*, *Patience*, and *Purity*. While each piece has its own distinct plot, there are numerous overarching narrative arcs predominantly concerned with virtue, morals, and ethics. As these reoccurring themes weave in and out of the disparate storylines, they culminate in *Sir Gawain*. When the titular character meets the Green Knight for the last time, he personifies Everyman, exemplifying the human response to temptation, in which the best intentions often fall short. He is the embodiment of the common human, and as he embarks on his journey, he never fails to err in the familiar ways, confused about his ultimate trials and almost oblivious to subversively perilous situations. He depicts the struggle concerning humans every day—the battle between adhering to social norms or following individual paths toward what is inwardly perceived as right. Even as Gawain withstands most of the temptations of the flesh brought upon him within the confines of the castle by day, he gives in to them at the banquet hall at night, and his greatest vice is his lack of humility revealed through his believed entitlement to his life.

As Gawain kneels before the Green Knight, bare necked and awaiting the repayment of his debt, his attempted deception has been discovered, and it becomes apparent that he has not learned his lesson. He cannot even accept the consequences for his actions, choosing to blame the tempters instead of realizing his own choice. Nevertheless, with a slap on the wrist, or more appropriately, a nick on the neck, he is forgiven and sent home. Gawain had not learned humility in the first encounter with the Green Knight, nor during his trials in the host's castle, and it is unclear if the Green Knight's mercy in the end left more than a physical mark on him. However, the Green Knight's actions demonstrate an understanding of human nature: While perfection is impossible, it is a willingness to learn and persevere that is necessary for even a modicum of success.

Sir Gawain is a Christian narrative, and as such, there are parallels to be drawn between it and Genesis in terms of human-animal relationships. In Genesis 1:26, God gave man dominion over all creatures, but that was in the state of purity. According to Thomas Aquinas (1952), "For his disobedience to God, man was punished, by the disobedience of those creatures which should be subject to him" (1:510). Further, Aquinas (1952) argues that

> in the state of innocence man would not have had any bodily need of animals; neither for clothing, since then they were naked and not ashamed, there being no inordinate motions of concupiscence, nor for food, since they fed on the trees of paradise, nor to carry him about, his body being strong enough for that purpose. (1:510)

The dominion humanity was given over animals in the state of purity is not equal to the kind of dominion humans claim over animals in the current state, after the Fall. In other words, the theft of one thing, fruit from the tree of knowledge, begets the further theft of life from animals—the infinite perpetuation of sin. In reading *Sir Gawain* as a pedagogical text, it can be argued that one contention the author makes through the hunting and feasting scenes is to insinuate that these activities go against the true letter of God's law. Thus, for those wishing to attempt to recreate the original state of innocence from sin, it is important to adhere to the proper treatment of animals as well as to the way the first humans lived in harmony with them. Even if avoiding these activities would cast one into the othered category of hermits, or on par with the vegetative Green Knight, these practices of abstinence were conceived as occupying the moral high ground.

According to Elizabeth Biebel (1998), contemporaneous authors, such as Geoffrey Chaucer, created similar divisions between characters:

> If the food consumption that occurs in the *Canterbury Tales* is examined as a whole, a method does begin to emerge. There is a pattern of pure, balanced or even vegetarian intake surrounding the genuinely good individuals in both the *General Prologue* and the separate tales that is countered by a meat-oriented diet evinced by a less upstanding cast of characters. (p. 22)

As the hunt and the resulting feasts precipitated social bonds and played into cultural norms during the Middle Ages, these were worldly affairs with which the spiritual person should not be concerned. These narratives occupy a similar murky space along the spectrum of concern for animals. While the religious doctrine being emphasized was not on par with ascetic disciplines that extoled abstinence for its own sake, the consideration espoused throughout *Sir Gawain* was no more for the animals being slaughtered than it had been traditionally for women during rape charges (in which the father's or husband's rights were at the forefront; see, Carter, 1985; Gourlay, 1996; Karras, 2005; Orr, 1994), as is illustrated in Gawain's bedroom scenes. In the role-reversed chamber chase, Gawain's concern is not for the wife, or for the preservation of her virtue or even body, but rather for his own and for that of his host. Unlike the Cathars who wanted to preserve their own souls as much as the souls of animals, who could potentially reincarnate as humans, or vice versa, the *Sir Gawain* author's primary care was for human virtue and its return to an idealized state of innocence.

Distancing oneself from the banquet table or the pleasures of a bed chamber, even if only in moderation, becomes the measure of self-virtue. In much the same way, Chrétien de Troyes's Perceval attempted to relinquish the round table in order to reach the Grail (Lacy, 2010); others, such as Lancelot and Arthur, could not do so because they were too tightly connected to and dependent upon earthly pleasures, including the courtly behavior that centered around feasts and the accompanying sins of the flesh. Over time, social behaviors remained writ large in favor of the latter group, but awareness brought with it a general discomfort with prevailing practices, and the aforementioned paradox expanded beyond the purview of a few men.

THE MEDIEVAL MEAT INDUSTRY AND BEYOND: A DIFFERENT SOCIAL NETWORK

Even as those who refrained from meat eating or animal exploitation remained well in the minority, the overt cruelty resultant of the majority's culinary preferences needed to be mitigated, at least on a superficial level. As Valéry Giroux and Renan Larue (2017) assert in regard to their "paradox of meat" theory,

> nous nous montrons de moins en moins indifférents au sort des vaches ou des moutons dans les élevages et de plus en plus soucieux de leur bien-être. La plupart d'entre nous souhaiteraient qu'ils soient bien traités. Pourtant, nous les mangeons, nous participons à leur exploitation et les faisons tuer dans des proportions à peine croyables.

> [We are less and less indifferent to the fate of cows or sheep in the livestock industry and more and more concerned about their well-being. Most of us wish that they are well treated. Yet we eat them, we participate in their exploitation and have them killed in unbelievable quantities.] (pp. 10–11)

This very amalgamation of seemingly contradictory sentiments emerged during the later Middle Ages, leading many to feel unease at the sight of butcheries or slaughterhouses. The process of displacing these establishments, however, would be exceedingly lengthy and complicated, achieved only after several hundred years of petitions and public outcry. The citizens of major cities, such as Paris or London (Garrioch, 1996; Perren, 2008), would be plagued by the stench and indelible visages of carcasses and penned up animals until well into the Age of Enlightenment that would free them from encountering such atrocities on a daily basis, even if it did not free the animals from having to endure them.

Butcheries were supported by the church as early as the ninth century, taking advantage of the natural resources available just outside major cities in lands owned by the monasteries. Additionally, workers and customers were both procured from within city lines, rendering the location of these establishments a matter of common sense. The meat from these animals was for private use by the members of the monasteries, but considering the numerous fast days, there was always an excess that could produce extra revenue, should the meat become available for general sale and consumption (Levasseur, 1900). While monetary rewards were at stake, it was also an enterprise of convenience. It was not long before wealthy families began to participate in the business, all but monopolizing it by the 11th century (Poëte, 1924). In the 12th century, the state, and consequently the crown, removed the killing of animals from the streets and sanctioned various butcheries where such undertakings would be allowed. They essentially controlled these establishments and granted access to those who would benefit the royal purse. For example, in Philippe Augustus's negotiations with a group of knights, he placated them with fish "selling" rights but not with "livestock" butchery that he reserved for those who directly benefitted him (Renaudin, 1867).

As the slaughterhouses continued to accrue revenue, they remained central features of Parisian life. Due to their highly religious lifestyles that bordered on the ascetic, some kings, such as Louis IX in the 13th century, attempted to curb their practices by prohibiting the slaughter of pigs or generally reducing meat production. But for the most part, these establishments grew and multiplied unhampered (Jussiau et al., 1999). Similar attempts were made in France throughout later centuries in which the monarchy attempted to eliminate—or at the very least limit—the slaughter and overall consumption of meat during holy days and throughout the duration of Lent, leading to a formidable underground countermovement brought about by the meat industry (Abad, 1999). England was no less affected by butchers and slaughterhouses in the public sphere, and different laws were enacted throughout the districts in order to curb their presence. Ultimately it was the industry's expansion that drew negative public attention and disdain (Boulton, 1987), even from the crown, the very entity that facilitated its creation. Unfortunately, the trade had grown too large to be controlled (Bourdieu et al., 2004), as evidenced by the numerous royal edicts issued against it between the 13th and 15th centuries (Beik, 1997; Jussiau et al., 1999; Vidalenc, 1952). Slaughterhouses continued in the face of various attempts to curtail them, as no single edict, even one issued by the king, could actually enact change within the industry (Watts, 2006, 2005). This practice has trickled down into modern times, in which the meat industry has remained empowered by its economic and consequent political power (Leonard, 2014; Nestle, 2013; Perren, 2006; Salamon & Siegfried, 1977). The tactics used by the meat industry to control consumer appetite and perception of the products consumed relied on the trivialization of animals in order to produce mass sales and consequently expand the industry (Stribbe, 2001). Nevertheless, despite the butchers' arguments against relocation and their success at remaining within city limits for hundreds of years, the state and the voice of the people eventually won out, the establishments became marginalized, and the slaughter of animals was removed from public spaces (Chagniot, 1988). The mere fact that so much energy was expanded throughout France in attempting to move the butcheries outside of city lines and out of public view (Contamine, 1978) reinforces the reality of the paradox: If it was such a sordid affair, since the industry depended on financial gratification, simply refraining from supporting the industry through the purchase of meat would have dissolved it faster than any royal edict. The public did not want to stop consuming meat but simply did not want to be privy to its origin.

CONCLUSION: MEAT EATERS AND EVERYONE ELSE

As butchers and their businesses were removed from the parameters of cities, they became some of the most irreputable entities in society, not unlike the meat eaters of medieval tales whose moral characters were brought into question as a consequence of their dietary choices and feasting practices. Nevertheless, people continued to consume meat in the same fashion as literary figures while patronizing the reviled establishments. Meat consumption continued to thrive just as well outside the city as it had within, and the industry's distance from the public arguably benefitted its trade, as people became further blinded from the repercussions of their meat eating. The animals who once fascinated in fairy tales, romances, and fables became completely disengaged from the cuts on the table.

Whether or not one ate meat has long been used as a measure of virtue, and the refusal to partake would cast one into a higher level. However, the reasons for which one refrained from meat eating were as important as the activity itself. Abstinence for its own sake as an outward demonstration of morality remained the most highly praised achievement, while other reasons, such as concern for animals' souls or the animals themselves, would relegate a person into heretical territories. Moreover, it was not solely one's motives that had to be sanctioned, but the intervals of participation in either consumption of or abstinence from meat. Year-round asceticism was met with suspicion, and refusal to integrate into social events would signal one's position in the outgroup, as evidenced by the many culinarily oriented celebrations held throughout the year as well as tales centered on hunting and feasting, such as *Sir Gawain and the Green Knight*. Once butchery became a fully lucrative business, meat eating became ubiquitously culturally acceptable, and the main battle people waged was in finding a medium between continuing to consume meat and not being forced to encounter the brutality of its existence. Historically, meat consumption has been used as a means of suppression, of both animals and of human virtue, as opposed to bringing these ideologies to the forefront through its abstinence, thus underscoring the dichotomy between morality and meat eating in the Middle Ages and beyond.

Notes

1. Malcolm Lambert (1998) argues that the Cathars were not connected to the Manichees but developed completely independently as a product of their own time.

2. All translations in this article are mine unless otherwise stated.

3. The Cathars were divided between regular believers, *credentes*, and those who had undergone Cathar official sacraments, the *pefecti*, or *bonhommes*.

References

Abad, R. Un indice de déchristianisation ? L'évolution de la consommation de viande à Paris en carême sous l'Ancien Régime. *Revue Historique, 301*, 237–275.

Adams, C. J. (1990). *The sexual politics of meat: A feminist-vegetarian critical theory*. New York, NY: Bloomsbury.

Adamson, M. W. (2004). *Food in medieval times*. Westport, CT: Greenwood Press.

Adhemar of Chabannes. (1829). In G. Waitz (Ed.), *Monumenta germaniae historica, scriptores* (Vols. 1–4). Hanover, Germany: Hahn.

Andrew, M., Waldron, R., & Peterson, C. (Eds.). (1993). *The complete works of the Pearl Poet* (C. Finch, Trans.). Los Angeles: University of California Press.

Aquinas, T. (1952). *Summa theologica* (D. J. Sullivan, Ed., & Fathers of the English Dominican Province, Trans.; Vols. 1–3). London, England: Encyclopedia Britannica.

Arbesmann, R. (1966). Fasting and prophecy in Pagan and Christian antiquity. *Traditio, 7*, 1–71.

Arnold, J. H. (2001). *Inquisition and power*. Philadelphia: University of Pennsylvania Press.

Bailey, C. (2007). We are what we eat: Feminist vegetarianism and the reproduction of racial identity. *Hypatia: A Journal of Feminist Philosophy, 22*(2), 39–59.

Baxter, R. (1998). *Bestiaries and their uses in the Middle Ages*. Gloucestershire, England: Sutton Publishing.

Bazell, D. M. (1997). Strife among the table-fellows: Conflicting attitudes of early and medieval Christians toward the eating of meat. *Journal of the American Academy of Religion, 65*(1), 73–99.

Beik, W. (1997). *Urban protest in seventeenth-century France: The culture of retribution*. Cambridge, England: Cambridge University Press.

Bellis, J. (2011). The dregs of trembling, the draught of salvation: The dual symbolism of the cup in medieval literature. *Journal of Medieval History, 37*, 47–61.

Bertuzzi, N. (2017). Veganism: Lifestyle or political movement? Looking for relations beyond antispeciesism. *Relations, 5*(2), 125–143.

Biebel, E. M. (1998). Pilgrims to table: Food consumption in Chaucer's *Canterbury Tales*. In M. Carlin & J. T. Rosenthal (Eds.), *Food and eating in medieval Europe* (pp. 15–26). London, England: Hambledon Press.

Bonaventure. (1988). The life of Saint Francis. In A. Linzey & T. Regan (Eds.), *Animals and Christianity: A book of readings* (pp. 28–34). New York, NY: Crossroad Press.

Boulton, J. (1987). *Neighborhood and society: A London suburb in the seventeenth century*. Cambridge, England: Cambridge University Press.

Bourdieu, J., Piet, L., & Stanziani, A. (2004). Crise sanitaire et stabilisation du marché de la viande en France, XVIIIe-XXe siècles. *Revue d'histoire moderne et contemporaine, 51*(3), 121–156.

Bourette, S. (2008). *Meat: A love story: Pasture to plate, a search for the perfect meal*. Berkeley, CA: Penguin Publishing.

Brown, M. A. (1998). The feast hall in Anglo-Saxon society. In M. Carlin & J. T. Rosenthal (Eds.), *Food and eating in medieval Europe* (pp. 1–13). London, England: Hambledon Press.

Bruckner, C. (2011). The fables of Marie de France and the mirror of princes. In L. Whalen (Ed.), *A companion to Marie de France* (pp. 209–236). Leiden, Netherlands: Brill.

Byrne, A. (2011). Arthur's refusal to eat: Ritual and control in the romance feast. *Journal of Medieval History, 37*, 62–74.

Camille, M. (1998). *The medieval art of love: Objects and subjects of desire*. London, England: Abrams.

Carter, J. M. (1985). *Rape in medieval England: An historical and sociological study*. Lanham, MD: University Press of America.

Chagniot, J. (1988). *Paris au XVIIIe siècle, Nouvelle Histoire de Paris.* Paris, France: Hachette.

Contamine, P. (1978). Les fortifications urbaines en France à la fin du Moyen Age: Aspects financiers et économiques. *Revue Historique, 260*, 23–47.

Eckert, K. D. (2013). Bad animals and faithful beasts in Bevis of Hampton. *Neophilologus, 97*(3), 581–589.

Evans, E. P. (1906). *The criminal prosecution and capital punishment of animals*. London, England: W. Heinemann.

Fabre-Vassas, C. (1997). *The singular beast: Jews, Christians and the pig*. New York, NY: Columbia University Press.

Farrier, S. E. (1995). Hungry heroes in medieval literature. In M. Adamson (Ed.), *Food in the Middle Ages: A book of essays* (pp. 145–159). New York, NY: Garland Medieval Casebooks.

Foucault, M. (1984). *L'usage des plaisirs*. Paris, France: Gallimard.

Garrioch, D. (1996). *The formation of the Parisian bourgeoisie, 1690–1830*. Cambridge, MA: Harvard University Press.

George, W., & Yapp, B. (1991). *The naming of the beasts: Natural history in the medieval bestiary*. London, England: Duckworth.

Giroux, V., & Larue, R. (2017). *Le véganisme*. Paris, France: PUF.

Goodich, M. (1998). *Other Middle Ages: Witnesses at the margins of medieval society*. Philadelphia: University of Pennsylvania Press.

Gourlay, K. (1996). Roses and thorns: The prosecution of rape in the Middle Ages. *Medieval Life, 5*, 29–31.

Grant, R. M. (1980). Dietary laws among Pythagoreans, Jews and Christians. *Harvard Theological Review, 73*(1–2), 299–310.

Griffin, N. S. (2017). *Understanding veganism*. London, England: Palgrave Macmillan.

Gui, B., & Douais, C. (1886). *Practica inquisitionis heretice pravitatis*. Paris, France: Alphonse-Picard, Librairie-Éditeur.

Hassig, D. (1995). *Medieval bestiaries: Text, image, ideology*. Cambridge, England: RES Monographs on Anthropology and Aesthetics.

Hassig, D. (1999). *The mark of the beast: The medieval bestiary in art, life, and literature*. London, England: Routledge.

Herek, G. M. (2004). Beyond "homophobia": Thinking about sexual prejudice and stigma in the twenty-first century. *Sexuality Research & Social Policy, 1*(2), 6–24.

Hoffman, R. C. (2000). Fishing and fish culture, western Christian. In W. M. Johnson & C. Hilberg, I. (Ed.). (1892). Jerome Epistulae. In *Corpus Scriptorum Ecclesiasticorum Latinorum* (Vols. 1–55). Vienna, Austria: Verlag der Osterreichischen Akademie der Wissensch.

Jambeck, K. K. (1992). The fables of Marie de France: A mirror of princes. In C. Maréchal (Ed.), *In quest of Marie de France: A twelfth-century poet* (pp. 59–106). Lewiston, NY: Edwin Mellon Press.

Jussiau, R., Montméas, L., & Parot, J. (1999). *L'élevage en France: 10.000 ans d'histoire*. Dijon, France: Educagri Éditions.

Karras, R. M. (2005). *Sexuality in medieval Europe: Doing unto others*. New York, NY: Routledge.

Kleinhenz (Eds.), *The encyclopedia of monasticism* (p. 475–478). London, England: Fitzroy Dearborn Publisher.

Lacy, N. J. (2010). The post-vulgate cycle: The quest for the holy grail and the death of Arthur. In *Lancelot-Grail: The Old French Arthurian vulgate and post-vulgate in translation series* (M. Asher, Trans; Vols. 1–10). Cambridge, England: D. S. Brewer.

Lambert, M. (1998). *The Cathars*. Oxford, England: Blackwell Press.

Lansing, C. (1998). *Power and purity: Cathar heresy in medieval Italy*. Oxford, England: Oxford University Press.

Larue, R. (2015). *Le végétarisme et ses ennemis: Vingt-cinq siècles de débats*. Paris, France: PUF.

Leonard, C. (2014). *The meat racket: The secret takeover of America's food business*. New York, NY: Simon and Schuster.

Levasseur, E. (1900). *Histoire des classes ouvrières et de l'industrie en France avant 1789*. Paris, France: Arthur Rousseau.

Mann, J. (2009). *From Aesop to Reynard: Beast literature in medieval Britain*. Oxford, England: Oxford University Press.

Mathews, D. (1992). k. d. Lang: Bold beginnings. *The Advocate, 52*, 35.

McCracken, P. (2017). *In the skin of a beast: Sovereignty and animality in medieval France*. Chicago, IL: University of Chicago Press.

Migne, J. P. (1853). *Patrologia Latina: Eckbertus abas schonaugiensis* (Vols. 1–221). Paris, France: Petit-Montrouge.

Minson, J. A., & Monin, B. (2012). Do-gooder derogation: Disparaging morally motivated minorities to defuse anticipated reproach. *Journal of Social Psychological and Personality Sciences, 3*(2), 200–207.

Moore, R. I. (1984). *The origins of European dissent*. Oxford, England: Wiley-Blackwell Press.

Moore, R. I. (2007). *The formation of a persecuting society: Authority and deviance in western Europe 950–1250*. Oxford, England: Wiley-Blackwell Press.

Müldner, G., & Richards M. P. (2005). Fast or feast: Reconstructing diet in later medieval England by stable isotope analysis. *Journal of Archaeological Science, 32*, 39–48.

Nestle, M. (2013). *Food politics: How the food industry influences nutrition and health*. Los Angeles: University of California Press.

Newman, M. G. (2009). Considerations on life and death: Medieval asceticism and the dissolution of the self. *Method & Theory in the Study of Religion, 21*(2), 177–196.

Omont, H. (1916). La collection Doat à la Bibliothèque nationale: Documents sur les recherches de Doat dans les archives du sudouest de la France de 1663 à 1670. *Bibliothèque de l'école des chartes, 77*(1), 286–336.

Orr, P. (1994). Men's theory and women's reality: Rape prosecutions in the English royal courts of justice, 1194–1222. In L. O. Purdon & C. L. Vitto (Eds.), *The rusted hauberk: Feudal ideals of order and their decline* (pp. 121–159). Gainesville: University Press of Florida.

Pegg, M. (2001). On Cathars, Albigenses, and good men of Languedoc. *Journal of Medieval History, 27*(2), 181–195.

Pegg, M. (2008). *A most holy war: The Albigensian crusade and the battle for Christendom*. Oxford, England: Oxford University Press.

Perren, R. (2006). *Taste, trade, and technology: The development of the international meat industry since 1840*. Burlington, VT: Ashgate Publishing.

Perren, R. (2008). Filth and profit, disease and health: Public and private impediments to slaughterhouse reform in Victorian Britain. In P. Y. Lee (Ed.), *Meat, modernity, and the rise of the slaughterhouse* (pp. 127–152). Durham: University of New Hampshire Press.

Pertz, G. (Ed.). (1839). *Gesta episcoporum Leodiensium* (Vols. 1–25). Hanover, Germany: Hahn.

Peters, E. (1980). *The Cathars: Heresy and authority in medieval Europe*. University Park: University of Pennsylvania Press.

Pluskowski, A. (2006). Holy and exalted prey: Hunters and deer in high medieval seigneurial culture. In I. Sidéra (Ed.), *La chasse pratiques, sociales et symboliques*, (pp. 245–255). Paris, France: De Boccard.

Poëte, M. (1924). *Une vie de cité*. Paris de sa naissance à nos jours. La jeunesse. Des origines aux temps modernes. Paris, France: Picard.

Preece, R. (2017). *Sins of the flesh: A history of ethical vegetarian thought*. Vancouver, Canada: University of British Columbia Press.

Regenstein, J. M., Chaudry, M. M., & Regenstein, C. E. (2003). The kosher and halal food laws. *Comprehensive Reviews in Food Science and Food Safety, 2*(3), 111–127.

Renaudin, E. (1867). *Paris exposition; ou, guide à Paris en 1867*. Paris, France: Delagrave.

Ricard, M. (2016). *A plea for the animals* (S. C. Kohn, Trans.). Boulder, CO: Shambhala Publications.

Roach, L. (2001). Hosting the king: Hospitality and the royal *iter* in tenth-century England. *Journal of Medieval History, 37*, 37–46.

Roberts, H. H. (2004). *Vegetarian Christian saints: Mystics, ascetics, and monks*. New York, NY: Anjeli Press.

Roquebert, M. (1970). *L'épopée cathare, 1198–1212: l'invasion, Toulouse*. Paris, France: Perrin.

Root, D. (1988). Speaking Christian: Orthodoxy and difference in sixteenth-century Spain. *Representations, 23*, 118–134.

Salamon, L. M., & Siegfried, J. J. (1977). Economic power and political influence: The impact of industry structure on public policy. *American Political Science Review, 71*(3), 1026–1043.

Salisbury, J. E. (1994). *The beast within: Animals in the Middle Ages*. New York, NY: Routledge.

Salter, D. (2001). *Holy and noble beasts*. New York, NY: Boydell and Brewer.

Shuffleton, G. (Ed.). (2008a). Sir Eustace. In *Codex Ashmole 61* (item 1). Kalamazoo, MI: Medieval Institute Publications.

Shuffleton, G. (Ed.). (2008b). Sir Isumbras. In *Codex Ashmole 61* (item 5). Kalamazoo, MI: Medieval Institute Publications.

Spencer, C. (1993). *The heretic's feast: A history of vegetarianism*. London, England: Fourth Estate Press.

Staples, J. (2017). Beef and beyond: Exploring the meat consumption practices of Christians in India. *Journal of Anthropology, 82*(2), 232–251.

Steiner, G. (2005). *Anthropocentrism and its discontents*. Pittsburgh, PA: University of Pittsburgh Press.

Steven of Bourbon. (1877). In A. L. de la Marche (Ed.), *Anecdotes historiques: Legendes et apologues tirés du recueil inédit d'Étienne de Bourbon, dominicain du XIII siècle*. Paris, France: Librairie Renouard.

Stribbe, A. (2001). Language, power and the social construction of animals. *Society and Animals, 9*(2), 145–161.

Sullivan, D. D. (2000). Cathars. In W. M. Johnson & C. Kleinhenz (Eds.), *The encyclopedia of monasticism* (pp. 251–253). London, England: Fitzroy Dearborn Publisher.

Sumption, J. (1999). *The Albigensian crusade*. London, England: Faber and Faber.

Sykes, K. (2011). Human drama, animal trials: What the medieval animal trials can teach us about justice for animals. *Animal Law, 17*, 273–311.

Tajfel, H. (1970). Experiment in intergroup discrimination. *Scientific America, 223*, 96–102.

Tajfel, H., Billig, M. G., Bundy, R. P., & Flament, C. (1971). Social categorization and intergroup behavior. *European Journal of Social Psychology, 1*(2), 149–178.

Théry, J. (2010). Les hérésies, du XIIeau début du XIVe siècle. In M. M. de Cevins & J. M. Matz (Eds.), *Structures et dynamiques de la vie religieuse en Occident (1179–1449)* (pp. 373–386). Rennes, France: PUR.

Tiller, K. (2007). The rise of Sir Gareth and the hermeneutics of heraldry. *Arthuriana, 17*(3), 74–91.

Tremlett, D. (1967). *Rolls of arms, Henry III: The Matthew Paris shields, c. 1244–1259*. Oxford, England: Oxford University Press.

Turner, R. (2017). Veganism: Ethics in everyday life. *American Journal of Cultural Sociology, 7*, 54–78.

Vidalenc, J. (1952). L'approvisionnement de Paris en viande sous l'ancien régime. *Revue d'histoire économique et sociale, 30*(2), 116–132.

Walsh, M. W. (2002). Medieval English "Martinmesse": The archaeology of a forgotten festival. *Folklore, 111*(2), 231–254.

Ward, J. (2002). *Women in medieval Europe, 1200–1500*. London, England: Longman.

Watts, S. (2005). Liberty, equality, and the public good: Parisian butchers and their rights to the marketplace during the French revolution. *Food and History, 3*(2), 105–117.

Watts, S. (2006). *Meat matters: Butchers, politics, and market culture in eighteenth-century Paris*. New York: University of Rochester Press.

Weis, R. (2000). *The yellow cross: The story of the last Cathars' rebellion against the Inquisition, 1290–1329*. New York, NY: Vintage Books.

Wheeler, B. (1994). "The prowess of hands": The psychology of alchemy in Malory's "Tale of Sir Gareth." In M. Shichtman & J. P. Carley (Eds.), *Culture and the king: The social implications of the Arthurian legend* (pp. 180–195). Albany: State University of New York Press.

Woolgar, C. M. (2011). Gifts of food in late medieval England. *Journal of Medieval History, 37*(1), 6–18.

The Anarchist Diet: Vegetarianism and Individualist Anarchism in Early 20th-Century France

CARL TOBIAS FRAYNE
University of Cambridge

Abstract: This article uncovers the historical connection between anarchism and vegetarianism in France. In doing so, it restores the significance of a little-known branch of the libertarian movement, namely individualist anarchism. Individualist anarchists sought to transform themselves by applying anarchist principles in their daily lives instead of waiting for a future revolution. Retracing the thoughts and deeds of these forgotten pioneers of the ecological and animal liberation movements, I show that vegetarianism is a striking illustration of anarcho-individualist prefigurative politics and that their aspiration to find their place within nature is as topical as ever.

Key words: anarchism, individualist anarchism, anarcho-individualism, history of vegetarianism, veganism, naturianism, Belle Époque

INTRODUCTION

There has been an unprecedented growth in the number of vegetarians and vegans in France in the past few years. In fact, the very word "vegan" entered the French language only recently, making its first appearance in a dictionary in 2013, 3 years after the creation of the first French vegan organization, the *Fédération végane*.[1] It is worth noting that, in contemporary French, one can distinguish between veganism as a diet excluding all animal foods—*le végétalisme*—and veganism as a way of life excluding all animal products—*le véganisme*. Vegetarianism excludes meat and fish but usually includes eggs and dairy.[2] According to a 2018 survey, it has been estimated that 5.2% of the population in France is now vegetarian, 5% of which is vegan.[3] The upsurge of vegetarianism is concomitant with the growth of animal rights advocacy in France in the past decade.[4] L214, one of the most influential animal protection organizations and known for placing hidden cameras in abattoirs, was founded in 2008. In 2015, the French National Assembly adopted a legislative amendment recognizing animals (whose legal status had not changed since the

1804 civil code) as "sentient beings" (*êtres sensibles*). Finally, 2016 witnessed the launch of an animal advocacy political party, *le Parti animaliste*.[5] It is fair to say that questions of vegetarianism and animal protection have never occupied such a prominent place on the French political agenda as they do today.[6]

In the modern West, vegetarianism, or rather "abstinence from meat," emerged in England between the late 17th and late 19th centuries.[7] It was part of a broader askesis of salvation and spiritual edification promoted by esoteric Christian and mystical sects.[8] The first vegetarian society was established in England in 1847 by members of the Bible Christian Church. The English animal and women's rights campaigner Annie Kingsford, vice president of the Vegetarian Church Society in 1873, was an important contributor to the rise of the vegetarian movement in France.[9] She wrote a seminal thesis on the benefits of a plant-based diet at the University of Paris in 1881, 1 year after the establishment of first French vegetarian organization, *la Société végétarienne de France*.[10] The word *végétarianisme* first entered the *Dictionnaire de la langue française* in 1877, with the broad definition "alimentation par les végétaux."[11] In 1906, an article from the newspaper of record *Le Figaro* referred to vegetarianism (*végétarisme*) and veganism (*végétalisme*) as fashionable diets.[12]

No comprehensive scholarly history of vegetarianism in France has yet been written. In 1998, André Méry, president of the *Association végétarienne de France*, wrote an overview of the evolution of the movement until the end of the 20th century (Méry, 1998; Ouédraogo, 1996). André Larue (2015, 2019), who authored a history of Western vegetarianism in 2015, recently published a book on abstinence from meat during the French Enlightenment. The sociologist Alexandra Hondermarck (2021) is currently working on a doctoral thesis on the sociological history of vegetarianism in France, which will be the first thorough academic study on the topic. This article contributes to shedding light on a virtually unknown episode of the history of vegetarianism in France, namely the connection between abstinence from meat and an oft-misunderstood branch of the anarchist movement, namely individualist anarchism. The history of anarcho-individualist veganism is practically unknown by the libertarian movement itself. In fact, when French anarchists began writing about environmentalism in the 1970s and veganism in the 1990s, no reference was made to their individualist predecessors of the first half of the 20th century. The main compilation of texts on anarchist vegetarianism in France is found in two supplements of the journal *Invariance*, published in 1993 and 1994.[13] The historian Arnaud Baubérot appears to be the only scholar who has investigated the subject in some depth in his history of naturism published in 2004 (see also Baubérot, 2013). The first part of this article provides a synopsis of anarchism and its defense of the animal cause before looking at the naturian movement. The second part examines individualist anarchists' motives for adopting a plant-based diet, many of which, as we shall see, are just as topical as ever. The concluding remarks will highlight the fact that veganism allows us to better understand a vastly understudied strand of anarchism, namely individualism.

FROM ANARCHISM TO NATURIANISM

The industrial revolution of the 19th century led millions of people to emigrate from the countryside to work in urban factories. Workers lived in extreme poverty. Indeed, their existence was deplorable: Degrading labor and squalid living conditions reduced them to a state of servitude and misery. Malnutrition, alcoholism, and disease were rife and only added to the ordeal of their 12-hour workdays. Along with Marxians and other socialists, anarchists were the main revolutionary forces opposing the capitalist order and denouncing the human degeneration it produced.

Anarchism is a political ideology and an existential orientation that opposes all forms of illegitimate authority and promotes individual freedom. Negatively, anarchism is synonymous with antiauthoritarianism. Coercive authority can come from gods, political leaders, teachers, judges, parents, or traditions and social conventions. Anarchists reject all systems of domination and exploitation. Historically, the state, the Church, and capitalism were viewed as the institutional loci of oppression. Positively, anarchism is a form of autarchism based upon a commitment to equality, justice, and solidarity; upon intellectual and moral self-government; and upon authentic self-expression and creative experimentation. When regarded as a historically sociopolitical tradition, anarchism is usually considered to have sprung from the European workers' movements in the second half of the 19th century along with the main political ideologies of modern society. As such, it was shaped by the industrial and scientific revolutions as well as by the Enlightenment and by Romanticism. Until the 1917 Russian revolution, anarchism was one of the leading radical political movements worldwide. Since the Second World War, during which all ideologies opposed to capitalism were squashed, the influence and diversity of anarchism has been largely underplayed.

Anarchist defenses of the animal cause in France emerged with the birth of the movement in the second half of the 19th century.[14] It is worth noting that many of them were put forth by women. In the late 1880s, the journalist Caroline Rémy (aka Séverine) wrote several articles condemning animal exploitation in the periodical *Le Cri du Peuple*, founded by Jules Vallès on the eve of the Paris Commune of 1871.[15] The poet and activist Marie Huot, founder of the Popular League Against Vivisection (1882), compared the domination of men over women to that of humans over animals.[16] Louise Michel, the French grande dame of anarchy, asserted that animals were sentient beings and decried the violence and cruelty with which humans treated them. Like many other anarchists, she drew a parallel between the exploitation of workers and that of nonhuman animals.[17]

The prominent geographer Élysée Reclus is one of the classical anarchists who reflected most deeply upon the animal question. He became a strict vegetarian in 1893, at the age of 63. For Reclus (1905), there are significant similarities between the process of human socialization and that of animal domestication. Mutatis mutandis, in both cases submission to authority is partly a matter of voluntary servitude. The devotee praying to their god is akin to a companion animal begging their carer for a treat (Reclus, 1897).

Reclus saw animals as having some degree of moral agency. As such, it is partly incumbent upon them to rebel and emancipate themselves from human dominion. That said, Reclus did not believe that domestication was necessarily bad. He distinguished exploitative relationships between humans and other animals from mutually beneficial ones. As with human associations, the latter can be based on cooperation, mutual aid, and camaraderie (even though they initially involve some degree of coercion). Ultimately, Reclus (1897) contends that human and other animals can work together as allies and learn from each other as companions.

After the harsh governmental repression that resulted from the infamous attentat period of 1892–1894, French anarchists sought to diversify their tactics. The mainstream of the movement joined syndicates and advocated the general strike as the primary revolutionary catalyst. In opposition, a fringe group that identified as individualist anarchists (*anarchistes individualistes*) believed that waiting for a hypothetical future revolution prevented people from changing their lives in the here and now. Even if a revolution as a sudden and radical rupture with the social order were to occur, it would not fundamentally change individuals' lives. Economic emancipation alone would not do away with deep-seated authoritarian prejudices such as gender or religious biases. Individualist anarchists wanted to prefigure the state of positive anarchy: They sought to transform themselves and their environment immediately and in their ordinary daily lives. To this end, they experimented with different forms of relationships, education, collective property, communal living, hygiene, and diet. Individualist anarchists were the strongest proponents of vegetarianism in anarchist circles.

The group of the naturians (*naturiens*) were part of this anarcho-individualist subculture. The naturian movement (aka naturianism) was launched by the charismatic painter and illustrator Émile Gravelle in Montmartre in 1894. Naturians believed that human beings living in modern industrialized society were undergoing a process of degeneration. In opposition to this dehumanizing drift, naturians strived to recover the state of nature and to live in accord with natural laws. While some, in tune with the mainstream of anarchism, believed that science could improve their lives, others rejected it altogether, alongside urbanization, mechanization, and indeed the whole of civilization. Thus, naturianism also constituted a critique of the alleged superiority of "civilized" cultures over "primitive" ones, thereby posing a challenge to the authority of Western countries over the rest of the world.

One can distinguish between two waves of naturianism. Early naturians, most active in the last decade of the 19th century, were millennialists who sought to return to a golden age. Their condemnation of modern society was proportional to their idealization of prehistory. The myth of the arcadia had replaced that of revolution. Early naturians were the first anarcho-primitivists. First-wave naturians were not vegetarians. In fact, some figureheads of the movement, notably Henri Beylie[18] and Henri Zisly,[19] were critical of vegetarianism. Nature, they argued, has made humans omnivores. Beylie believed that humans were meant to be predators and that animals would proliferate exceedingly if they were not killed for food (Zisly, 1911). He thought that plant-based diets were fitting for the summer whereas meat was to be consumed in the winter. Zisly (1903, 1905) distinguished natural foods (vegetables, honey, milk, meat, etc.) from civilized ones (all processed foods, sugar, alcohol, etc.) and claimed that meat gave humans greater strength. In his view, animals and plants were both part of nature and both suffered in their own way when killed for food. Although he believed that it would be best if humans and other animals could live in peace, he claimed that vegetarians were "nature fanatics" (Zisly, 1905). Zisly became more sympathetic toward vegetarianism as years passed and even became a member of the Société végétarienne de France in 1905.

It is the second generation of naturians, the neo-naturians, who embraced vegetarianism (as well as veganism [végétalisme] and raw veganism [crudivégétalisme]). Neo-naturianism emerged before the First World War, but really took root in the 1920s with Henry Le Fèvre's journal Néo-naturien (1921–1927). Less radical than their predecessors, neo-naturians yearned for a simpler existence, free from superficial and superfluous needs and possessions. They sought to lead more rustic lives, finding more natural alternatives to housing, transport, relationships, and so on. Close to the naturist movement, they promoted outdoor activities, physical exercise, simple clothing, and nudism. Veganism was at the heart of the neo-naturian quest for natural lifestyles.

VEGETARIANISM IN INDIVIDUALIST ANARCHISM

Explicit anarchist advocacy of vegetarianism began at the dawn of the 20th century. In 1901, two articles (Adrien, 1901; Végétus, 1901) from the prominent anarchist newspaper Le Libertaire argued in favor of vegetarianism, and Reclus (1901) wrote a famous piece on the subject for La Réforme alimentaire, the publication of the French Vegetarian Society. In the same year, the feminist writer and activist Léonie Fournival (aka Rolande), who had adopted a plant-based diet during her 2-year stay with English anarchists in London, joined the naturians and founded the group Les végétariens de Paris. Libertad, Paraf-Javal, and friends of the seminal individualist journal l'anarchie began promoting plant-based diets from 1905, but it is from the 1910s that vegetarianism and veganism began to truly flourish in libertarian circles. Several individualist journals published articles on the question of these meat-free diets (e.g., Nada, 1912). Notably, naturist and hygienist doctors provided scientific arguments in favor of vegetarianism in L'Idée libre, edited by cofounder of l'anarchie André Lorulot (e.g., Guelpa, 1912). Vegetarianism was also a commonly debated topic during anarchist gatherings and conferences. A note from a meeting of the anarchist group of the 15th arrondissement that took place in the winter of 1914 reports that its participants discussed the many benefits of vegetarianism: "The anarchists present only spoke of questions related to the vegetarian diet. They unanimously noted the benefits of this diet for one's health, as well as for the development of one's intellect and willpower."[20] Sophie Zaïkowska[21] and her partner Georges Butaud,[22] central figures of neo-naturianism, were among the keenest individualist advocates of vegan and raw food diets (Butaud, 1930). They were also the main instigators of libertarian colonies in France.

Libertarian colonies (milieux libres) were a way for workers to escape from urban factories as well as a reaction to the antianarchist laws that had been passed as a result of the terrorist attacks of 1892–1894. In France, the first two libertarian colonies were founded in 1903 in the northeast of the country. They were spaces in which anarchist ideas could be applied, tested, and refined. They also gave the general public a glimpse of what an anarchist society could be like and portrayed its proponents in a new light, far from the stereotypical images of hateful terrorists circulated by the media. Although there were only a few dozen actual colonists, several hundred people visited the *milieux libres*. Colonists sought to be as self-sufficient as possible. To this end, they practiced voluntary simplicity, which consisted primarily in the radical minimization of one's needs for material goods and the adoption of a vegetarian or vegan diet.[23] Several naturians lived in libertarian colonies, notably Zisly and Beylie who were among the first colonists at the *Clairière de Vaux* (1902–1907), founded by Butaud and Zaïkowka.

In 1911, Butaud and Zaïkowska established a second *milieu libre* in Bascon (Aisne), which became exclusively vegan in 1914.[24] It was the longest-lasting *milieu libre* in early 20th-century France. It remained a libertarian colony until 1931 and then became a vegetarian and naturist holiday center until 1951. From 1918 on, Zaïkowska and Butaud gave fortnightly talks on veganism in Paris. In 1919, they founded the *Société Végétalienne Communiste*, whose manifesto described veganism as: "une base necessaire du développement individuel et social" (Butaud, 1919). In 1922, Butaud instituted the *Foyer végétalien*, first in Nice and then in Paris, which acted as the model for other vegan community centers around France.[25] The couple contributed to the *Néo-naturien* and launched their own journal, *Le Végétalien* (1924–1929), of which Zaïskowska helmed by herself after Butaud's death in 1926. She continued their vigorous vegan propaganda in years to come and wrote the entry *Végétalisme* in Sébastian Faure's *Anarchist Encyclopaedia* (1925–1934).

Louis Rimbault was another significant individualist anarchist promoter of veganism.[26] He was one of the first members of the Bascon colony, where he lived for a couple of years with his wife Clémence alongside Butaud and Zaikowska. In the early 1910s—probably the time during which he became vegan—he established a *milieu libre* in Pavillons-sous-Bois (Seine-et-Oise) with a dozen comrades, including his brother, Marceau Rimbault, a contributor to *l'anarchie*, and Octave Garnier, future member of the Bonnot Gang. From 1922, his vegan campaigning intensified: He wrote several articles for the *Néo-naturien*, gave talks at the *Foyer végétalien* in Paris, and went on a tour giving conferences on veganism all over France with the Breton naturian Hervé Coatmeur. His veganism became gradually more intransigent: He called meat eaters "walking graveyards" that "fed on blood" (Levebvre, 1963; Rimbault, 1923, 1924). In 1924, Rimbault established another *milieu libre*, a "vegan city" called *Terre Libérée* in Luynes (Indre-et-Loire), which was intended to be the continuation of the vegetarian experimentation of the Bascon colony. This exclusively and strictly vegan colony had explicit pedagogical goals: It was meant to be "a practical vegan school intended to show that the vegan individual can be self-sufficient" (Rimbault, 1926).[27] It was geared toward individuals who already followed a plant-based diet and who wanted to keep exploring and studying the health benefits of plant-based diets. Rimbault coined the term *naturarchie* to illustrate his vision of veganism as a holistic natural lifestyle.[28]

The restoration and preservation of health in the face of the physical and moral degeneration produced by industrial civilization was the upmost consideration for most vegan anarchists. Indeed, many were those who justified veganism solely on naturist and hygienist medical terms. For hygienists, health is achieved by living in accord with the laws of nature (e.g., Neuens, 1897, p. 18). Disease arises when one transgresses those laws. A healthy body is one that is able to withstand disease (Baubérot, 2004). Diet was seen as the principal means of strengthening the immune system (others included the proper use of water, air, sunlight, rest, and physical exercise; Cornet, 1909). Some also claimed that a plant-based diet had curative virtues. Such was the case of Rimbault, who built a preventorium and a health center for the sick at *Terre Libérée*, where he invented what he believed was an optimally nutritious meal, *La Basconnaise*, a seasonal vegan salad composed of some 34 ingredients, and which could be adapted to the individual's personal dietary needs.[29] Zaïkowska (1929a, 1929b), who eventually made the *Basconnaise* the basis of her diet, wrote that it was her health problems that first led her transition from vegetarianism to veganism. The Breton anarcho-syndicalist Charles Fouyer (1927) claimed that his articular rheumatisms had completely disappeared after spending only 6 months on a vegan diet in Bascon. We are told that 8 years after the colony had embraced veganism, no one had fallen badly ill: "except for a few minor and passing health problems, [colonists] did not suffer from any real illnesses."[30] Veganism was thus regarded as the diet of regeneration.

It is important to point out that vegetarianism and veganism were not always limited to abstinence from meat and fish or from all animal products (as in present-day usages of the term). When it did not imply the exclusive consumption of fruit and vegetables, vegetarianism was linked to a broader hygienist and naturist lifestyle that also excluded processed foods and intoxicants, notably alcohol, tobacco, and sugar.[31] These were regarded as addictive and debilitating substances that kept workers in a state of weakness and servitude. Conversely, vegetarianism was viewed as the diet that would help people recover their physical and mental abilities. As Jules Méline wrote in the *Encylopédie anarchiste*: "[Vegetarianism is] a dietary system that excludes all that jeopardizes one's physical and mental equilibrium, and, consequently, affects one's vigor, [namely] meat, fish, spirits, fermented beverages, . . . chocolate, coffee, etc."[32] Thus, in addition to health promotion, veganism was adopted as therapy and disease prevention. For many individualist anarchists, veganism was no less than the quest for the ideal—or the most natural—human diet.

Veganism, for individualist anarchists, was not merely a question of diet or healthy lifestyle. It contributed to one's personal and social emancipation in other important ways. As Butaud (1922) wrote: "One should not keep considering veganism solely as a therapeutic system. Veganism is part of the doctrine of free inquiry that will transform the world." First, veganism enabled a person to gain economic freedom. Individualists believed that people enslaved themselves with artificial needs. As Butaud (1912) argued:

> One of the tendencies of individualism is to do away with false needs, to make things simpler, less costly, and to reject all that is unnecessary so that it may be easier for the individual to flourish and to maintain a healthy body.

Like Epicureans, they sought to distinguish natural and necessary needs from unnatural and unnecessary ones. Animal source foods and animal products were instances of unnecessary goods that kept one dependent upon the capitalist system and the ultra-consumerist mindset it fostered. During a conference, a speaker gave the recipe for what was supposed to be a wholesome meal made up of corn, oatmeal, cacao, and calcium phosphate, which cost only 25 cents (almost half the price of a 1-kilo loaf of bread at the time and half the price of a baguette today; c. 0.65 euro cents).[33] Individualists such as Butaud, Zaïkowska, and Rimbault were convinced that veganism was the key to monetary independence, autonomy, and self-sufficiency. Also, veganism was a way to practice anarchy in the here and now: "[Les végétaliens] sont des anarchistes en action, qui ne coopèrent en rien que ce soit, par notre méthode de vie, aux forces sur lesquelles repose le principe d'État ou de simple autorité" (Rimbault, 1926). It was yet another way to fight against the social order: "Veganism is not merely a question of dietary hygiene . . . it is a formal practice of non-cooperation against all forces on which the State and its satellites rely: Church, Money, Army, Salaried Work, Justice System" (Rimbault, 1926). In addition to health, veganism was a means of self-sufficiency and revolt against society.

As mentioned earlier, vegetarianism has historically been closely linked to various esoteric sects (Spencer, 1993). Some anarchists also seem to have found in it a spiritual conduit. This can be illustrated, for instance, by the quasi-monastic atmosphere at the *Foyer végétalien* in Paris. The *Foyer végétalien* organized various activities such as gymnastics and literature classes, weekly talks and debates, as well as feasts. It had six beds for the homeless and comrades in need. It also included a restaurant that served daily vegan meals at a low cost. On its walls one could read oddly juxtaposed naturist and anarchist precepts such as "Do not drink wine, do not smoke . . . learn Esperanto" (Gascoin, 1928, p. 183). There was an overtly religious overtone to these vegan gatherings, such that some commented upon the ritualistic feel of communal meals (Gascoin, 1928, p. 183). Butaud (1924) noted "the religious have understood quite well that sharing food bring[s] men closer together." Elsewhere, he wrote that veganism brought about redemption (Butaud, 1925): "The Church offers salvation through self-sacrifice for God. Veganism and naturism offer serenity and forgiveness for your crimes if you contribute to their dissemination." He even described the core individualist belief in self-transformation, which he viewed as uniting all vegans, in quasi-religious terms:

> The social question is no longer a matter of power, it is a question of individual transformation, and all vegans, regardless of their living conditions, of their social background, and even of their personal ethic, are united by a common calling. (Butaud, 1924)

For individualists like Butaud, veganism was partly grounded in spirituality. "The real vegan is a mystic," wrote an anonymous contributor to the individualist journal *l'Insurgé* in 1926.[34] Veganism fostered hope in a new world of free, regenerated, and conscious individuals.

Even when it was not explicitly linked to spiritual expression, veganism had an important symbolic and ritualistic value. When awaiting their death sentence, the *bandits tragiques*, or members of the so-called Bonnot Gang, held fast to a strict askesis: They remained vegan, kept on training their bodies and minds, and still refrained from consuming intoxicants (Michon, 1913, p. 187). This shows that such practices were valuable in and of themselves, not merely for some kind of future emancipation. In addition, it suggests that they had taken on a ritualistic dimension of their own. They were a way for individualists to preserve their dignity and to remind themselves that they were members of a select group of conscious individuals (Bauberot, 2004). Naturist and hygienist practices may thus be regarded both as means of consolidating the individualist identity and as a form of spiritual exercise. Moreover, they probably gave comrades a sense of working toward a cause that was greater than themselves, thus allowing them to simultaneously assert their marginality and to transcend their individuality. In sum, in addition to being a central element of the process of self-regeneration, naturist practices, of which veganism was the core, were part and parcel of the good life, as well as a way to symbolically identify with an individualist elite that prefigured anarchy (Dequeker, 1914).

Veganism had broader moral implications for anarchists' self-development. According to a 1924 survey of members of the *Foyer végétalien*, some linked veganism to pacifism and nonviolence as well as kindness and solidarity, while others saw in it the most efficient way to lead a simpler, happier, and more natural life (Butaud, 1924, p. 24). As a 24-year-old respondee by the name of Bourguigneau contended: "The individual who practices veganism moves closer to nature. They achieve greater personal growth and better health. They become happier and better to others" (Butaud, 1924, p. 21). Another respondee, Charlotte Davy, stated: "All vegan, simpler life, less bloody humanity, more goodness . . . what disruption of popular mentality, what a moral revolution!" (Butaud, 1924, p. 27). Veganism was a springboard for moral edification.

Although the regeneration of one's health along with the quest for personal emancipation (be it economic, moral, or spiritual) were the primary motives for converting to veganism, individualist anarchists also expressed concern for animal suffering and opposed animal exploitation. Many argued that animal life was valuable in and of itself. Butaud denounced the state of servitude of domesticated animals and spoke in favor of agricultural machines that would suppress animal slavery. Rimbault (1922) decried the "necrophiliac business" of meat production and the cruelty it involved: The animal slaughtered for human consumption was always "overworked, exhausted, famished, brutalized, [and] terrorized." Libertad drew an unequivocal parallel between workers' exploitation and that of animals: "By eating animal flesh you become complicit in numberless murders that are of no benefit to you. You are victims that let themselves be fed with the blood of other victims" (Colomber, 1912, pp. 92–93). The individualist propagandist and member of *l'anarchie* Rirette Maîtrejean (1913/1988) concluded: "[Individualist anarchists] cannot bear the sight of slaughtered meat on their plate. The motto 'Be good to animals' is engraved on their heart" (p. 11). It is thus clear that individualist anarchists were concerned with the freedom and well-being of nonhuman animals.

Adopting a plant-based diet was one of the main ways in which individualists sought to live in harmony with nature. The ruthless exploitation of humanity over nature was sometimes described as yet another form of domination, especially in naturian texts. Though not the principal argument for veganism, ecological concerns were nonetheless present in several individualist writings. Even for someone like Rimbault (1922), for whom adopting a plant-based diet was primarily a matter of health, veganism meant respecting and taking care of the more-than-human world:

> The vegan individual cultivates their vegetables. He makes *basconnaise* by collecting one leaf at a time on each plant, and for each plant that needs to be extracted, he will grow many others so as to restore Nature's equilibrium through his work. (Rimbault, 1928, p. 59)

Veganism allowed individualists to reconsider their place on earth. As Butaud stressed: "[Veganism] is not merely a diet, but a social framework that allows the individual to live in accord with natural laws" (as cited in Zaïkowska, 1929a). Vegan anarchists did not merely follow natural laws for the sake of personal growth; it was a way to reconcile themselves with the rest of the natural world.

Finally, it should be noted that veganism was not embraced unanimously by individualists. In fact, it was occasionally a source of conflict rather than a rallying point. Dietary difference was one of the main reasons for the dissolution of Rimbault's first colony in Pavillons-sous-Bois, which could not afford the expenditure incurred by the purchase of nonvegan food products (Rimbault, 1924). At the *milieu libre du Quai de la Pie*, vegetarians and omnivores ate their meals separately (Zisly, 1914). When living together in the urban colony of Romainville, members of *l'anarchie* quarreled over dietary issues. Lorulot wanted to enforce a strict vegetarian diet that Rirette Maîtrejean and Victor Serge refused to adopt. Similarly, Butaud argued with Beylie at the Vaux colony over oysters that the latter had bought from a communist cooperative.[35] Many individualists, such as the leading propagandist E. Armand, were in favor of veganism but did not want to impose it on anyone. They thought that the rigid dietary restrictions advocated by individuals such as Butaud, Zaïkowska, Lorulot, and Rimbault were dogmatic. Indeed, their obsession with hygiene and healthy eating was sometimes seen as a form of orthorexia nervosa. The question of diet thus created divisions in anarchist ranks between those who wanted to remain omnivorous or flexitarians and those who swore only by a strict vegan diet.[36]

CONCLUSION

Individualist anarchists were promoting veganism as an autonomous diet and lifestyle long before the creation of the first vegan society in the United Kingdom in 1945, not to mention that of the French *Fédération végane* in 2010. For individualist anarchists, veganism was first and foremost a matter of personal emancipation through preserving one's health, gaining economic independence, and working toward moral regeneration. It was part and parcel of their aspiration to lead a simpler life, free from unnecessary possessions, and more in line with their instincts. Some individualists also defended the inherent value of animal life and opposed all forms of animal exploitation. Finally, anarchists did not think so much in terms of the ecological impact of the production of animal-based foods but rather in terms of their desire to live in harmony with nature. Influenced by the broader naturist and hygienist movements, anarcho-vegans' primary aim was to recover a natural way of life in opposition to the alienation and degeneration produced by industrial civilization.

Despite having had little impact on the rest of the anarchist movement and still less on society at large, neo-naturians and other individualist vegans can legitimately be considered the forgotten precursors of the modern ecological and animal liberation movements. Moreover, anarcho-individualist vegans show us a different conception of anarchist political struggle, which contrasts with the clichéd image of the thug or the terrorist. Their lives and deeds give us a glimpse into their vision of positive anarchy. Individualist anarchists did not believe that economic emancipation and revolution could truly liberate people. In their view, the only way forward was that self-transformation in the here and now that would eventually ripple through the rest of society. Veganism was one such concrete practice of anarchist prefiguration. In Butaud's (1922) words: "Enlightened individualists who practice veganism transform society by transforming themselves."

Notes

1. The word "vegan" was originally coined in 1944 by Donald Watson, who founded the U.K. Vegan Society in 1945. In France, *véganisme* and *végane* were first added to the *Dictionnaire Hachette* in 2013, then to the dictionaries *Robert* and the *Larousse* in 2015. According to a 2014–2015 Istitut National du Cancer study, there are approximately 90,000 vegans in France (see https://www.federationvegane.fr/documentation/combien-de-veganes/).

2. *Larousse* defines *véganisme* as a "mode de vie alliant une alimentation exclusive par les végétaux (végétalisme) et le refus de consommer tout produit (vêtement, chaussure cosmétique, etc.) issu des animaux ou de leur exploitation." *Végétalisme* is defined as a "régime alimentaire excluant tout aliment d'origine animal." Finally, *végétarisme* is defined as a "régime alimentaire excluant toute chair animal (viande, poisson), mais qui admet en général la consommation d'aliments d'origine animale comme les œufs, le lait et les produits laitiers (fromage, yaourts)."

3. Rates in other European countries include: Germany 5.6%, Spain 3.8%, United Kingdom 8% (Synthèse des résultats à partir de l'étude "Panorama de la consommation végétarienne en Europe," réalisée par le CREDOC pour FranceAgriMer et l'OCHA en 2018, October Edition, 2019).

4. The modern animal rights movement is called the antispeciesist movement (*movement antispécisite*) in France.

5. Note that the *Parti animaliste* is a welfarist organization. It does not advocate the abolition of animal exploitation and ethical vegetarianism. Rather, it promotes the improvement of animals' living conditions and the reduction of meat consumption mainly for ecological and health reasons.

6. Animal rights activism is not necessarily corelated to vegetarianism. Political scientist Christophe Traïni (2012, pp. 12–13) distinguishes three groups in animal rights organizations, namely those who defend companion animals, those who defend free-living animals, and those who oppose animal exploitation more generally. Ethical vegetarianism is practiced mainly by members of the last group.

7. The word "vegetarian" was first used in England in the mid-19th century.

8. Notably behmenism, the Philadelphians, and the Bible Christian Church. For further discussion on the development of modern Western vegetarianism, see Ouédraogo (2000).

9. *L'Alimentation végétale de l'homme*. Kingsford was one of the first English women to obtain a doctoral degree in medicine. She was also the only person at the time who graduated without having experimented on animals.

10. The first vegetarian society in the Western world was founded in the United Kingdom in 1847, followed by the United States (1850), Germany (1867), and Austria (1879). The first vegetarian cookery book was written by Martha Brotherton in 1812.

11. The word *végétariaisme* became more popular than the anglicism *végétarianisme*. In the 1890s, dictionaries included both words as well as the word *végétalisme*. For example, the *Grand Dictionnaire universel* (1890) defined *végétarisme* as a "doctrine diététique consistant dans l'abstention de tout aliment qui ne peut s'obtenir que par la destruction d'une vie animale" and "végétalisme" as a "régime des personnes qui se nourrissent exclusivement de végétaux."

12. Parisette. (1906, April 15). La vie de Paris. *Le Figaro*.

13. "Naturiens, Végétariens, Végétaliens et Crudivégétaliens dans le mouvement anarchiste Français," *Invariance*, suppléments au n. 9 (July 1993 and January 1994).

14. The geographer Philippe Pelletier (2015–2016) is the main French scholar who has looked at the connection between animal liberation and anarchism. He edited two anthologies on the subject.

15. Séverine directed the journal from 1885 to 1888, making her the first female publication manager of a major daily newspaper in France (see Couturiau, 2001).

16. In 1886, Huot interrupted a lecture on a treatment against rabies as it involved animal experimentation (see Bory, 2013).

17. For further discussion on early anarchist defenses of the animal cause, see Pelletier (2016).

18. Henri Beylie (Félix Beaulieu; 1870–1944) was born in Paris, where he worked as a banker and an accountant. He joined the *naturiens libertaires* in 1895 and coedited *La Nouvelle Humanité*, which later became *Le Naturien* (1895–1898), alongside Henri Zisly. He married Clémentine Bontoux in 1898. He participated in the establishment of the *Ligue antimilitariste* with Paraf-Javal and Libertad in 1902. He gravitated toward being a communist anarchist from 1905 onward.

19. Henri Zisly (1872–1945) was born in Paris to working-class parents living in free union. At age 17, he was already active in anarchist circles. He coedited *La Nouvelle Humanité*, which later became *Le Naturien* (1895–1898), with Henri Beylie. He married the milliner Marie Lucie Dusolon in 1908. He wrote in numerous individualist journals, including articles on naturism and vegetarianism for *l'anarchie*. He launched a naturist periodical *La vie naturelle* (1907–1920) and wrote the entries *Naturianisme*, *Naturocratisme*, and *Naturophilie* in the *Encyclopédie anarchiste*. He participated in the foundation of the *Fédération anarchiste* in 1936.

20. Archive de la Préfecture de Police. January 6, 1914, BA 1506.

21. Sophie Zaïkowska (1874–1939) was born in Vilna (Russian Empire, present day Vilnus, Lithuania). She was one of the most active female individualists in the early 20th century. She self-identified as a feminist individualist anarchist. She moved to France in 1898 after having studied physical and natural sciences (specializing in nutrition) in Geneva, Switzerland. She wrote in numerous anarchist journals, including *L'Éducation libertaire* (1900–1902), *l'Autarcie* (1903), and *La vie anarchiste* (which she directed in 1920).

22. Georges Butaud (1868–1926) was born in Marchienne-au-Pont, Belgium, into the petite bourgeoisie. He worked as a stonemason in Switzerland before moving to Vienne (Isère), where he launched the journal *Le Flambeau* (1901–1902) and began collaborating with E. Armand, Henri Zisly, and Sophie Zaïkowska on the foundation of a libertarian colony. He was the most

active proponent and instigator of the *milieux libres* (Vaux, 1902–1907; Bascon, 1911–1951; Saint-Maur, 1913–1914). He wrote several articles for *l'anarchie* between 1910 and 1911.

23. It is interesting to note that some anarchist vegans left Europe in hopes of founding libertarian colonies in freer and more fertile lands such as Tahiti and South America, especially Brazil (see Rimbault, 1924).

24. *La Revue naturiste*, September 1922.

25. Zaïkowska, Végétalisme, *Encyclopédie anarchiste*.

26. Louis Rimbault (1877–1949) was born in Tours and was one of eight children in a poor family with an alcoholic father. He worked as a locksmith and as a mechanic. He began frequenting the illegalist and individualist milieus in the 1910s. He spent 2 years in jail after having been associated with the *Bandits tragiques* in 1911. He became vegan around the same time—a lifestyle he kept on promoting. An accident that occurred at the colony *Terre Libérée* in 1932 left him paraplegic until his death.

27. Although there were supposed to be 20 permanent residents at the colony, there were only five for most of its existence, namely Louis Rimbault; his wife, Clémence Rimbault; their adopted daughter, Léonie Pierre; and Gabrielle Lallemand and her daughter, Solange. Visitors were numerous (300 during the first 10 months following the foundation of the colony).

28. For further discussion on Rimbault, see Baubérot (2014).

29. Zaïkowska, Végétalisme, *Encyclopédie anarchiste*.

30. *La Revue Naturiste*, September 1922.

31. For Zaïkowska, for instance, vegans abstained from eating sugar and drank nothing but water (Zaïkowska, Végétalisme, *Encyclopédie anarchiste*).

32. Méline, Végétarisme, *Encyclopédie anarchiste*.

33. Archives de la Préfecture de police de Paris, April 30, 1912, BA 1499.

34. *L'Insurgé*, n. 52, May 1, 1926.

35. Bulletin mensuel de la colonie communiste "Le Milieu libre de Vaux," April-May, 1904.

36. There were also petty disagreements between vegan individualists, especially between Rimbault and friends of the *Néo-naturien* and Butaud and Zaïkowska and followers of the *Végétalien*.

References

Adrien. (1901, August 24–31). Le végétarisme et la question sociale. *Le Libertaire*.

Baubérot, A. (2004). *Histoire du naturisme: Le mythe du retour à la nature*. Rennes, France: Presses universitaires de Rennes.

Baubérot, A. (2013). Les naturiens libertaires ou le retour à l'anarchisme préhistorique. *Mil neuf cent. Revue d'histoire intellectuelle*, 31.

Baubérot. (2014). Aux sources de l'écologisme anarchiste: Louis Rimbault et les communautés végétaliennes en France dans la première moitié du XXe siècle. *Le Mouvement social*, 246.

Bory, J-Y. (2013). *La douleur des bêtes*. Rennes, France: Presses universitaires de Rennes.

Butaud, G. (1912, June 12, 15). *La vie anarchiste*.

Butaud, G. (1919, December 1–15). Société végétalienne communiste. *Pendant la mêlée*.

Butaud, G. (1922, November 8). *Le Néo-naturien*.

Butaud, G. (1924, December). Banquet des amis du foyer. *Le Végétalien*.

Butaud, G. (1925, February). Le bénéfice de la propagande. *Le Végétalien*.

Butaud, G. (1930). *Le végétalisme*. Ermont, France: Publication du Végétalien.

Colomber, A. (1912). *À nous deux, patrie!* Paris, France: Édition de l'Insurgé.

Cornet, C. (1909). Les lois de la santé. *Hygie*, 23.

Couturiau, P. (2001). *Séverine, l'insurgée*. Monaco: Édition du Rocher.

Dequeker, C. (1914, January 1). *La vie anarchiste*.

Fouyer, C. (1927, December). *Le Végétalien*.

Gascoin, E. (1928). *Les religions inconnues*. Paris, France: Gallimard.

Guelpa. (1912, July 1). Désintoxication organique et régime végétarien. *L'Idée libre*.

Hondermarck, A. (2021). *Une nébuleuse végétarienne: Sociologie historique du mouvement végétarien (1880–1940)*. Paris, France: Institut d'études politiques. Doctoral thesis in progress.

Larue, A. (2015) *Le végétarisme et ses ennemis*. Paris, France: Presses universitaires de France.

Larue, A. (2019). *Le végétarisme des lumières*. Paris, France: Classiques Garnier.

Levebvre, A. (1963, September). *Le milieu libre de bascon, texte dactylographié de la conférence faite à la société historique de Château-Thierry*.

Maîtrejean, R. (1988). *Souvenirs d'anarchie*. Baye, France: La digitale. (Original work published 1913).

Méry, A. (1998). Éléments d'histoire du végétarisme en France. *Association végétarienne de France*, 2.

Michon, E. (1913). *Essai de psychologie criminelle: Un peu de l'âme des bandits*. Paris, France: Dorbon-Ainé.

Nada, P. (1912, January). Végétarisme. *La vie anarchiste*.

Neuens, N. (1897). *Bains atmosphériques*. Namur, Belgium: A. Voitrin.

Ouédraogo, A. P. (1996). Le végétarisme. Esquisse d'une histoire sociale. *INRA Sciences Sociales*, 2.

Ouédraogo, A. P. (2000). De la secte religieuse à l'utopie philantropique. Genèse sociale du végétarisme occidental. *Annales, Histoire, Sciences Sociales*, 55.

Pelletier P. (2015–2016). *Anarchie et cause animale* (Vol. 1 and 2). Paris, France: Les éditions du Monde Libertaire.

Pelletier, P. (2016). L'anarchisme et l'animal. *Pour*, 231.

Reclus, E. (1897, January). La grande famille. *Le Magazine international*.

Reclus, E. (1901, March 5). À propos du végétarisme. *La Réforme alimentaire*.

Reclus, E. (1905). *L'homme et la terre* (Vol. 1). Paris, France: Librairie universelle.

Rimbault, L. (1922, April 4). Le problème de la viande. *Le Néo-naturien*.

Rimbault, L. (1923, December 15–1924, January). *Le Néo-naturien*.

Rimbault, L. (1924, February). Libération économique. *Le Néo-naturien*.

Rimbault, L. (1926). Lettre à E. Armand, 18 août 1926. IFHS. Fond Armand, 14 AS 211.

Rimbault, L. (1928). *Secrets bienfaits de la maladie, les soins exécutant, médecine et médecins, ce que le visage révèle*. Luynes, France: Éditions de Terre libérée.

Spencer, C. (1993). *The heretic's east*. Hanover, NH: University Press of New England.

Traïni, C. (2012). Between disgust and moral indignation. *Revue française de science politique*, 62, 12–13.

Végétus. (1901, September-October 5). Un mot sur le végétarisme. *Le Libertaire*, 84.

Zaïkowska, S. (1929a). La vie et la mort de Georges Butaud. *Le Végétalien*.

Zaïkowska, S. (1929b). Recettes végétaliennes, *Le Végétalien*.

Zisly, H. (1903). Réflexion sur le végétarisme. *Le Libertaire*, 25.

Zisly, H. (1905, November). Nature et civilisation. *L'Ordre naturel*.

Zisly, H. (1911). Mouvement naturien et néo-naturien. *La vie naturelle*, 5.

Zisly, H. (1914, April-May). Pâcques communiste. *Les Réfractaires*.

PART IV

Historical Controversies: Vivisection

Vivisection, Virtue Ethics, and the Law in 19th-Century Britain

A. W. H. BATES
University College, London, England.

This historical study of early 19th-century opposition to vivisection suggests that the moral persona of the vivisector was an important theme. Vivisectors claimed they deliberately suppressed their feelings to perform scientifically necessary experiments: Where there was reason, there could be no cruelty. Their critics argued they were callous and indifferent to suffering, which was problematic for medical practitioners, who were expected to be merciful and compassionate. This anthropocentric debate can be located within the virtue ethics tradition: Compassion for animals signified a humane character. The 1876 Vivisection Act facilitated experimentation by separating the practice of vivisection from that of medicine.

KEY WORDS: vivisection, virtue ethics, law, 19th century, medicine

Historiographic interest in the opponents of vivisection increased with the renewed awareness of animal interests in the mid-1970s that was epitomized by Peter Singer's (1995) work on animal liberation (French, 1975; Turner, 1980; Harrison, 1982, pp. 82–122). Subsequent studies located antivivisection activity in the context of 19th-century social movements, particularly feminism and socialism (Lansbury, 1985; Elston, 1987; Kean, 1995, 1998; Miller, 2009). Most scholarship on 19th-century vivisection and medicine has concentrated on the two decades between 1870 and 1890, and especially on the debate between antivivisectionists and career scientists around the Cruelty to Animals Act 1876, which Richard French (1975) used as a case study of the attitude of Victorian society to scientific medicine (Feller, 2009; Boddice, 2011). In a pioneering essay on vivisection in the early 19th century, Anita Guerrini (2008) characterized the debate as a predominantly anthropocentric one, in which the suffering of animals and their rights or interests were less important than the effects of vivisection on the experimenter's morals and reputation (Boddice, 2007).

In this article, I wish to develop our understanding of the ethical objections to animal experimentation that were put forward in the early 19th century, particularly by doubters within the medical profession. I shall argue that the law's emphasis on the wantonness of cruelty encouraged experimenters to justify their work with reference to its anticipated outcome, since a rational purpose precluded their actions being cruel. Utilitarian arguments that the medical benefits of vivisection outweighed any unpleasantness or suffering were effective against claims that experimentation was unnecessary, but they failed to address the criticism that participation in vivisection was a sign, or cause, of a callous temperament. Physicians were concerned that links with vivisection would deter patients, and medical experimenters tried to show that they could carry out their work without compromising their moral sensibility. By framing the anticruelty debate in terms of the character of the experimenter, I shall examine the contribution of virtue ethics, a subject that has hitherto received little attention in studies of the 19th-century debate on vivisection.

Virtue ethics differs from utilitarian or deontological ethics in its concern with agents rather than actions. It asks how a virtuous person would behave in a particular situation and emphasizes character and motives instead of rules and outcomes. Though it is one of the oldest ethical systems, described in Aristotle's *Nicomachean Ethics*, it had declined in importance by the 18th century, which saw the ascendancy of utilitarianism and deontology. Medicine, however, retained an attachment to the virtues, particularly concerning the moral character of its practitioners (Percival, 1803). One virtue relevant to experimental medicine was that of humanity toward animals, which the anatomist James Lawson Drummond regarded as "doing good for its own sake" (Drummond, 1831, p. 183). As experimentation began to replace patient-based studies, practitioners questioned whether it was ever acceptable for a physician to experiment on living animals. Some contended that to perform vivisection was to show oneself as callous: a particularly damaging charge for those whose patients expected compassion and mercy from them. In response, experimenters argued that they experimented reluctantly, only after deliberately suppressing their sensibilities (an act that required the virtues of fortitude and courage), but critics dismissed this as demoralization. I suggest that the suspicion with which patients and professionals regarded the character of the vivisector was an important factor in promoting self-regulation by medical practitioners in Britain in the early and middle 19th century.

ANTICRUELTY LAW AND ANIMAL EXPERIMENTATION

After repeated attempts in the early 19th century by members of the English Parliament to introduce anticruelty bills, Richard Martin's Cruel and Improper Treatment of Cattle Act finally became law in 1822. Martin—"Humanity Dick"—was well known for his animal welfare campaigning, but the bill was of little interest to most members of the House of Commons, who greeted it with mocking laughter (Niven, 1967, p. 61). That there was sufficient concern over the treatment of livestock for it to be debated at all was partly due to demographic changes: The burgeoning conurbation of London brought well-to-do citizens into proximity with cockpits and cattle markets and they found what they saw disturbing. Especially worrying for an urban bourgeoisie unsettled by the French Revolution were the ungovernable lower classes, who were thought to treat animals cruelly because they either lacked feeling or actually enjoyed seeing them suffer. Parliament's interest in anticruelty laws was an attempt to moderate these vicious tendencies, a motive that historians of the antivivisection movement have also ascribed to those voluntary associations, such as the Society for the Prevention of Cruelty to Animals (SPCA), that were set up to bring prosecutions under Martin's act (SPCA, 1832; French, 1975; Guerrini, 2008). The argument that cruelty to animals led to violence against humans (Linzey, 2009) made its suppression a matter of self-interest, but this link was questioned: One reason the House of Commons hesitated for so long over anticruelty laws was that they could not agree whether "sports" such as bear-baiting were signs of incipient savagery or safe outlets for high spirits (Niven, 1967, pp. 57–58).

Whatever the truth of the claim that people who treated animals cruelly would harm humans if given the opportunity, it was not predicated upon the animals' moral status or capacity to suffer. In anticruelty law, the chief concern was not the suffering of the victim but the intentions of the perpetrator. Martin's act characterized cruelty as "wanton": It was indifferent to suffering caused for any rational purpose but punished violence perpetrated in an uncontrolled manner. The act left the public to decide when there was a case to answer; since there was no funding for its enforcement, prosecutions depended upon private citizens coming forward to press charges (Hughes & Lawson, 2011). The SPCA and other groups took up the challenge, though wantonness was difficult to prove as acts with a rational motive, however heartless, were not wanton: For example, a man who whipped a goat pulling a cart was found not guilty because he claimed he beat the goat "to make it go" (Anonymous, 1839). Through a combination of litigation and education, anticruelty societies set out to put a stop to casual, unthinking cruelty among the urban poor by "compel[ling] them to think and act like those of a superior class" ("Society for the Prevention of Cruelty to Animals," 1824).

Martin's act did not mention medical or physiological experiments on animals and was not drafted with these in mind; he probably did not become aware of the issue until 1824, when the French physiologist François Magendie gave a widely reported vivisection demonstration in London's Windmill Street anatomy school ("On Experiments," 1837). The publication of his experiments, in which he allegedly nailed a greyhound to a table, unleashed strong anti-French feelings that led to a public outcry in which Martin took up the antivivisection cause (Olmsted, 1944, p. 137). The Continental vogue for experimentation was alien to British medicine, which was based on observations made on patients: Experiments on living animals were uncommon (it was estimated that in the 1820s fewer than 1,000 a year were performed in the whole British Empire), and British medical men were said to have a "horror" of them (Magendie, 1824, p. 261; Etherington, 1842, p. 80).

After Magendie's visit, the secretary of the SPCA corresponded with leading medical men to solicit support for "a board . . . of the profession, to whom all proposed experiments must be submitted" (Mushet, 1839, p. 209). Their original responses have not survived, but several calling for animal experiments to be restricted were published in the national press ("Society for Preventing Cruelty to Animals," 1825). Undistinguished provincial practitioners, concerned that their profession would acquire a "bad name," also declared their opposition: 28 medical men from Newcastle upon Tyne and 38 from Bath signed testimonials against animal experimentation ("Physiology," 1825; Etherington, 1824, p. 111). Some were criticized for opposing vivisection merely in order to "curry favour" with concerned layfolk ("Physiology," 1825), but this made commercial sense as patients were prepared to boycott doctors who vivisected: For anticruelty activists this was a matter of principle, but poorer folk feared being experimented on themselves ("Correspondence on Field Sports," 1838).

Most early-19th century anticruelty campaigners were willing to liaise with the medical profession to decide what experiments were acceptable. A notable exception was Lewis Gompertz, who founded the Animals' Friend Society (AFS) in 1833 after he was expelled from the SPCA. He did not regard scientific necessity as justification for cruelty (he wanted the wording of Martin's act changed from "cruelly and wantonly" to "cruelly *or* wantonly"), and he offered a cash reward for evidence leading to the conviction of surgeons or students who "cut up Dumb Animals Alive" (Gompertz, 1992, p. 147). In reply, Thomas Wakley, editor of the *Lancet*, simply observed that anticruelty law did not cover medical experiments (Chippendale, 1839). The AFS under Gompertz campaigned for a change in the law to include the domestic animals that experimenters usually used. Though the Cruelty to Animals Act of 1835 was passed extending legal protection to cats and dogs, this made little difference as medical vivisection was unlikely to be thought "wanton" by any magistrate ("Amendment of the Laws," 1834).

NECESSITY AND HUMANITY

At the time of Magendie's London experiments the British medical profession was a loosely defined group with more than a dozen licensing bodies. There was no official position on animal experimentation, but medical men, concerned by the demonstrative vivisection popular in France, articulated various objections to it. The principal methodological criticism raised in the medical journals was that animals differ so greatly from humans physiologically that results could not reliably be extrapolated between them ("Observations Pathologiques," 1825; Knox, 1839). If animals were sufficiently similar to humans for results to be transferable, they ought also to be conscious of pain, so to some critics it seemed that vivisection, which was typically performed to assess responses mediated through the nervous system, was "criminal" if animals were physiologically similar to humans, and "objectless" if they were not (Lordat, 1854). It was not usual, however, for early-19th century vivisectors to concern themselves with animal pain at all, and the argument had little influence on them: Like Darwin, they could accept that "the lower animals, like man, manifestly feel pleasure and pain, happiness and misery" and still consider vivisection justifiable (Regan & Singer, 1989, p. 27).

Though British medical practitioners agreed that Magendie's demonstrations had "drawn odium" upon their profession (they regarded them as unnecessary and therefore cruel), few declared themselves unequivocally against vivisection: "Necessary" experiments that might significantly advance knowledge were usually regarded as acceptable and proponents of experimentation cited William Harvey's work on the circulation of blood and John Hunter's on aneurysms as examples of what could be achieved. Writing in the 1860s, the physician Andrew Wynter (1869) considered Hunter's work alone worth "the destruction of a whole hecatomb of dogs" (p. 68). In most cases, it was not necessary to offer such a precise utilitarian calculus, but enthusiasts for vivisection could always anticipate some benefit to justify their work. In his monograph *Vivisection Investigated and Vindicated*, the physician George Etherington (1842) described some recent animal experiments that he considered had yielded medically useful results, though humanitarians may have disagreed: For example, multiple injections of creosote were given to a series of dogs in order to demonstrate its properties as a poison. A difficulty for opponents of vivisection who were untrained in medicine was that it was hard to gainsay professional opinion without having their objections dismissed as the kind of ill-informed sentimentalizing favoured by "old ladies of both sexes" (Wynter, 1869, p. 66); womanish thought was supposedly based on the emotions rather than intellect and was therefore inappropriate in scientific contexts.

After his failed attempt at prosecution, Gompertz concluded that justification of experiments by their anticipated benefits had rendered the law "nugatory": Experimenters always predicted that their own work would yield worthwhile results, and so the justification of necessity became "the cheat of humanity" ("Necessity the Cheat of Humanity," 1841). Etherington, in defense of vivisection, agreed with him: "The worst moral character, never performs an act without thinking upon and having a motive in performing it" (1842, p. 72). Throughout the 19th century, groups such as the London Anti-Vivisection Society continued to assert that medical experiments were being performed "needlessly, and therefore cruelly," but there was no realistic prospect of bringing a successful prosecution as long as the experimenters were the arbiters of necessity ("Our Programme," 1890).

Vivisectionists kept the risk of prosecution to a minimum with strategies for self-regulation such as adherence to written guidelines and approval from peers. When criticizing the Continentals, British medical men made it clear what types of experiment—for example, speculative studies and public demonstrations—they considered unnecessary. The relatively few Englishmen who did vivisect—most notably Marshall Hall, James Blundell, James Hope, and Charles J. B. Williams—distanced themselves from criticism by experimenting privately, publishing their work only in professional journals, and following an apparently predetermined line of investigation. Hall repeated some of Magendie's experiments, in one of which he vivisected a dog and then made him vomit, whereon, according to Hall's (1828) own account, "a portion of lung was driven through the thoracic opening with violence and a sort of explosion" (p. 601). He was criticized in the medical press for this type of work (Manuel, 1990), but continued to experiment without encountering significant public opposition. Hall was responsible for some of the earliest published criteria for demonstrating that experiments were justified: The required information must not be obtainable by observation alone and the experiment had to have a distinct and definite object, could not be a repeat, had to cause the least possible suffering to the least sentient animal, and had to be properly recorded and witnessed (Hall, 1831, pp. 2–7). Though they made little impact at the time, these recommendations were influential in the drafting of the 1876 Cruelty to Animals Act.

Foreign experimenters preferred a more demonstrative approach that was unpopular with their English peers. The visit of another controversial French physiologist, Eugène Magnan, to London in 1874 revived the prospect of prosecution for cruelty, after medical men led by Thomas Jolliffe Tufnell, the president of the Irish College of Surgeons, intervened to stop Magnan's public vivisection of a dog ("Prosecution at Norwich," 1874). An attempt by the (now Royal) SPCA to prosecute the organizers failed (Magnan promptly returned to France), but the magistrates made it clear they thought the action was justified by refusing to award defense costs (Wolfensohn & Lloyd, 2003, p. 8). This was the closest a vivisectionist had come to being prosecuted for cruelty, and the legal position of experimenters was seen to require clarification. In 1875, Parliament set up a Royal Commission to consider the problem: the first step toward the 1876 Cruelty to Animals Act (French, 1975, pp. 112–158).

THE CRUELTY TO ANIMALS ACT

The 1876 act removed the word "wantonly" from the definition of cruelty but since, in the words of Mr. Justice Day, "cruelty must be something which cannot be justified," in practice the requirement that cruelty must be wanton remained (Candy, 1890). Like the controversial 1832 Anatomy Act, the 1876 Cruelty to Animals Act, also known as the Vivisection Act, was permissive rather than regulatory. It required experimenters to hold a license but these were liberally awarded within the scientific community: By 1891, 676 had been granted, a large proportion with special certificates dispensing with the requirement for anesthesia. The National Anti-Vivisection Society (NAVS), founded as the Victoria Street Society in 1875 by Frances Power Cobbe, branded the act "an utter failure," because it resulted in more experimentation than if vivisection had remained unlicensed, and called for it to be repealed ("Our Programme," 1890; Candy, 1891; "Plain Truth," 1891–1892). In the opinion of the NAVS, experimenters had used their "professional esprit de corps . . . to secure for themselves prolonged immunity from state interference with their atrocities" ("Plain Truth," 1891–1892). There was no successful prosecution during the 110 years the act remained in force.

Since Martin's law was never used to regulate vivisection, the apparent increase of it after the 1876 act needs to be accounted for. If, as its critics claimed, the 1876 act encouraged vivisection, what had been the prior barrier to it occurring? It was not the prospect of prosecution, since this had hardly seemed feasible until the Magnan case in 1874. An important aspect of the Cruelty to Animals Act was that the support of a professor of physiology, medicine, anatomy, or a related discipline was necessary (unless the applicant himself held such a post) to obtain a license to experiment. This gave formal recognition and authority to a new class of experimental physiologists, whose professional body, the Physiological Society, was founded in the year the act became law. Their vade mecum was the recently published *Handbook for the Physiological Laboratory* (Klein, Burdon-Sanderson, Forster, & Brunton,1873), a primer for neophytes that contained instructions for hundreds of experiments, but made no explicit reference to the administration of anesthesia. The act placed the responsibility for recommending licensees with the presidents of the notoriously unrepresentative medical royal colleges, but there was no role for ordinary practitioners, some of whom had been critical of the act, and were now said to be "afraid" to speak out for fear of disapproval from the leaders of their profession (Morris, 1886, p. 80). The act also forbade the admission of lay observers to vivisection demonstrations and ensured it was difficult for them to find out where they took place, since experimenters, who were required to make returns to the secretary of state, could ask that their names and addresses be omitted from the published lists. In 1892, Reverend F. O. Morris suggested that admitting the public to experiments would actually prevent cruelty since, unlike the professionals, their sensibilities had not been blunted by familiarity (Anonymous, 1891–1892). One example suggests that the public was a stricter judge of what was acceptable: Nottingham University College was initially granted a license for vivisection, but it had to be withdrawn after local protests ("Nottingham University College and Vivisection," 1891–1892).

The NAVS was concerned that the new cadre of licensed vivisectors was so indifferent to suffering that experimentation would be "the simple, natural thing to do to any helpless creature in their hands" ("Editorial," 1881–1882). Physiologists may not have treated patients themselves, but they could set a bad example to those who did. If even the most distinguished scientists, wrote Lewis Carroll (1875), were careless of the suffering they caused, "what will be the temper of mind of the ordinary coarse, rough man . . . of whom the bulk of the medical profession . . . is made up?" The NAVS blamed vivisection for what it saw as a trend toward medical experimentation on human subjects: The chemist and microbiologist Louis Pasteur proposed experimenting on condemned criminals, the dermatologist Jonathan Hutchinson delayed the treatment of a patient with a painful disease to better demonstrate the case, and the microbiologist Robert Koch experimented on paupers; all actions, it was said, to which no vivisectionist could logically object (Anonymous, 1881–1882; "Two Views of the Vivisector," 1881–1882; "Items of Interest," 1890).

Professional physiologists might experiment without fear that this would deter potential patients, but they were nonetheless careful to portray themselves as reluctant vivisectors. According to one account of their work, the real sacrifices were being made not by the animals, but by the experimenters: "We have heard a considerable number of physiologists declare unanimously, that all vivisection tires them exceedingly; sometimes so shatters them, that it requires all their power of will to carry the process through to the accomplishment of the aim" ("Two Views of the Vivisector," 1881–1882). This claim shows that the experimenters' moral character and sensibilities were still an important issue. From a utilitarian perspective, the case for vivisection would actually have been stronger if, in addition to acquiring knowledge from it, the operators had enjoyed their work rather than suffering for it. By stating that they undertook experiments reluctantly at the cost of great personal effort, physiologists were defending their personal virtue: They suffered for the benefit of others, while their antivivisection opponents were oversentimental hypocrites who profited from medical experimentation, but did nothing to encourage it.

VIRTUE ETHICS AND VIVISECTION

In the *Fortnightly Review* of 1882, the physician William Benjamin Carpenter (1882) argued that the morality of a pain-giving act lay not in the act itself, nor in its result, but in the motive for the act. This was firmly in the tradition of 19th-century medical ethics, which emphasized the virtues proper to medical practitioners. Some of these virtues were common to all persons who might call themselves ladies or gentlemen, a class whose "honour and humanity are unimpeachable" ("Surgical Experiments on Living Animals," 1839), but medics claimed some adaptation to their profession: While an honorable character was indispensable, it was possible that an excess of humanity might lead to oversensitivity that would hamper their work. For example, it might cause a surgeon from proceeding with a painful operation, so medics permitted themselves what John Hunter somewhat unfortunately termed a "necessary inhumanity." The finesse of the virtue ethics approach lay in choosing which virtues to cultivate, and to what degree, especially when two virtues appeared to conflict. For example, it was "proverbial" that medical men needed to balance tenderness and resolution, because an excess of tenderness might beget a debilitating squeamishness, while too much moral resolve could become habitual callousness ("Body-Snatchers," 1862; Steintrager, 2004, pp. 64, 124).

Medical gentlemen derived many of their moral tenets, as did lay antivivisection campaigners, from the Christian tradition. Though the main Christian denominations in Britain made no formal pronouncements on the treatment of animals (Stevenson, 1956; Li, 2000; 2012), mercy and compassion were transferable guiding principles: To evangelicals such as William Hamilton Drummond (1838) they were virtues that reflected the divine mercy and there was an obligation on all Christians to practice them (pp. 15, 17). The same virtues were the staple of secular literature such as gentlemen's manuals, which offered readers who aspired to social and moral advancement advice on correct manners and sentiments, including the proper attitude toward animals: neither cruel and heartless nor overly sentimental. In general, moral rectitude was judged on a person's character and motivation, rather than adherence to inflexible rules of action. Drummond (1838) accepted that just as eating animals or destroying vermin could be acceptable for reasons of health and cleanliness, so vivisection was justified if prompted by laudable desires such as improving health or acquiring knowledge (pp. 23, 148).

The debate on human cadaveric dissection that took place in the early 1830s shows parallels with that on vivisection (the public assumed that anatomists vivisected, despite their protests to the contrary) and the arguments for and against each were regarded as to some extent interchangeable (Wynter, 1869, p. 67; Brayfytte, 1891–1892). Dissection and vivisection were condemned not because of any suffering caused, but for the coldheartedness and self-indulgence of their practitioners, and both were the subject of public scandals; the much-publicized murders for dissection in Edinburgh and London between 1829 and 1831 led to the 1832 Anatomy Act that regulated the supply of cadavers and formalized pauper dissection: the anatomical equivalent of the 1876 Vivisection Act. The public response to the anatomy scandals was ambiguous, depending to some extent on the perceived motivation of the anatomist. In some quarters, anatomy, and by synecdoche the profession of medicine, came to be regarded with opprobrium: Medical students and their teachers were accused of callous indifference and it was suggested they were motivated by ambition, greed, or even carnal desire (Richardson, 2001). However, as the Anatomy Act drew the public's attention to the chronic difficulty in obtaining cadavers and the extreme lengths to which anatomists had to go, anatomists gained respect for risking their reputations in order to obtain the material necessary to teach medical students. While there was clearly a utilitarian argument in play (it was worth dissecting cadavers to train skillful surgeons), the anatomists' conduct was presented as virtuous—what Chaplin (2008) has called the "heroic anatomist"—because they set aside their personal aversion and stoically endured the horrors of the dissecting-room (Bates, 2010, p. 21).

Like anatomists, vivisectors defended their moral character by emphasizing the fortitude and self-control needed for their work. Claims that they deliberately suppressed their natural sensibilities were, however, problematic (quite apart from the proposition that it could be virtuous to suppress a virtue) because an alternative, adverse construction was possible. The behavior of an individual who reluctantly participated in vivisection for the best motives was difficult to distinguish from that of someone so morally indifferent that he gave it no thought. It was certainly possible to be cruel without realizing it, though such ignorance was typically associated with the laboring classes: According to Dr. Rolleston, the president of the British Association for the Advancement of Science, children and "persons in the lower order" were often unthinkingly cruel to animals, but not so "men of science," if only because experimentation was too "tedious and toilsome" to be undertaken recklessly ("The British Association for the Advancement of Science," 1863). The argument that scientists were indisputably morally well-adjusted failed to convince medical professionals, one of whose chief concerns was that a doctor who vivisected animals would be unmoved by suffering patients. Dr. Robert Hull (1842–1843), who wrote against vivisection in the *London Medical Gazette*, agreed with the surgeon John Abernethy that no doctor who vivisected was fit to attend a family. The *Protestant Magazine* concurred and printed a "caution to parents" advising them to refuse the services of any practitioner who was guilty of vivisection ("A Caution to Parents," 1844). This was not a "slippery slope" argument, since it supposed that vivisectionists were already deficient in the compassion that patients expected: As Kant had written, "we can judge the heart of a man by his treatment of animals" (Regan & Singer, 1989, p. 24).

A criticism of vivisection first raised in the 17th century was that normal function could not reliably be investigated because the response of a tormented animal did not represent the normal state (Rupke, 1990, p. 22). This durable methodological objection acquired new force in the 19th century as an indictment of experimentalists' good conduct and self-restraint, since inappropriate vivisection looked like a clumsy, ill-considered effort to wrest Nature's secrets from her by force: the antithesis of reasoned philosophical enquiry. Some writers compared it to judicial torture in that it both yielded untrustworthy information and discredited the inquirer (Drummond, 1838, p. 145; "Christianity and Its Effect," 1839). According to Karl Marx (1846), its use in medicine was of doubtful value and an affront to "humanity" (p. 121).

The appeal to humanity was not dependent upon the status of animals or their exact capacity for suffering: It was the character of the vivisector that mattered. The British medical press responded to Magendie's visit by attacking his character and motivation; his supporters countered with a testimonial to his kindly bedside manner ("Bills to Prevent Cruelty to Animals," 1826). The gravest accusation against him was that he found experimentation pleasurable, a perhaps not unreasonable claim in the light of an account provided by one medical eyewitness to his demonstrations in Paris: "he really likes his business . . . when loud screams are uttered, he sometimes laughs outright" (Olmsted, 1944, pp. 221–222). No British vivisector was seen to take such pleasure in his work: Hall performed similar studies to Magendie, but by demonstrating appropriate motives, declaring his distaste for the business, and adhering to his own ethical rules, he showed that his approach was neither reckless nor self-indulgent. The persona of the reluctant vivisector enabled him to perform similar experiments to the "satanic" Frenchman without significant public or professional opposition.

While there is no means of determining how many experiments were performed before the 1876 Cruelty to Animals Act, comparatively few appeared in the British medical literature (most of those reported after 1820 were performed in France or Germany) and they were said in the medical press to be "proverbially rare" (Etherington, 1842, p. 17). Since there was no law to prevent vivisection, it is probable that concerns within the medical profession were the most effective deterrent to potential experimenters. The few who did proceed met with far less criticism in the British press than did Continental physiologists, because they were careful to show that they approached vivisection morally prepared and correctly disposed. Like anatomists, they were to some extent able to turn to their advantage the apparent insensitivity required for their task by suggesting that deliberate suppression of sentimentality was proof of self-discipline and determination.

There were, however, concerns for the character of those who persevered in their work. To witness or, worse, to perform vivisection, was thought to be "demoralizing," a word coined to describe the moral decline during the French Revolution that left the revolutionaries, according to stories in the British press, in a state of bloodthirstiness that did not baulk at cannibalism (Bates, 2008). Fears of similar events in Britain had been behind Martin's anticruelty legislation and the anticruelty societies' efforts to stem viciousness by encouraging what Darwin (1871) called the "virtue" of "humanity to the lower animals" (Vol. 1, p. 101). The early-19th century fashion for social mobility, which found positive expressions in projects for self-improvement and the betterment of the lower classes, brought with it anxiety at the prospect of moral deterioration. If men and women could progress by means of education they could also, if exposed to demoralizing influences, regress to an uncivilized state. For students of the natural sciences, theories of biological degeneration (regression of races to primitive forms and recrudescence of suppressed animal characteristics) were particularly suggestive of the possibility of a return to barbarism (Knox, 1855).

Medical men were understandably averse from acquiring an enthusiasm, however well intentioned, that could lead to moral insensibility. There was a longstanding, though apocryphal, notion that anatomists and butchers were forbidden to serve on coroners' juries because their trades destroyed their moral competency (Stevenson, 1954), and vivisection was feared to have a similar effect, especially on impressionable young students. According to the professor of anatomy James Lawson Drummond (1838–1839), "little was to be expected" of young men exposed to vivisection, a concern echoed by Lord Carnarvon, the SPCA's president, who claimed that because, in time, the vivisector's "feelings of compassion for suffering [would become] entirely obliterated," the majority of the medical profession wanted it restricted by law (SPCA, 1837, pp. 19–20). Despite their stereotypical portrayal in literature as callous and undisciplined, medical students generally shunned vivisection, and it was little used in British medical schools, where some teachers shared anatomist Josef Hyrtl's view that no one who could look on vivisection calmly would make a good physician ("Hyrtl, Prof. of Anatomy," 1881–1882).

SOME CREDIT FOR HUMANITY

In responding to Martin's act, medical enthusiasts for, and critics of, vivisection made quite different assumptions. For vivisectionists, the decision to experiment was typically a utilitarian judgment in which the predicted benefits to medicine made their work a necessity. By contrast, opponents of vivisection tended to claim that anyone who experimented on living animals was likely to be callous and insensitive, character traits more usually associated with the lower classes, whose cruelty was unthinking, and certainly undesirable in a medical practitioner. The definition of cruelty under Martin's act prompted lay antivivisection campaigners to direct their efforts toward showing that experimentation on living animals was wanton—an almost impossible goal since they needed to prove the experiments were unnecessary and the experimenters reckless or malicious. By contrast, medical opponents of vivisection focused on two concerns: That practitioners willing to experiment on live animals were so deficient in compassion that their fitness to treat patients was compromised, and that habitual involvement in vivisection blunted the moral sensibilities. By the latter half of the 19th century, this was the view of many humanitarians, who felt that animal experimentation was, as Queen Victoria confided to her private secretary: "horrible, brutalising, unchristianlike" and "one of the worst signs of wickedness in human nature" (Fulford, 1976, p. 185; Gardiner, 1923, p. 403). With its focus on the pain experienced by animals, the 1876 Vivisection Act did little to address fears that vivisection "saps our moral sense," "blunts our sympathy," and promotes "ruthlessness and oppression" (MacGregor-Mathers, 1890).

When choosing a physician, patients tended, as they still do, to value virtues such as compassion, kindness, and humanity above scientific acumen (Stammers, 2013), and to be less concerned with specific actions than with the motives underpinning them (Hursthouse, 2001, p. 48). Early-19th century medical self-regulation also focused on character rather than compliance with rules (there was no specific legislation governing medical practice until 1858), and practitioners were expected to meet the moral standards of genteel society. The acceptability of vivisection depended upon whether compassion and mercy were more praiseworthy than determination and commitment to scientific progress. While it is difficult to estimate how many experiments were prevented by the profession's regard for its moral reputation, the limits on experimentation were predominantly self-imposed ones. Virtue ethics did not offer a decisive argument against vivisection—the pursuit of knowledge provides a virtuous motive for the vivisectionist—but the figure of the "mad" scientist, prepared to transgress boundaries in the single-minded search for knowledge, evoked public anxiety as well as admiration (Bates, 2010, pp. 161–172), and few medical men in practice were prepared to press on with experimentation at the risk of appearing self-indulgent or callous. The controversial and outspoken anatomist Robert Knox shunned vivisection, and his refusal to experiment on animals earned him "some credit for humanity" in the medical press ("Dr Knox," 1844).

In defense of their own humanity, experimenters presented themselves as reluctant vivisectionists, who suppressed their innate sensibility for the sake of medical progress. The frontispiece of Etherington's *Vivisection Investigated and Vindicated* (1842) depicted female vivisectors (there is no record of any contribution to animal experimentation by British women in the 19th century), as if to reassure the reader that vivisection was compatible with the emotional sensitivity that was considered a female characteristic. Less subtle apologists, critical of the idea that *"the virtuous person will accept emotions as justifications"* (Merriam, 2008), dismissed antivivisectionists as "effeminate" (i.e., oversentimental). The argument that vivisectionists were self-controlled rather than insensitive succeeded to the extent that in Britain they did not face the accusations of cruelty and self-indulgence that were directed at their Continental counterparts, though nationalistic sympathies must also have helped. However, the predominance of *public* statements from medical practitioners against vivisection (those who did experiment maintained a low profile) suggests that the virtues of compassion and mercy were more attractive to potential patients than fortitude and moral resolve. The question of whether a vivisector could be a compassionate doctor was rendered less significant by the emergence of physiology as a distinct discipline at the time of the 1876 Cruelty to Animals Act. The argument that vivisection demoralized did not disappear—its' effect on the morals of those who performed it remained an issue for some groups such as Quakers (Glahalt, 2012)—but it no longer carried the force it had when vivisection was seen as the responsibility of medical practitioners.

References

Amendment of the laws to prevent cruelty to animals. (1834). *Animals Friend*, 2, 11–15.
Anatomy Act, 2 & 3 Will. IV. c. 75 (1832).
Anonymous. (1839). *Animals Friend*, 7, 51.
Anonymous. (1881–1882). *Zoophilist*, 1, 244.
Anonymous. (1891–1892). *Animals Guardian*, 2, 33.

Bates, A. W. (2008). "Indecent and demoralising representations": Public anatomy museums in mid-Victorian England. *Medical History, 52,* 1–22.

Bates, A. W. (2010). *The anatomy of Robert Knox: Murder, mad science and medical regulation in nineteenth-century Edinburgh.* Brighton, England: Sussex Academic Press.

Bills to prevent cruelty to animals. (1826). *Parliamentary History and Review,* 756–775.

Boddice, R. (2007). *A history of attitudes and behaviours toward animals in eighteenth- and nineteenth-century Britain: Anthropocentrism and the emergence of animals.* Lampeter, Wales: Edwin Mellen.

Boddice, R. (2011). Vivisecting major: A Victorian gentleman scientist defends animal experimentation, 1876–1885. *Isis, 102,* 215–237.

Body-snatchers. (1862, July). *Church and State Review,* 87.

Brayfytte. (1891–1892). Experimental physiology: What it is, and what it asks. *Animals Guardian, 2,* 39–42.

British Association for the Advancement of Science. (1863). *Medical Times and Gazette,* 258–260.

Candy, G. (1890). The legal definition of cruelty in relation to the animal world. *Animals Guardian, 1,* 5.

Candy, G. (1891). Should the vivisection act of 1876 be repealed? *Animals Guardian, 1,* 49–50.

Carpenter, W. B. (1882). The ethics of vivisection. *Fortnightly Review, 31,* 237–246.

Carroll, L. (1875). Some popular fallacies about vivisection. *Fortnightly Review, 23,* 847–854.

A caution to parents. (1844). *Protestant Magazine, 6,* 57–58.

Chaplin, S. (2008). *The heroic anatomist: Dissection and the stoic ideal.* Retrieved from http://www.rcpe.ac.uk/library/listen/

Chippendale, J. (1839). Experiments on animals. *Lancet, 1,* 357–358.

Christianity and its effect upon man's treatment of animals considered. (1839). *Church of England Magazine, 6,* 294–296.

Correspondence on field sports & and surgical experiments on living animals. (1838). *Animals Friend, 6,* 21.

Cruel and Improper Treatment of Cattle Act, 3 George IV. c. 71 (1822).

Cruelty to Animals Act, 5 & 6 Will. IV. c. 59 (1835).

Cruelty to Animals Act, 39 & 40 Vict. c. 77 (1876).

Darwin, C. (1871). *The descent of man and selection in relation to sex.* London, England: John Murray.

Dr Knox, of Edinburgh. (1844). *Medical Times, 10,* 245–246.

Drummond, J. L. (1831). On humanity to animals. *Edinburgh Philosophical Journal, 13,* 172–183.

Drummond, J. L. (1838–1839). On humanity. *London Medical Gazette, 24,* 160–163.

Drummond, W. H. (1838). *The rights of animals, and man's obligation to treat them with humanity.* London, England: John Mardon.

Editorial. (1881–1882). *Zoophilist, 1,* 190.

Elston, M. A. (1987). Women and antivivisection in Victorian England, 1870–1900. In N. A. Rupke (Ed.), *Vivisection in historical perspective* (pp. 259–273). London, England: Croom Helm.

Etherington, G. (1842). *Vivisection investigated and vindicated.* Edinburgh, Scotland: P. Richard.

Feller, D. A. (2009). Dog fight: Darwin as animal advocate in the antivivisection controversy of 1875. *Studies in History and Philosophy of Biological and Biomedical Sciences, 40,* 265–271.

French, R. D. (1975). *Antivivisection and medical science in victorian society.* Princeton, NJ: Princeton University Press.

Fulford, R. (1976). *Darling child: Private correspondence of Queen Victoria and the German Crown Princess of Prussia, 1871–78.* London, England: Evans Brothers.

Gardiner, A. G. (1923). *The life of Sir William Harcourt*. London, England: Constable.

Glahalt, H. R. (2012). Vivisection as war: The "moral diseases" of animal experimentation and slavery in British Victorian Quaker pacifist ethics. *Society and Animals, 20*, 154–172.

Gompertz, L. (1992). *Moral inquiries on the situation of man and brutes*. Fontwell, England: Centaur Press.

Guerrini, A. (2008). Animal experiments and antivivisection debates in the 1820s. In C. Knellwolf and J. Goodall (Eds.), *Frankenstein's science: Experimentation and discovery in romantic culture, 1780–1830* (pp. 71–86). Aldershot, England: Ashgate.

Hall, M. (1828). On the mechanism of the act of vomiting. *Lancet, 2*, 600–602.

Hall, M. (1831). *A critical and experimental essay on the circulation of the blood*. London, England: R. B. Seeley & W. Burnside.

Harrison, B. (1982). *Peaceable kingdom: Stability and change in modern Britain*. Oxford, England: Clarendon Press.

Hughes, G. & Lawson, C. (2011). RSPCA and the criminology of social control. *Crime, Law and Social Change, 55*, 375–389.

Hull, R. (1842–1843). On vivisection. *London Medical Gazette, 32*, 864.

Hursthouse, R. (2001). *On virtue ethics*. Oxford, England: Oxford University Press.

Hyrtl, prof. of anatomy, Vienna, on vivisection as demonstration to students. (1881–1882). *Zoophilist, 1*, 145.

Items of interest. (1890). *Animals Guardian, 1*, 34–35.

Kean, H. (1995). The "smooth, cool men of science": The feminist and socialist response to vivisection. *History Workshop Journal, 40*, 16–38.

Kean, H. (1998). *Animal Rights: Social and Political Change since 1800*. London, England: Reaktion.

Klein, E., Burdon-Sanderson, J., Forster, M., & Brunton, T. L. (1873). *Handbook for the physiological laboratory*. London, England: J. & A. Churchill.

Knox, R. (1839). Some observations on the structure and physiology of the eye and its appendages. *Lancet, 1*, 248–251.

Knox, R. (1855). Some remarks on the Aztecque and Bosjieman children, now being exhibited in London. *Lancet, 1*, 357–360.

Lansbury, C. (1985). *The old brown dog: Women, workers, and vivisection in Edwardian England*. Madison: University of Wisconsin Press.

Li, C. (2000). A union of Christianity, humanity and philanthropy: The Christian tradition and prevention of cruelty to animals in nineteenth-century England. *Society and Animals, 8*, 265–285.

Li, C. (2012). Mobilizing Christianity in the antivivisection movement in Victorian Britain. *Journal of Animal Ethics, 2*, 141–161.

Linzey, A. (2009). *The link between animal abuse and human violence*. Brighton, England: Sussex Academic Press.

Lordat, J. (1854). Mental dynamics in relation to the science of medicine. *Journal of Psychological Medicine and Mental Pathology, 7*, 252–263.

MacGregor-Mathers, S. L. (1890). The roots of cruelty. *Animals Guardian, 1*, 27.

Magendie, F. (1824). *An elementary compendium of physiology; for the use of students* (E. Milligan, Trans.). Philadelphia, PA: James Webster.

Manuel, D. (1990). Marshall Hall (1790–1857): Vivisection and the development of experimental physiology. In N. A. Rupke (Ed.), *Vivisection in Historical Perspective* (pp. 78–104). London, England: Routledge.

Marx, K. F. H. (1846). *The moral aspects of medical life* (J. Mackness, Trans.). London, England: John Churchill.

Merriam, G. (2008). *Virtue ethics and the moral significance of animals.* (Unpublished doctoral thesis). Rice University, TX.

Miller, I. (2009). Necessary torture? Vivisection, suffragette force-feeding, and responses to scientific medicine in Britain c. 1870–1920. *Journal of the History of Medicine and Allied Sciences, 64,* 333–372.

Morris, F. O. (1886). *The curse of cruelty. A sermon [on ps. xxxvi. 6] preached in York Minster.* London, England: Elliot Stock.

Mushet, D. (1839). *The wrongs of the animal world.* London, England: Hatchard & Son.

Necessity the cheat of humanity. (1841). *Animals Friend, 9,* 16.

Niven, C. D. (1967). *History of the humane movement.* London, England: Johnson Publications.

Nottingham University College and vivisection. (1891–1892). *Animals Guardian, 2,* 117.

Observations pathologiques propper a éclairer plusiers points de physiologie par F. Lallemand. (1825). *London Medical and Physical Journal, 53,* 238–245.

Olmsted, J. M. D. (1944). *François Magendie.* New York, NY: Schuman.

On experiments on living animals. (1837). *London Medical Gazette, 20,* 804–808.

Our programme. (1890). *Animals Guardian, 1,* 2.

Percival, T. (1803). *Medical ethics, or a code of institutions and precepts adapted to the professional conduct of physicians and surgeons.* Manchester, England: S. Russell.

Physiology. (1825). *Medico-Chirurgical Review, 3,* 198–200.

"Plain truth" past and present. (1891–1892). *Animals Guardian, 2,* 6–9.

Prosecution at Norwich. (1874). *British Medical Journal, 2,* 751–754.

Regan, T. & Singer, P. (Eds.) (1989). *Animal rights and human obligations.* Englewood Cliffs, NJ: Prentice-Hall.

Richardson, R. (2001). *Death, dissection, and the destitute.* London, England: Phoenix Press.

Rupke, N. A. (Ed.) (1990). *Vivisection in historical perspective.* London, England: Routledge.

Singer, P. (1995). *Animal liberation.* London, England: Pimlico.

Society for preventing cruelty to animals. (1825, June). *Morning Chronicle,* 3.

Society for the prevention of cruelty to animals. (1824). *Evangelical Magazine and Missionary Chronicle, 2,* 357–358.

SPCA. (1832). *Sixth report and proceedings.* London, England: W. Molineux.

SPCA. (1837). *Eleventh report and proceedings.* London, England: Philanthropic Society.

Stammers, T. (2013). The NHS—no place for conscience. *Catholic Medical Quarterly, 63,* 12–14.

Steintrager, J. A. (2004). *Cruel delight: Enlightenment culture and the inhuman.* Bloomington: Indiana University Press.

Stevenson, L. G. (1954). On the supposed exclusion of butchers and surgeons from jury duty. *Journal of the History of Medicine and Allied Sciences, 9,* 235–238.

Stevenson, L. G. (1956). Religious elements in the background of the British anti-vivisection movement. *Yale Journal of Biology and Medicine, 29,* 125–157.

Surgical experiments on living animals. (1839). *Animals Friend, 7,* 61–62.

Turner, J. (1980). *Reckoning with the beast: Animals, pain, and humanity in the Victorian mind.* Baltimore, MD: Johns Hopkins University Press.

Two views of the vivisector. (1881–1882). *Zoophilist, 1,* 194.

Wolfensohn, S. & Lloyd, M. (2003). *Handbook of laboratory animal management and welfare.* Oxford, England: Blackwell.

Wynter, A. (1869). *Subtle brains and lissom fingers.* London, England: Robert Hardwicke.

"The New Superstition, the New Tyranny": The Ethics and Contexts of John Cowper Powys's Antivivisection

FELIX TAYLOR
The Queen's College, Oxford, England

Abstract: This article examines the antivivisectionist writings of British novelist and philosopher John Cowper Powys (1872–1963) during the 1930s and 1940s. Powys's opposition to the widespread practice of animal experimentation, both in his fiction and his contributions to activist newspapers, has been noted by critics to have prefigured the modern animal rights movement. On the surface, his writings on the subject display an unnuanced and impassioned outrage, yet on closer inspection, they form a logical piece of Powys's idiosyncratic worldview and to some extent reflect the arguments of "new age" antivivisection campaigns of his time.

Key Words: Powys, vivisection, animal experimentation, theosophy, Autobiography, Morwyn, dogs, animism, philosophy, new age

John Cowper Powys (1872–1963) is an overlooked figure in the landscape of British literature and letters. His almost 20 novels, several poetry collections, many "how-to" philosophy manuals, and reams of correspondence and diaries have been persistently avoided by mainstream critics. "He is so far outside the canon," wrote Margaret Drabble (2006), one of Powys's rare champions, "that he defies the concept of a canon." Perhaps best remembered these days for his five "Wessex" novels published between 1929 and 1936 (so called for their Dorset and Somerset settings and their debt to Thomas Hardy), Powys carved out a unique niche in the novel form collecting themes of pastoralism, (his self-declared) "sexual perversion," Celtic mythology, and an elemental view of the natural world into what he termed his "life philosophy." An understudied piece of this sprawling and multifaceted vision is Powys's opposition to the widespread practice of animal vivisection. Noted by several critics to have prefigured the modern animal rights movement, Powys's writings on the subject display on the surface an unnuanced and impassioned outrage.[1] With closer consideration, however, they form a logical piece of his idiosyncratic worldview and to some extent reflect the arguments of "new age" antivivisection campaigns of his time.[2]

Although etymologically "vivisection" implies the dissection of live animals, the word was used during the 19th and early 20th centuries (usually only by its opponents) to refer to animal experimentation more broadly. By the time Powys was first made aware of the idea—at Corpus Christi, Cambridge, in the 1890s—the practice was rare in Britain compared to continental Europe, yet it was gaining in notoriety: John Ruskin had resigned his chair at Oxford in 1885 in protest of the university's stance on vivisection and the Humanitarian League was founded in 1891, which opposed the avoidable infliction of pain on sentient beings (Bates, 2017, p. 71). A. W. H. Bates (2017) has made the case that early opposition to vivisection took a "virtue-centred" approach and was first spearheaded by the very doctors who were performing these experiments, supposedly in the name of science (p. 1). Groups protesting vivisection were formed throughout the second half of the 19th century: the Victoria Street Society was born in 1875 (later to become the National Anti-Vivisection Society, known as NAVS) followed by the British Union for the Abolition of Vivisection (BUAV) in 1898. Both were set up by Frances Power Cobbe, soon to be a giant of the women's suffrage movement. In fact, it was the disproportionate number of women involved in animal advocacy during this period that led to the gendered dichotomy of "rational" male scientists versus the "emotional" female antivivisectionists.[3] Yet despite fervent public opposition, the number of animals vivisected in Britain continued to rise through the end of the 19th century and into the 20th. The First Royal Commission on Vivisection in 1875 (which led to the 1876 Cruelty to Animals Act) reported around 300 experiments, while in 1945, the figure was estimated to have reached more than 1 million (National Anti-Vivisection Society, 2012).

An ethical consideration for animals is apparent in Powys's view simply by reading his major novels. Several antagonists or unlikeable characters express support for vivisection—and on some occasions are themselves practicing vivisectors. "Hell's Museum" is the name given to the house in *Weymouth Sands* (Powys, 1934/2000, p. 86) owned by the vivisector Dr. Brush, and in *Wolf Solent* (Powys, 1929), the protagonist Wolf returns to his rural childhood home and notices the phantom appearance of a newly erected slaughterhouse, "fenced off from the road with some unnatural and sinister precaution" (p. 26). "I suppose *you* eat them?" asks Wolf's companion as they pass (Powys, 1929, p. 26).[4] Following his move to North Wales with his partner Phyllis Plater in 1935, the horrors of vivisection prompted Powys to write his most polemical and allegorical novel, *Morwyn, or the Vengeance of God* (Powys, 1937). He and Phyllis visited what Powys (1995) describes as a "VIVISECTION shop" in Wrexham with its "horrible 'ads' of shocking cruelty"—presumably some form of public demonstration or protest because he mentions a young man "who came from Headquarters" (p. 220).[5] The resulting book charts a descent into hell from an opening in the Eglwyseg Rocks above Llangollen. The narrator, his romantic interest Morwyn, and her vivisector father are plunged deep into the earth by a "meteoric body" (Powys, 1937, p. 11) and find themselves in the presence of Gilles de Rais, Nero, and the Marquis de Sade, all of whom boast about the pleasure they derive from acts of sadistic cruelty. In the very bowels of the underworld, large television screens have been rigged up to broadcast every vivisection happening across the globe.

Part IV: Historical Controversies: Vivisection

Beyond grappling with the issue in fiction, Powys (as we can see from his trips to Wrexham) was also an active member of the antivivisection movement during the 1930s and 1940s. He and Phyllis became members of the BUAV after their return from America in 1934, and his exclamatory opinions in his *Autobiography* (1934) were advertised and discussed in issues of *The Animal's Defender*, the monthly newspaper of the NAVS (Taylor, 2019). Half a chapter is also devoted to Powys's stance in Evalyn Westacott's *A Century of Vivisection and Anti-Vivisection* (1949), Powys having met Westacott through NAVS. His *Autobiography* is quoted from extensively, alongside an article Powys wrote for the BUAV's newspaper *The Abolitionist* titled "Vivisection and Moral Evolution" in which he takes umbrage with the commonly deployed phrase "in the interests of Science":

> This sinister phrase . . . ought to be enough to startle us, enough to rouse us to what is happening. . . . There is only one ground to take in this matter; and that is the ground of simple conscience. The thing is cruel and abominable. Therefore it is wrong. That it *is* both cruel and wrong can be seen in the way that ordinary conscientious men and woman *shrink from thinking about it*. They feel in their hearts that these fanatics of Science are doing something that they themselves would shudder to do. (Westacott, 1949, p. 592)

The tone is in keeping with the arguments Powys previously made against vivisection: that it is fundamentally immoral and that this incontrovertible fact—self-evident due to our avoidance of the subject in conversation—needs no further justification. In a similar passage from his *Autobiography*, Powys again supplies an ardent, and to his mind irrefutable, defense:

> I am . . . totally unable to understand the meaning of the word "conviction." My knowledge that the practise of vivisection, for example, is a crime against everything that is noblest in our race, is not a conviction, *it is my life*. . . . "With my whole being I *know*," I answer them, "that the vivisecting of dogs is evil!" That is really how we all know that all is evil is evil. You can find reasons to defend anything. (Powys, 1934, p. 201)

On the surface there appears to be very little substance to these kinds of impassioned statements. Yet Powys had been a public lecturer for the first three decades of his adult life (an extension lecturer in America from 1905 to around 1930), and so performance and rhetoric were his natural modes for expressing his opinion on any given subject. It was even common while lecturing for Powys to attempt "intermittent stabs at the abomination of vivisection" given with "spasmodic delivery" (Powys, 1934, p. 522), further suggesting that these opinions often came to him spontaneously and unformed. Statements such as those quoted above, however, mirror the familiar arguments and rhetoric of antivivisectionists of the time, based on the promotion of kindness and prevention of cruelty.[6] Vivisectors in Powys's mind are cruel and sadistic (such as those in *Morwyn*) and derive pleasure from inflicting torture on animals, a popular view of critics from the late 19th century onward, although one without sufficient evidence: Doctors carrying out these experiments seemed generally to dislike what they did but considered it a necessary part of their profession (Bates, 2017, pp. 6–7). Similarly, Powys's disdain for the utilitarian justification for vivisection—that animal suffering is necessary for the advancement of medical science—was a familiar position for Victorian antivivisectionists; the experimental method challenged the belief in scientific moral progress (Turner, 1980, pp. 96–97).

That Powys knew that vivisection was wrong with his "whole being" can be viewed less as an emotional response than as an expression of his "life philosophy." Powys was a philosopher who took seriously the formation of a particular and personal worldview, and a central theme in Powys's philosophy is the devotion to what he calls a "magical view of life" opposed to sterile, scientific rationality (Powys, 1930, p. 9). This was a familiar intellectual position for many writers and artists of the 1920s and 1930s, many of whom were reacting to the postwar surge in industrialization and technological advancement, yet Powys's commitment to an animistic, and, some have argued, *panpsychist* picture of the world leaves him in a category of his own (Gore, 2019). "Every living organism," Powys (1934) declares, "has its own peculiar universe, not quite like any other" (p. 55). To express this quasimystical union between the "animate" human self and the primal "inanimate" other, he came up with the concept of the "ichthyosaurus ego" (Powys, 1930, p. 9) in *The Defence of Sensuality*, a method of psychological withdrawal into the "subhuman" to discover what he terms the "peace of the ultimate" (Powys, 1930, p. 282). It is then a simple leap to connect Powys's idea of a universal consciousness with his sympathy toward animals (dogs especially), and it follows his abhorrence for vivisection.

Pain, however, was a complex issue for Powys, one that cannot be overlooked when discussing his position on experimentation. For the first 50 years of his life, he claimed to have experienced a peculiar tendency toward "Sadism," or what he refers to as his "Viciousness" (Powys, 1934, p. 8), the deriving of pleasure from the suffering of other creatures. As a child living in Shirley, Derbyshire, he would take great delight in removing tadpoles from a nearby pond, mutilating them, and "slaughtering [them with] a yellow hammer" and would even wander over the countryside near Sherbourne "looking for something to tear to pieces" (Powys, 1934, p. 137), though after these early years (until, he assures his readers, about 1922) he restricted this "most dangerous of vices" (p. 8) to his thoughts alone. How then to reconcile Powys's consuming urge to witness pain in humans and animals with the compassion he expresses for dogs in scientific experiments? He was not wholly convinced by a friend's suggestion that the two urges stemmed from the same source, but on the contrary, this attention to intense suffering appears to have provided him with a great faculty for empathy (Krissdóttir, 2007, p. 327). David A. Cook (1974) has noted that Powys was "imaginatively aware of pain to a remarkable degree" (p. 43) and demonstrably extended this position to include nonhuman animals in both his fiction and his activism, suggesting that his antivivisectionism may have in fact have been strengthened by his sadistic urges. "Dogs are as sensitive to pain as we are," (Powys, 1937, p. 88) he writes in *Morwyn*, a novel in which he recognizes the "steriliz[ing]" (p. 125) nature of sadism; indeed, he brands vivisection as "scientific sadism," a "perversion" of the life force (p. 125).

In wider British culture, the suffering of animals was also a concern for an array of "new age" societies and groups devoted to the study of the occult and alternative spiritualities. Many expressed an opposition to vivisection, and while Powys did not have any sustained contact with any of these communities, his unorthodox and often eccentric view of humankind's spiritual place in the material world recalled some of their core tenets, particularly those of the pseudoreligion known as theosophy. Theosophists believed that beneath the world's religions and mythologies lay a "Secret Wisdom," an ultimate truth that required diligent investigation and personal self-discovery to unearth. Like other heterodox spiritual systems of the time, it attempted to tread a path between the rigid dogmatism of mainstream Christianity and the stifling materialism of the "rational" scientific view. In fact, between these opposing poles, theosophy leant more toward materialism, claiming that mind was matter and matter simply "crystallized spirit" (Blavatsky, 1948, p. 11), thereby eschewing the standard Christian division of body and soul. All biological life shared a universal spirit, one that was linked through evolution. "I may well remind you," wrote the Theosophical Society's founder H. P. Blavatsky (1948), "that there may well be other spiritual laws, operating on plants and animals as well as on mankind, although, as you do not recognize their action on plants and animals, you may deny their existence" (p. 17). Bodily suffering presented a tough problem to crack for theosophists, but, viewed through an evolutionary lens, thinkers like Blavatsky and Annie Besant concluded that the realities of physical pain in all creatures (caused by the likes of war, famine, and animal experimentation) might be used to rally essential social change.

The animism that gradually became a part of Powys's view of the world during the early 20th century echoes much of theosophy's teachings. By the 1930s, Powys had turned his back on conventional religion and worshiped instead using his own complex philosophy of physical and mental sensation, regarding all material things as unified yet existing in their own subjective universes. He rejected "Thou shalt love thy neighbour as thyself" in favor of his own commandment: "Thou shalt be merciful and pitiful and considerate *to all living organisms*" (Powys, 1934, p. 376). Theosophy's insistence that behind the world's mythologies and religions lay a universal truth, combined with a willingness to co-opt animals into its spiritual system, chimes with Powys's own belief that truths could be extracted from tradition via imaginative reinterpretation. Powys even advances a clear distinction between mythology (specifically Welsh mythology, which featured prominently in his thinking throughout his life) and animal experimentation: "I . . . regard the magic of the *Mabinogion*," he writes, "as a nearer approach to the secret of Nature than anything you could learn by vivisecting dogs" (Powys, 1934, p. 287).

It is likely, given Powys's involvement in the antivivisection press, that he was aware of the theosophical stance against animal experimentation. Bates (2017) has noted that many prominent theosophists were vegetarians, including the president of the Theosophical Society herself Annie Besant (successor to Blavatsky, d. 1891), and that the society shared the aims and values of the Victoria Street Society to such a degree that the two were practically "sister movements" (pp. 86–87). Powys was also familiar with the key theosophical doctrines, introduced to him while at Corpus Christi, Cambridge, by family friend Ralph Shirley (Powys, 1934, p. 186). He read A. P. Sinnett's *Esoteric Buddhism* (1883), a core text aimed at explaining theosophy to the general public, and recounts irritating his Anglican father by expounding at length upon Besant's *Seven Principles of Man* (1892; Powys, 1934, p. 252, p. 50). Powys's writings were also frequently lumped in together with Blavatsky's in the pages of antivivisectionist newspapers (Taylor, 2019).

While the ethics behind Powys's stance against vivisection align with the theosophical belief in "the unity of living organisms" (Viswanathan, 2011, p. 445), his zealous antiscientism ultimately distinguishes him from Besant's movement. The appeal of theosophy for many of its adherents, argues Gauri Viswanathan (2011), was that it "provided scientific principles to be invoked in the fight against science" (p. 444), whereas Powys's advocation for a "magical view of life" (and with it a sinking into oneself to escape modern society) left little space for scientific progress. Vivisection represented for Powys the ugly pinnacle of modern rationalism—dispassionate, utilitarian, and objective—without consideration for the suffering inflicted on nonhuman animals:

> Vivisection is the new superstition, the new tyranny, the new incarnation of the powers of evil. Like all abominable wickedness that has once got into the saddle, this vivisecting science has now begun to brand as "sentimental," as "emotional," as "idealistic," as "unpractical" the deep honest realistic human instinct that it is deliberately seeking to kill. (Powys, 1934, p. 640)

But more than this, animal experimentation was to Powys a profoundly immoral act that shook the very foundations of what it means to be human. "This wickedness contradicts and cancels the one single advantage that our race has got from what is called evolution," he writes, "namely the development of *our sense of right and wrong*" (Powys, 1934, p. 640). The practice was antithetical to what Powys saw as what is most noble and good in humankind, a crime worse than violence, murder, and rape because it is carried out under the cold, rational banner of scientific progress. Antivivisection remained a theme in his work throughout the rest of his life. On its completion in 1937, Powys considered his novel *Morwyn* to have been "the most valuable & the best thing" he had ever written: "If all my writings were to be destroyed this is the one . . . that I would most *regret*" (Powys, 1995, p. 231).

Notes

1. See, for example, Ryder, 2000, p. 269. Powys's novel *Morwyn* is listed as one of the few novels of the 20th century "to touch the cause of animal protection."

2. I have elsewhere provided an overview of Powys's involvement with the British antivivisection movement during the first half of the 20th century. See Taylor, 2019.

3. See Donald, 2020, pp. 179–222. This imbalance persists today in the sphere of animal advocacy, notably in the numbers of vegetarians and vegans.

4. Powys seems to have adopted a vegetarian diet at various stages of life, although periods of ill health (and eccentricity) led to stranger and more restrictive food choices such as exclusively bread and milk, or simply olive oil.

5. Powys also mentions a similar antivivisection meeting that he attended the year after in 1937. See Powys & Hanley, 2018, p. 58.

6. Current arguments against animal experimentation have shifted beyond this limited moral framework and onto an "evidence-based" focus. A growing body of data suggests that animal

tests "have not proved beneficial" and has led to the question of whether animals are actually suitable models for investigating human disease (Linzey & Linzey, 2018, p. 27).

References

Bates, A. W. H. (2017). *Anti-vivisection and the profession of medicine in Britain: A social history*. Basingstoke, England: Palgrave Macmillan.

Blavatsky, H. P. (1948). *The key to theosophy (abridged)*. London, England: Theosophical Publishing House.

Cook, David A. (1974). The "autobiography" of John Cowper Powys: A portrait of the artist as other. *Modern Philology, 72*(1), 30–44.

Donald, Diana. (2020). *Women against cruelty: Protection of animals in nineteenth-century Britain*. Manchester, England: Manchester University Press.

Drabble, Margaret. (2006, August 12). The English degenerate. *The Guardian*. Retrieved from: www.theguardian.com/books/2006/aug/12/featuresreviews.guardianreview14

Gore, Taliesin. (2019). A panpsychist reading of *Wolf Solent* and *A Glastonbury Romance*. *The Powys Journal, 29*, 77–98.

Hanley, James, & Powys, John Cowper. (2018). *Powys and Lord Jim: The correspondence between James Hanley and John Cowper Powys 1929–1965* (C. Gostick, Ed.). Mappowder, England: The Powys Press.

Krissdóttir, Morine. (2007). *Descents of memory: The life of John Cowper Powys*. London, England: Overlook Duckworth.

Linzey, Andrew, & Linzey, Clair. 2018. *The ethical case against animal experimentation*. Urbana: University of Illinois Press.

National Anti-Vivisection Society. (2012, July 24). *The history of the National Anti-Vivisection Society*. Retrieved from: www.navs.org.uk/about_us/24/0/299/

Powys, John Cowper. (1929). *Wolf solent*. New York, NY: Simon and Schuster.

Powys, John Cowper. (1930). *In defence of sensuality*. London, England: Golancz.

Powys, John Cowper. (1934). *Autobiography*. London, England: John Lane at the Bodley Head.

Powys, John Cowper. (1937). *Morwyn, or the vengeance of God*. London, England: Cassell.

Powys, John Cowper. (1995). *Petrushka and the dancer: The diaries of John Cowper Powys 1929–1939* (M. Krissdóttir, Ed.). Manchester, England: Carcanet.

Powys, John Cowper. (2000). *Weymouth sands*. London, England: Overlook. (Original work published 1934)

Ryder, Richard D. (2000). *Animal revolution: Changing attitudes towards speciesism*. Oxford, England: Berg.

Taylor, Felix. (2019). John Cowper Powys and the anti-vivisection movement. *The Powys Journal, 29*, 57–76.

Turner, James. (1980). *Reckoning with the beast: Animals, pain and humanity in the Victorian mind*. Baltimore, MD: Johns Hopkins University Press.

Viswanathan, Gauri. (2011). "Have animals souls?": Theosophy and the suffering body. *PMLA, 126*(2), 440–447

Westacott, Evalyn. (1949). *A century of vivisection and anti-vivisection*. Ashingdon, England: C. W. Daniel.

Boycotted Hospital: The National Anti-Vivisection Hospital, London, 1903–1935

A. W. H. BATES
University College, London, England

The National Anti-Vivisection Hospital opened to patients in 1903, the only district hospital in London not financed by state-controlled funds, which refused it support because of its principles. For three decades the hospital treated the local poor and conscientious objectors to vivisection, who were assured that staff pledged not to experiment on animals or patients. After an overambitious building program, the hospital ran into financial difficulties, and the King's Fund refused to help unless all references to antivivisection were removed from its statutes. Thus it reopened as Battersea General in 1935, continuing to serve the borough until 1972.

KEY WORDS: antivivisection, charity, hospital, King's Fund, London

THE HOSPITAL'S ORIGIN AND PURPOSE

What exactly was an antivivisection hospital? The question was asked at an inquest into the death of a child, Mabel Florence Jones, in 1908. She had been treated at the National Anti-Vivisection Hospital in Battersea, one of the poorest suburbs of London ("The Case of Mabel Florence Jones," 1909). The coroner asked the medical officer: "I see in your hospital's annual report the words, 'No experiments on patients.' What do they mean?" ("No Experiments on Patients," 1908). The hospital's secretary (chief administrator), G. W. F. Robbins, explained that it meant no experiments for the sake of knowledge rather than the sake of patients. The coroner asked if this implied that other hospitals *did* experiment, to which Robbins answered, "Not in the least" ("No Experiments on Patients," 1908). Local people, however, believed they did, and the antivivisection hospital, which required all staff to sign a pledge not to experiment on animals or humans, presented itself as a safe haven from such horrors ("Child's Death," 1908).

Thanks to the dogged antivivisectionist Stephen Coleridge, everybody thought they knew where London's vivisectionists worked: In 1901, he published *The Metropolitan Hospitals and Vivisection*, with its "blood-red band" against the names of the great teaching hospitals, such as Barts, Guy's, the London, Mary's, and St Thomas's. According to Coleridge, these "vivisecting" hospitals also had a callous attitude to patients: when they boasted of "an adequate supply of clinical material for purposes of instruction," he told his readers, they meant "the prostrate bodies of the sick" (Coleridge, 1901). He knew that money was being raised by the National Anti-Vivisection Society (NAVS) for a new hospital where all experimentation would be banned, and his pamphlet was intended to divert the "stream of charity" away from the laboratories of London's teaching hospitals. These hospitals had influential friends, like the doyen of hospital fundraising, Sir Henry Burdett, who complained about "those peculiar people who have chosen to associate themselves with the National Anti-Vivisection Society [of which Coleridge was secretary] and to set themselves in opposition to such great charitable movements as the Hospital Sunday Fund and King Edward's Hospital Fund" ("Anti-Vivisection Methods," 1902).

The NAVS had been raising money for a hospital since 1896, and in 1897 set up a fund with Lords Coleridge (Stephen's father) and Hatherton, Dr. Abiathar Wall of the London and Provincial Anti-Vivisection Society, Ernest Bell of the NAVS, and Rev. Augustus Jackson as trustees. Helped by donations from the Dowager Countess of Portsmouth, the fund grew rapidly. In 1900, they paid £7,000 for a large house known as Lock's Folly, which opened as a hospital in 1903 with "eight beds, three cots, and four medical officers, one of whom is also chairman of the hospital" ("Hospital in a Lawsuit," 1936). Its prospectus promised: "No Vivisection in its Schools. No Vivisectors on its Staff. No Experiments on Patients" (Anti-Vivisection Hospital, 1903).

South London was chronically short of hospital beds, and the local poor, who made up 90% of the new hospital's patients, had few alternatives; nevertheless, Robbins boasted that "the special effect of our principles upon the sick poor is to attract them to our Hospital in which they seem to have complete confidence, as is proved by the rapid increase in our work" (Robbins, 1907). The hospital's annual report described it as "a standing protest against cruel experiments on animals, and a concrete demonstration that these are not necessary for the succour of the maimed or the healing of the sick," and assured patients that "the whole of the medical, surgical and administrative staff are pledged against vivisection," and that treatments prepared using live animals were "absolutely shut out" (King's Fund, 1912).

HOSPITAL FUNDING

There was never any doubt that a voluntary hospital *could* treat the sick without experimenting on animals—most already did. The question was whether an openly antivivisection hospital could survive financially. Public donations to hospitals were usually channeled through three central funds: King Edward's Hospital Fund (the King's Fund), the Hospital Sunday Fund (derived from church collections), and the Saturday Fund (a workers' levy). If these failed to support the hospital, its survival was in danger (Prochaska, 1992). In 1906, the Anti-Vivisection Hospital applied to the King's Fund, whose inspectors noted the "steadily increasing amount of work done" and agreed that it "supplies a want," but they concluded that "the anti-vivisection basis upon which the Institution is founded is in itself considered a sufficient reason for withholding help" (Visitors' Report, 1906). The King's Fund, whose £140,000 annual distribution gave it great influence over practices and standards, did not give any reason for withholding a grant, but Sydney Holland, the chairman of the London Hospital (one of the fund's biggest beneficiaries), told Robbins that they were refusing to help because the premises were unfit for a hospital (Holland, 1907). This was wrong in fact—the hospital continued in the same buildings until 1972— and was at variance with the fund's own records, which stated that their objection was to the hospital's antivivisection charter. The conservative *Medical Times* noted that "patients are not bound to go to the hospital" and added:

> We are unable to understand why such a dead set has been made against the hospital. Enormous influence is being brought to bear to crush [it] with such success that the Distribution Committees of the great Hospital Funds in London have been induced to refuse . . . funds. ("The National Anti-Vivisection Hospital," 1908)

The journal suggested that, as with other special interest hospitals, such as the London Homoeopathic and National Temperance, the experiment should be allowed to take its course and be judged by its results.

The King's Fund's committee was far from impartial, as it included doctors sympathetic to vivisection as well as others, like its chairman Lord Lister, who performed it themselves, and Coleridge was characteristically forthright about this: "These great funds had got into the hands of persons who deliberately disposed of them to forward the views they personally held" ("Editorial," 1907). However, as the Anti-Vivisection Hospital was conceived and promoted as an alternative to supporting the funds, to allow donors who objected to vivisection to give without "sacrificing their consciences," it was, by approaching the funds itself, trying to have its cake and eat it ("Editorial," 1904).

The Sunday Fund told the hospital it had been refused an award because "the best treatment known" (i.e., antisera) was not given and the "Governing Body dictates the forms of treatment to be used by its medical staff" (Currie, 1907). The latter was, however, true of most voluntary hospitals, which typically had no medical governors. The National Anti-Vivisection's board, which included three doctors and a dentist, had more medics than most, though these were of course antivivisectionists like Lizzy Lind af Hageby, whose infiltration of the laboratories at University College in London precipitated the notorious Brown Dog affair. The Sunday Fund also claimed, improbably, that patients did not understand what antivivisection meant, to which the hospital replied that "the poorer class in Battersea, who appreciate our Hospital . . . well understand its title. Possibly the statue of the brown dog erected there conduces to this knowledge" (Pomeroy & Bowie, 1907).

The Brown Dog affair was an antivivisection cause célèbre that led to riots on the streets of Battersea between 1907 and 1909, as medical students attempted to demolish the council's provocative—the British Medical Association thought libelous—bronze statue of a terrier "done to death" in the laboratories of University College. Battersea's menfolk came out in force to defend the dog and "guard" the hospital, and one rather fanciful account had them forcibly preventing an injured student—whose objection to the hospital's ethos had conveniently evaporated when he needed its help—from entering its doors (Mason, 1997, p. 55; Lansbury, 1985; DeMello, 2012, pp. 183–186; Cain, 2013). These "town versus gown" fights channeled the "pent-up hatred felt by certain classes towards medical science and medical men" who, "brutalised by vivisection," experimented on those weaker than themselves ("The 'Brown Dog' Disturbances," 1907). Given the furor they generated, the Sunday Fund's claim that local people did not know or care what antivivisection meant was hardly credible.

Rioting medical students reinforced the stereotype that those prepared to experiment on animals were uncaring; as a correspondent to the King's Fund later wrote:

> The disgraceful scene... made by the medical students [at an antivivisection meeting] fills one with the utmost contempt and loathing for these cowardly "butchers"... if these creatures are our coming medical men, then I say—God help their unfortunate patients! (George, 1930)

The Antivivisection Hospital's raison d'être was to promote medical compassion: its antivivisection rule did not directly save any animals—only a tiny minority of medical practitioners ever vivisected, and district hospitals had little time for it—but the rule affirmed the hospital's commitment to humane medicine. Signing the pledge was a significant step: Dr. W. R. Hadwen told antivivisectionists in 1907 that medical practitioners who spoke out "had to learn what it meant to be heterodox," and it was said that "no one with pronounced anti-vivisectional principals would be elected to the Medical Staff of the larger London Hospitals... and his promotion unlikely" ("Anti-Vivisection Meeting in Cheltenham," 1907; Pomeroy & Bowie, 1907). Not surprisingly, medical practitioners who had misgivings about vivisection were reluctant to speak up: "A young Doctor told a lady that he hated Vivisection, but did not dare express it, or he would have been hooted out of the Profession" (Bradley, n.d.).

In 1908, the Sunday Fund did give the hospital £440, but only in the hope that they "would mend their ways, purge their methods, and, in fact, fall into line" (Hospital Board, 1908). It was, Burdett wrote, "pretentious humbug" to employ modern methods developed by experiments on animals and then boast of being antivivisection ("The Anti-Vivisection Hospital," 1909). In reply, Robbins challenged him to name a remedy whose development had depended on vivisection. This was an invitation to an argument that, though it had remained popular over the years with both sides, was always unproductive, since even if it were agreed that a particular medical advance had resulted from vivisection (which it never was), it was practically impossible to prove that it could *only* have been made in this way and not by some other means.

The previous year, 1907, the King's Fund's committee, with the Prince of Wales (the future George V) in the chair, had met in private and agreed that the hospital "should not be visited in future in consequence of its work being based on considerations which are not exclusively directed to the welfare of the patients," adding that this "should not be published" since "if communicated to the hospital it would at once involve a discussion" (King's Fund, 1907). The desire to prevent a discussion suggests the fund lacked confidence in their ability to convince the public, who seemed increasingly supportive of the "Anti-Vivi."

SENTIMENT AND SCIENCE

The hospital board was careful not to make patients choose between sentiment and science. After its staff participated in the 1911 British Union for the Abolition of Vivisection march, Robbins wrote to the press to clarify that the hospital, which now had 28 beds, did not oppose "legitimate and beneficent forms of laboratory research unconnected with Vivisection such as microscopical investigation of pathological specimens and bacteriological examinations . . . necessary to the interests of medical progress" (Hospital Board, 1911). Thereafter, it remained somewhat aloof from the antivivisection societies. In the same year it opened a 12-bed "cancer research department," equipped with the latest electric "light and colour bath" (Special Board, 1911; Hospital Board, 1914). The board was fond of such gadgets, though they seem to have been largely for show: The outpatient department boasted "the Buisson Institute for hydrophobia," but no cases of this rare condition ever turned up, and inspectors found the special Buisson bath languishing under a pile of rubbish (Visitors' Report, 1908).

The hospital's death rates were "exceedingly low"—4.2 per 1,000 compared with the London Hospital's 9.5—though Robbins wisely told the King's Fund that this was not "a statistic which we would wish to press or labour," probably because the nature and complexity of the procedures performed in each hospital was not taken into account (Visitors' Report, 1908). Some inpatient deaths led to criticisms at inquests, suggesting that competent junior staff were hard to find, perhaps because they feared for their careers, though there is no record of any complaints from patients, though surely the hospital's critics would have seized on them had any been made. Battersea's "working men and women" valued their hospital and organized dances, concerts, and boxing tournaments to raise money, with both provivisectionists and antivivisectionists working together for "so worthy a cause in helping the very poor" (Hospital Board, 1922; Bench, 1912a, 1912b).

The King's Fund accepted that patients were treated according to the latest principles and that no attempt was made to exclude treatments that might have been developed by experiments on animals, yet still the fund gave grants to other "alternative" hospitals but not to the Anti-Vivisection Hospital. An internal memo recorded that:

> The Distribution Committee decided not to give their arguments—which were that the ~~principles~~ restrictions at the Temperance and Homoeopathic hospitals are adopted because they are believed to be in the interests of the patients: those at the Antivivisection Hospital in the interests of the animals. (Maynard, 1912)

Had they seen the memo, the antivivisectionists might well have said that their principles *were* in the interests of patients, since their staff was more compassionate. Patients seemingly preferred doctors who did not experiment on animals: for example, teaching hospitals concealed, rather than advertised, the presence of vivisectionists in their schools.

Whatever one thought of them, the National Anti-Vivisection Hospital took its principles seriously: In 1912, an extraordinary committee meeting was convened to investigate the actions of its resident medical officer, Dr. Maurice Bayly, who had performed a major operation for breast cancer on a dying patient. There was no suggestion that the unconscious patient had suffered, and her family made no complaint, but Bayly admitted he had been so "anxious to perform the operation" that he had practiced on a dying woman. This was the kind of experiment that led patients to lose confidence in hospitals, and Bayly, whose conduct had been otherwise excellent, was severely reprimanded for failing to meet the hospital's standards, and he left shortly afterward (Emergency Committee, 1912; Hospital Board, 1912). In 1926, a nurse was dismissed for her "callous and brutal" treatment of patients, and a visiting doctor was not admitted because he refused to sign the antivivisection pledge. A would-be honorary surgeon who tried to water down the pledge was not appointed, and a doctor who treated two patients with antisera without authorization was asked to resign (Hospital Board, 1926–1927). Vaccines and antisera prepared from live animals were specifically banned by the hospital's regulations.

CHARITABLE SUPPORT

The hospital's supporters argued that it was the funds' boycott, rather than the hospital's principles, that was against patients' interests. In 1914, one wrote to the King's Fund: "It can hardly be right that solely on account of the question for or against vivisection, the poor of a populous district should be left without the aid of a Hospital" (Culme-Seymour, 1914). Fortunately, the hospital had sufficient income from legacies and donations to remain solvent and even expand, leaving the King's Fund looking increasingly narrow-minded. In 1922, Richard Morris, the local member of parliament, called on the fund to ask why they would not assist a voluntary institution that was "doing the work of a general hospital"; were they, he asked, "prejudiced by the views of orthodox medical men on the fund"? (Memorandum, 1922).

The Anti-Vivisection Hospital's chairs came from varied professional and political backgrounds and included the libertarian economist Joseph Hiam Levy (until 1905), John Prince Fallowes, Rector of Heene (1905–1911), the Liberal politician Sir George William Kekewich (1911–1914), hereditary peer Lord Tenterden (1914–1926), solicitor Alderman Robert Tweedy Smith (1926–1927), insurance broker S. C. Turner (1927–1928) and member of parliament, novelist, theologian, and sometime fascist Lord Ernest Hamilton (1928–1935). Its supporters were equally varied, from the radical Progressive Party borough council and local trades unions to wealthy aristocrats—most notably, in its early years, Lady Portsmouth, whose death in 1906 deprived it of a generous supporter (Hospital Board, 1906). The stereotype of the antivivisection supporter as a wealthy widow with animals for company was not without foundation: By the 1920s, over 70% of the governors were female, and the board later planned a charity appeal to 10,000 widows (Hospital Board, 1933).

In 1922, an inspection of the hospital, which theoretically had 52 beds, found only 11 occupied. A new outpatient building, completed in 1915 at a cost of £15,000, remained empty for want of equipment, and the old department still advertised "RABIES SCARE BUISSON BATH TREATMENT," although the bath was not even connected to the gas supply (Perry & Fry, 1922). The postwar period had been difficult for many voluntary hospitals, as people had less money for charitable giving, and antivivisection was a declining cause. The antivivisectionists' aging demographic was, however, a rich source of legacies. A bequest of £7,361 wiped off the hospital's wartime debt, a large building program was begun to accommodate "ever-increasing applications for admission," and the whole hospital was renovated "with every essential modern appliance and made as perfect as possible" (King's Fund, n.d.). In 1929, the hospital received a further windfall of over £38,000 from three large bequests (Hospital and General Purposes Committee, 1929).

By the late 1920s, the hospital was treating over 400 inpatients and 40,000 outpatients a year, but its reputation was damaged by a dispute that began in 1927 when a former honorary surgeon, J. F. Peart, made a series of accusations. The hospital's ban on antisera was well known, and Peart claimed that one of his patients had died of tetanus as a result. Furthermore, he told the King's Fund, the hospital "discouraged" the use of vaccines, two patients had died due to the use of infected catgut, and "there were two unqualified persons on the Staff" (Peart, 1927). He accused "women members of the board of management" of interfering with medical affairs and communicated his concerns to the *Lancet* and *British Medical Journal*, which printed detrimental reports. In its defense, the hospital maintained that Peart had been aware of alternative arrangements for giving antiserum—by sending patients who asked for it to other hospitals—since as long ago as 1922.

There are reasons to be skeptical about Peart's allegations. The hospital minutes record that he was dismissed after an argument with the matron. His statement that the hospital was antivaccination was not substantiated by other sources, the board's interference with clinicians was no greater than at other hospitals, and the deaths due to infected catgut were more likely due to poor technique than policy. Peart clearly wanted to cause as much damage as possible, and wrote, on the advice of the King's Fund, to London County Council, which stopped ambulances from bringing patients to the hospital (Cox, 1927).

In response, the hospital board unwisely contacted the council to "confirm that in cases of tetanus and diphtheria and all else medical officers are authorized to take all steps necessary for the preservation of life" (Hospital Board, 1928). It is not clear how long this compromise had been in effect, but the damage was done, as the hospital appeared either unsafe or hypocritical, depending on whether or not antiserum had actually been in use. Some supporters, such as the absolutist British Union for the Abolition of Vivisection, deplored this concession to expediency, and resignations of governors followed. The council took 4 years to reinstate the ambulance service, at which time the hospital secretary told the King's Fund:

> In the opinion and practice of the medical staff there is nothing in our constitution or Articles of Association which limits them in treating patients under their care in any

way different from that which they practice in other Hospitals in which they work. They maintain that sera are not the products of Vivisection." (Cox, 1932)

This admission removed any pretense that the hospital's practices were different from the norm, which further alienated its supporters while making no difference to the King's Fund's boycott (Woolven, 1932).

BOYCOTTED HOSPITAL

By the early 1930s, the hospital's financial position was unsustainable. Eight board members resigned and the sale of £4,300 in stocks failed to clear its debts (Hospital Finance Committee, 1933). Late in 1934, the mortgaged hospital received an ultimatum from Barclays Bank. Lord Ernest wrote to the King's Fund to suggest: "You, as custodians of the largest British hospital fund, should take the hospital over as the Battersea General Hospital, without the objectionable title of 'Antivivisection,'" since it would be a "calamity" for Battersea if it closed down (Hamilton, 1934). This was a marked concession for a committed antivivisectionist, but Lord Ernest felt this was the only way to save the hospital to which he was devoted. Realizing that the King's Fund's objective was to overturn the antivivisection charter, Coleridge tried to press them into assisting immediately, as forcing the hospital to close would be "playing it very low" (Hogg, 1934).

The fund, however, refused, bringing upon itself a raft of criticisms for misusing its influence, failing to uphold its original purpose of honoring Queen Victoria ("whose utter detestation of Vivisection was expressed in perfectly definite terms"), ignoring the fact that that its income of £240,000 a year included donations from people "suspicious" of vivisection, and failing to point out when collecting money "that the Fund was only for the orthodox" (Blackwood, 1935; "Closing a Hospital," 1935). When the hospital's money ran out, its nurses worked for nothing and local people gave up their savings ("Battersea General Hospital," 1935). There was a plan to petition the Prince of Wales (the future Edward VIII) to intervene, and Lord Ernest wrote to the Prince informing him that "all Battersea is in a ferment," which predictably made no impression ("Battersea General Hospital Fighting for Life," 1935; Thomas, 1935). After meeting representatives of the King's Fund (at Ascot races), His Royal Highness "fully realised that it would have been impossible to go back on the previous decisions of the Council, which are based on logical reasons" (Werner, 1935). In an internal memo, the chairman of the fund's distribution committee, Edwin Cooper Perry (1935), wrote: "Let it die, as it will of inanition if we go on saying nothing." He may have been referring to the bad publicity, but "it" could just as well have meant the hospital. Later that year, Cooper Perry was knighted for services to charity.

In defeat, Lord Ernest vented his spleen to the press, condemning the "fanatical bigotry," which had "killed" the hospital. "If this hospital was in one of the smart well-dressed districts of London there would be no difficulty at all. . . . But we are situated in a poor district on the wrong side of the river for fashionable sympathy" ("Malice Charge," 1935) The hospital finally closed in June 1935, and the remaining 50 inpatients were "whisked off" in ambulances to other hospitals ("Alteration of a Hospital's Objects," 1935).

A King's Fund inspection at the end of 1935 found the hospital fit for purpose and concluded that it had come to grief because of overspending: There were debts of £45,000 "due to a recent extension from 56 beds to 100, at a cost of £30,000 of which £26,000 was met by loans" (Distribution Committee, 1935). A number of factors, they felt, had conspired to prevent the hospital from paying its debts: declining interest in antivivisection, disillusionment with the equivocation about its antiserum policy, and higher taxation ("Boycotted Hospital," 1935). In addition, the hospital's policy of paying local people fair rates had kept running costs high, and the antivivisection charter made it hard to recruit junior staff and necessitated paying more for those prepared to sign up (Parkes, 1936; Report of Inspection, 1938).

Lord Ernest stepped down as chair in favor of Sidney Parkes, a London builder and sports promoter who disconcertingly promised that his plan to restore the hospital's fortunes would be "absolutely legal" (Hospital Board, 1935). Five board members resigned within a year of his appointment, and though he effected "every possible economy"—from reducing the use of X-ray film to requiring members of the board to pay sixpence for tea and cake—debts continued to grow. Parkes had personally guaranteed a £6,500 bank loan, but there seemed no prospect of repaying it and he resigned in January 1936, "anxious to be relieved of this responsibility," and having discovered the hard way that "the Hospital had lost a great deal of income through abandoning anti-vivisection" (Hospital Finance Committee, 1937). After its charter was changed, the medical staff were obliged to resign and reapply for their jobs without the anticruelty clause. One who did not do so was Alexander Bowie, the hospital's first chair, who wrote to the board:

> I remember that we began with one little girl patient. But it soon grew till the number was 100. I appointed the first house physician, a woman, the first nurse and the first medical staff. The hospital was obviously needed, and it has been successful so far as the treatment of patients is concerned. ("Hospital in a Lawsuit," 1936)

It was also successful in demonstrating that there was enough support from patients and donors to make an antivivisection hospital a going concern. The determination of the medical establishment to crush it was an indication that they found this public demand for a hospital run without cruelty something of an embarrassment.

ACKNOWLEDGMENTS

This work was partially supported by Wellcome Trust grant number 104505/Z/14/Z. The author would like to thank the Wellcome Trust for a short-term research grant; Professor Joe Cain and the staff of the Department of Science and Technology Studies at University College, London, the staff of the London Metropolitan Archive, Dan Mitchell of University College London Special Collections, and Annie Lindsay of University College London Hospital Archives.

References

Alteration of a hospital's objects. (1935). *British Medical Journal, 2*, 1055.

Anti-Vivisection Hospital. (1903). [Flyer]. London Metropolitan Archives (hereinafter LMA; A/KE/260/001). London, England.

Anti-vivisection meeting in Cheltenham (1907, November 23). *Cheltenham Looker-On*, p. 15.

Anti-vivisection methods. (1902). *Hospital, 32*, 244–245.

Battersea General Hospital. (1935, June 23). *South Western Star*.

Battersea General Hospital fighting for life (1935, June 15). *South Western Star*, p. 9.

Bench, J. (1912a, March 26). [Letter to H. R. Maynard]. LMA (A/KE/260/001).

Bench, J. (1912b, March 26). [Letter to King's Fund]. LMA (A/KE/260/001).

Blackwood, J. (1935, July 9). [Letter to H. R. Maynard]. LMA (A/KE/245/04).

Boycotted hospital: Battersea ceases to be anti-vivisectionist. (1935, November 20). *News Chronicle*.

Bradley, T. W. (n.d.) *Torture in laboratories and hospitals*. Wellcome Library, London (SA/RDS A3).

Cain, J. (2013). *The brown dog in Battersea Park*. London, England: Euston Grove Press.

Child's death. (1908, December 31). *Sheffield Evening Telegraph*, p. 2.

Closing a hospital. (1935, June 7). *South Western Star*.

Coleridge, S. (1901). *The diversion of hospital funds: A controversy between the Hon. Stephen Coleridge and the* British Medical Journal. London, England: National Anti-Vivisection Society.

Cox, M. H. (1927, August 12). [Letter to Harry W. Woolven]. LMA (A/KE/260/001).

Cox, M. H. (1932, March 17). [Letter to the Medical Superintendent]. LMA (A/KE/260/001).

Culme-Seymour, M. E. (1914, June 1). [Letter to H. R. Maynard.] LMA (A/KE/260/001).

Currie, E. H. (1907, July 15). [Letter to G. W. F. Robbins]. LMA (A/KE/260/001).

DeMello, M. (2012). *Animals and society: An introduction to human-animal studies*. New York, NY: Colombia University Press.

Distribution Committee. (1935, December). [Minute book]. LMA (A/KE/245/04).

Editorial. (1904, June 13). *Exeter and Plymouth Gazette*, p. 3.

Editorial. (1907, October 1). *The Times*, p. 10.

Emergency Committee. (1912, August 2). [Minute book]. LMA (HO6/BG/A/01/002).

George, R. M. (1930, May 22). [Letter to the Treasurer, King's Fund]. LMA (A/KE/260/002).

Hamilton, E. (1934, December 19). [Letter to H. R. Maynard]. LMA (A/KE/260/002).

Hogg, T. H. D. (1934, May 28). [Letter to the Treasurer, King's Fund]. LMA (A/KE/260/002).

Holland, S. (1907, December 23). [Letter to G. W. F. Robbins]. LMA (A/KE/260/001).

Hospital and General Purposes Committee. (1929, June). [Minute book]. LMA (H6/BG/A9/1).

Hospital Board. (1906, October 4). [Minute book]. LMA (H6/BG/A1/1).

Hospital Board. (1908, August 6). [Minute book]. LMA (H6/BG/A1/1).

Hospital Board. (1911, December 6). [Minute book]. LMA (HO6/BG/A/01/002).

Hospital Board. (1912, September). [Minute book]. LMA (HO6/BG/A/01/0020).

Hospital Board. (1914, June). [Minute book]. LMA (HO6/BG/A/01/002).

Hospital Board. (1922, May). [Minute book]. LMA (H6/BG/A1/3).

Hospital Board. (1926, March, April-1927, March). [Minute book]. LMA (H6/BG/A1/4).

Hospital Board. (1928, July 12). [Minute book]. LMA (A/KE/260/001).

Hospital Board. (1933, June). [Minute book]. LMA (H6/BG/A1/5).

Hospital Board. (1935, June). [Minute book]. LMA (H6/BG/A1/6).

Hospital Finance Committee. (1933, April). [Minute book]. LMA (A6/BG/A4/1).

Hospital Finance Committee. (1937, December). [Minute book]. LMA (A6/BG/A4/1).
Hospital in a lawsuit. (1936, December 28). *Evening News*.
King's Fund. (n.d.). [Memorandum]. LMA (A/KE/245/04).
King's Fund. (1907, December 16). LMA (A/KE/260/001).
King's Fund. (1912). [Memorandum]. LMA (A/KE/260/001).
Lansbury, C. (1985). The old brown dog: Women, workers, and vivisection in Edwardian England. Madison: University of Wisconsin Press.
Malice charge by chief of hospital: King Edward's Fund attacked. (1935, 31 May). *Daily Mirror*.
Mason, P. (1997). *The brown dog affair: The story of a monument that divided the nation*. London, England: Two Sevens Publishing.
Maynard, H. R. (1912, May 24). [Letter to G. W. F. Robbins]. LMA (A/KE/260/001).
Memorandum. (1922). LMA (A/KE/260/001).
"No experiments on patients," but "every kind of operation." (1908, December 31). *Nottingham Evening Post*, p. 8.
Parkes, S. (1936, January). [Notes of interview]. LMA (A/KE/245/04).
Peart, J. F. (1927, February 28). [Letter to H. R. Maynard]. LMA (A/KE/260/001).
Perry, E. C., & Fry, F. (1922, July 22). [Report to King's Fund]. LMA (A/KE/260/001).
Perry, E. C. (1935, May 30). [Memorandum]. LMA (A/KE/245/04).
Pomeroy, E. A. G., & Bowie, A. (1907, August 27). [Letter to Currie]. LMA (A/KE/260/001).
Prochaska, F. K. (1992). *Philanthropy and the hospitals of London: The King's Fund, 1897–1990*. Oxford, England: Clarendon Press.
Report of Inspection. (1938, February). LMA (A/KE/512[5]).
Robbins, G. W. F. (1907, November 11). [Letter to H. R. Maynard]. LMA (A/KE/260/001).
Special Board. (1911, June 14). [Minute book]. LMA (HO6/BG/A/01/002).
The "brown dog" disturbances. (1907). *Medical Press and Circular, 85*, 593.
The Anti-Vivisection Hospital. (1909, September 23). *Hospital*, p. 677.
The case of Mabel Florence Jones. (1909). *Lancet, 173*, 124–126.
The National Anti-Vivisection Hospital. (1908, January 11). *Medical Times*, p. 24.
Thomas, G. (1935, June 11). [Letter to H. R. Maynard]. LMA (A/KE/245/04).
Visitors' report. (1906). LMA (A/KE/260/001).
Visitors' report. (1908). LMA (A/KE/260/001).
Werner, H. (1935, June 22). [Letter to H. R. Maynard]. LMA (A/KE/245/04).
Woolven, H.G. (1932, July 18). [Letter to H. R. Maynard]. LMA (A/KE/260/001).

Animal Research, Safeguards, and Lessons from the Long History of Judicial Torture

ADAM CLULOW
University of Texas at Austin

JAN LAUWEREYNS
Kyushu University, Japan

For animal research, the precautionary principle was written into public policy through the so-called three R's of replacement, reduction, and refinement. These guidelines, as developed by Russell and Burch six decades ago, aimed to establish safeguards against the abuse of animals in the pursuit of science. While these safeguards, which started from the basic premise that science itself would benefit from a reduction of animal suffering, seem compelling at first, the three R's have in practice generated a degree of confusion while opening up loopholes that have enabled researchers to effectively dismiss some of the more inconvenient aspects of ethical concerns. Such problems have been discussed in detail by multiple authors. Here, we suggest a different approach by arguing that a clear parallel can be drawn between the shortcomings evident in the current three R's model and the flawed practice of early modern judicial torture, in which a set of elaborate safeguards that were designed to prevent abuses served instead to create the same combination of confusion and easily exploited loopholes. In the case of judicial torture, attempts to refine the system from within produced limited results, and effective change only took place when individual legal systems succeeded in enforcing clear absolutes. We explore the implications of this for the regulation of animal research by pointing to the need for achievable absolutes, based on a clear, evidence-based, and publicly deliberated rationale, in order to facilitate and improve research ethics.

Key words: animal research, three R's, precautionary principle, judicial torture, achievable absolutes

INTRODUCTION

The regulation of animal research varies widely across countries. While individual governments have developed their own sets of safeguards, several lines converge. First, there is a clear consensus that certain animals deserve a certain amount of protection, or what is often termed "humane" treatment. Second, there exists among scholars and policymakers a preferred framework that aims to provide a structure for this protection. This framework is clearly detailed in Article 4 of Directive 2010/63/EU (2010), which refers to the "principle of replacement, reduction and refinement":

> 1. Member States shall ensure that, wherever possible, a scientifically satisfactory method or testing strategy, not entailing the use of live animals, shall be used instead of a procedure.
> 2. Member States shall ensure that the number of animals used in projects is reduced to a minimum without compromising the objectives of the project.
> 3. Member States shall ensure refinement of breeding, accommodation and care, and of methods used in procedures, eliminating or reducing to the minimum any possible pain, suffering, distress or lasting harm to the animals. (pp. 39–40)

These points draw directly from the principles first articulated in Russell and Burch's (1959/1992) landmark study *The Principles of Humane Experimental Technique*, which was published in 1959. In this, they defined replacement as the "substitution for conscious living higher animals of insentient material"; reduction as the "reduction in the numbers of animals used to obtain information of a given amount and precision"; and refinement as "any decrease in the incidence or severity of inhumane procedures applied to those animals which still have to be used" (Russell & Burch, 1959/1992, p. 62).

The influence of this foundational text has meant that the three R's are not only very widely accepted but have become "fundamental to the philosophy underlying the guidelines and legislation that regulate animal experimentation" (Buchanan-Smith et al., 2005, p. 379). They have also come to define the way universities and commercial laboratories manage and regulate animal research via their own policies and procedures. This near universal recognition has meant that their basic language and the framework they developed have been adopted by advocates on both sides of the debate, with opponents of animal research citing the three R's with equal frequency and fervor (Goldberg, 2010; Olsson, Franco, Weary, & Sandøe, 2012; Roelfsema & Treue, 2014; Tannenbaum & Bennett, 2015).

It is not difficult to understand why the three R's have proved so appealing for so many researchers, scholars, and activists concerned with the use of animals in research. The principles developed by Russell and Burch were intended to improve the praxis of science with animals through a principled approach aimed at reducing animal suffering. In their view, the two goals were compatible. The reduction of animal suffering would in fact contribute to the progress of science, or, phrased in simpler terms, the better the care for the animals, the better the data.

In the abstract, it was a message that resonated with different groups. The three R's provided a concrete and readily accessible variant of the precautionary principle, setting in place clear safeguards against the risk of animal abuse. The promise of the framework seemed both substantial and compelling (Holm, 2018). The reduction of animal suffering can be a profoundly motivating goal for animal rights' activists, and, by extension, a very real public concern. Even more appealing, the implied direction of the precaution seemed, in mathematical terms, simple and precise, leaving only the option of *less*.

This positive picture is tarnished, however, by a series of interconnected problems. While they offer an intuitive appeal, the three R's have in fact created new uncertainties while failing to prevent ill-use (e.g., Bailey & Taylor, 2016; Balls, 2010; Bayne & Turner, 2019; Freshwater, 2015; Glasziou et al., 2014; LaFollette & Shanks, 1996; Lauwereyns, 2018; Rollin, 2017; Singh et al., 2016). Sometimes it is not clear which of the three R's should get priority, or in what order they should be applied. In practice, many researchers seem content to concentrate their efforts exclusively on refinement while neglecting replacement and reduction (Balls, 2010; Lauwereyns, 2018; Phillips et al., 2014). At the same time and even as they endorse the framework put forward by Russell and Burch, many researchers, scholars, and animal ethicists often pay surprisingly little attention to its actual content. When there is a genuine effort applied toward replacement, researchers approach it inconsistently and in a manner at odds with the original text. As one example, replacement for Russell and Burch was about replacing animals with nonsentient materials (e.g., plants, artificial simulations; this was "absolute replacement") or replacing animals with nonsentient animal tissue (e.g., a brain slice in a dish; what they termed "relative replacement"; as cited in Lauwereyns, 2018, p. 15). In contrast, most researchers working today understand replacement as, potentially, switching from a nonhuman primate to a rodent without acknowledging the departure from the original principles or offering a clear rationale (e.g., Roelfsema & Treue, 2014). This discrepancy between discourse and praxis suggests the three R's no longer function as effective guidelines.

Equally worrying, the safeguards put in place by the three R's have failed to prevent the continued authorization of a range of experiments that involve significant and largely unjustifiable harm to animals (e.g., Bailey & Taylor, 2016). One problem is that Russell and Burch never questioned the validity of research objectives, working from the premise that if there was knowledge to be gained from a particular experiment then it was a matter of how, not whether, to conduct the research. In this way, they started from the notion that experiments must be carried out, but, if replacement was not possible, these should be designed to reduce animal suffering. Put another way, Russell and Burch did not engage in harm-benefit analysis; that is, they did not consider opportunity costs with respect to the time, effort, and money to be invested in research (Lauwereyns, 2018). Finally, the three R's have not ended the continued waste of animal research (e.g., Glasziou et al., 2014; Singh et al., 2016), with poor research practices continuing to result in the loss of animal lives to trivial or useless outcomes.

Such issues have created an impasse in which the three R's have been unsuccessful in providing effective safeguards capable of ensuring animal welfare, even while acquiring a massive institutional weight. One possible way around this impasse is by looking backward toward a historical regime, namely the system of judicial torture that dominated European legal practice for centuries. Strikingly, this comparison reveals not only a range of parallel features but also a potential path out of the current situation.

On the surface, this may seem like a curious, or even futile, approach. The concern for the care and use of animals in research sits at the interface between research ethics and animal ethics and is, by its nature, highly specific. Even though researchers have used animal models to replace humans in biomedical and behavioral research at least since Alcmaeon of Croton several millennia ago (Franco, 2013), the current level of attention and effort toward a principled ethical approach is relatively new, and the legislation referenced at the beginning of the article only emerged in recent decades.

What, then, do we hope to gain from a comparison with the history of judicial torture? First, we aim to identify certain parallels that have not been noted previously by scholars but that exist between the regime of animal research that prevails today and the system of judicial torture that dominated continental courts across Europe for close to 6 centuries before its eventual abolition in the late 18th century. Second, we believe that there is something to be learned here and that an examination of the past may enable us to suggest paths forward (Dougherty, Scheck, Nelson, & Narens, 2005). In the closing section, we argue that the experience of early modern torture points to the value of achievable absolutes in preventing potential abuses while suggesting possible mechanisms to enforce them.

One caution should be noted. We should be clear immediately that we are not comparing animal research to torture per se. That may be a debate but it is not one that we are concerned with here. Instead, our focus is on the ways in which large-scale systems attempt to minimize abuses by erecting appropriate safeguards and some of the problems that can be generated in the process.

Historical Parallels Between Animal Research and Judicial Torture

Russell and Burch's (1959/1992) foundational text started from three interconnected points. First, they argued that animal testing has generated vast benefits for humanity. For them, it "is a truism, though one that cannot too often be repeated, that we owe to animal experimentation many if not most of the benefits of modern medicine and countless advances in fundamental scientific knowledge" (Russell & Burch, 1959/1992, Chapter 1). Second, they recognized that, if unregulated, abuses could and would take place. And third, they were adamant that these abuses could be prevented by creating clear principles or safeguards that would minimize distress to animal test subjects. The goal of the framework was thus the "removal of inhumanity" through the development of guidelines for animal research (Russell & Burch, 1959/1992, Chapter 4). This would enable animal testing to continue to generate the scientific benefits necessary for progress while minimizing any potential negative outcomes, which in turn would serve to boost the research itself via a virtuous cycle of continual improvement.

This three-part framing has become a standard and much-repeated part of defenses of the three R model (Lauwereyns, 2018). Proponents of animal research—particularly the most controversial types involving nonhuman primates (e.g., Phillips et al., 2014; Roelfsema & Treue, 2014)—continue to reach for similar arguments decades after Russell and Burch's first framing. Typically, these commence with broad statements about the greater good of biomedical research, which has, in the words of prominent proponents of this view, "played a vital role in many of the medical and scientific advances of the past century" (Phillips et al., 2014, p. 801) by forming one of "two main fields of human endeavor that have propelled mankind forward" (Roelfsema & Treue, 2014, p. 1200). But having established this greater good, they acknowledge as well that there are genuine ethical concerns surrounding the possibility of abuses. However, any conflict can be resolved by implementing "animal protection laws . . . built on the broad consensus across science, politics, and society that a certain amount of research on animals is necessary and justifiable. This consensus includes the 3R principles . . . of Replace, Refine, and Reduce," which will provide clear safeguards against abuse (Roelfsema & Treue, 2014, p. 1200). In this way, such formulations mirror the basic logic first expressed by Russell and Burch.

This general situation offers a striking parallel to the regime of judicial torture as it developed in Europe from roughly 1200 to 1800. This system, which first appeared in northern Italy and then spread across the continent more generally, hinged on the "use of physical coercion by officers of the state in order to gather evidence for judicial proceedings" (Langbein, 2006, p. 3). It stemmed from what is commonly referred to as the European law of proof, which was a set of standards that derived from a renewed focus on and adaptation of Roman law. This required two clear eyewitnesses in order to establish guilt of a crime. If these were not present, then a confession from the accused was needed to provide evidentiary certainty, as circumstantial evidence, however compelling, was not considered adequate to convict. Since there were many cases in which the required two eyewitnesses were not available, torture became a way to generate a confession, the so-called "queen of proofs" that was necessary to reach a guilty verdict (Peters, 1999, p. 41). This reliance on sanctioned torture underpinned legal codes, such as the *Constitutio Criminalis Carolina*, which was issued for the Hapsburg Empire in 1532, or the 1570 Criminal Ordinance (*Criminele Ordonnantiën*), which exerted an enduring influence even in those territories that had broken away from Spanish control. It also spawned lengthy treatises written by prominent legal thinkers across Europe that were designed to elaborate and refine the system. The combination of the two combined to generate a massive textual edifice built around the use of judicial torture.

Like proponents of the three R's, defenders of judicial torture started from a familiar triumvirate of three points. They argued first for the indispensable nature of judicial torture, which was necessary to sustain order in society. A prominent Dutch legal thinker, Ulrik Huber (1939, pp. 457–458), summed up this broad defense by noting that "the common weal and tranquility of nations could not be preserved if we were to leave unpunished all crimes which could not be fully proved." If this was the case, the failure to use torture "would be incomparably greater than the hardship arising from its use, and, consequently the good in torture is much greater than the evil." Given this fact, there could be only one conclusion: "It must follow that it has been accepted with the general concurrence of the nations, and all their private citizens, so that he to whom it occurs has no complaint against anybody." But like other legal thinkers from this period, Huber recognized as well that any reliance on torture to produce confessions could generate its own abuses. For this reason, it was essential to follow what he called the "precepts of the law in regard to torture," which would mitigate any potential negative outcomes.

Such reasoning was a standard part of discussions of early modern torture. While it is easy to dismiss early modern judicial torture as an irrational or essentially barbaric institution deployed without proper consideration of its perils or pitfalls, this was not the case. Instead, from the beginning, legal scholars recognized the inevitability, if not properly regulated, of abuses. In the words of another prominent Dutch scholar, Antonius Matthaeus, "torture is a frail institution . . . and one which cheats the truth" (as cited in Stoop, 1996, p. 556). The result was a basic unease that was built into the system from its inception. This in turn generated a set of clear principles or safeguards that were designed to regulate the practice of torture so as to prevent any possibility of misuse.

For the drafters of legal codes, and the scholars who interpreted them, torture could only be used when a set of precise conditions were met. The list was long but at the top were two basic principles. First, torture could only be used to investigate a serious crime in which the potential punishment extended to death or serious physical punishment (Langbein, 2006, p. 13). Second, torture should only be authorized when the evidence was already so clear that there was little doubt that the suspect was in fact guilty. In the words of Huber (1939), torture could only be used if the "accused, though not fully convicted, is pressed with such violent presumptions, that the Judge has hardly any doubts but that he is guilty" (p. 458). This meant that torture was to be authorized only when there was such clear-cut evidence that the guilt of the suspect was readily apparent. Such conditions were written into law in the 1570 Criminal Ordinance, which stated that torture could only be used "when the thing is so clear, and the proof so apparent, that nothing seems to be wanting but the confession of the prisoner to convict him without doubt" (as cited in Peters, 1999, p. 37). If this high evidentiary bar was not reached, then torture should not be used. Beyond these two basic provisions were a list of lesser conditions that had to be met before torture could authorized. One Italian writer, Sebastian Guazzini, laid out 19 separate prerequisites for the use of such techniques (Henry, 1821, pp. 251–259). If one followed the letter of the law, such writings combined to establish an extremely high bar, creating a situation in which torture could only be used in precisely delimited situations in which a set of stipulated prerequisites were present. If these tests were not met, then torture should be replaced with another technique of interrogation.

THE FAILURE OF SAFEGUARDS

Such safeguards, whether for animal research or judicial torture, look convincing on the surface, presenting a picture in which the basic dynamic seems pointing always and irreversibly to less. To use the language of the three R's, both regimes take replacement as their core principle. For Russell and Burch (1959/1992), replacement was always the default and animal testing should only be used when there was no alternative. Wherever possible, absolute replacement was the "absolute ideal," the one principle that "is always a satisfactory answer" (Russell & Burch, 1959/1992, Chapter 4). Put another way, animal research should only take place if a precise test was met: that the prospective gain in knowledge could not be obtained in any other way. If this test was not met, then replacement by another technique of experimentation had to happen. Similarly, judicial torture could only be authorized in highly specific situations in which it was indispensable to confirm the guilt of the suspect. Too little evidence would mean replacement with another technique, as would too much, in which case guilt could be established without the use of torture.

And yet, despite such reassuring claims, these safeguards provided little safety. There is ample evidence that abuses continue to take place despite the presence of the framework provided by the three R's. The abuses range from circumventing animal-subjects research requirements to other aspects of research misconduct such as data fabrication that compromise the three R's indirectly (e.g., Godecharle, Fieuws, Nemery, & Dierickx, 2018; Hvistendahl, 2013). Equally important, the three R's are also frequently violated in ways that are not always recognized as malfeasance in the scientific community—principally in the form of waste, with animals used in vain (e.g., Glasziou et al., 2014; Li et al., 2018; Singh et al., 2016). In recent years, irreproducibility has become a major issue in biomedical research, leading to what has been termed "the translational research crisis" (i.e., the problem that many basic research findings with animal models do not live up to the promise of therapeutic efficacy; Schulz, Cookson, & Hausmann, 2016). By its nature, any irreproducible finding must be understood as essentially useless. Within the framework of the three R's, any animal sacrificed for an irreproducible finding may rightfully be considered a victim of abuse. The causes of irreproducibility are complex and include poor experimental design, statistical analysis, and reporting standards as well as conceptual flaws. Here, the bad scientist may not have any intention to commit abuses while still failing to reduce animal suffering in the pursuit of knowledge—or publications (Smaldino & McElreath, 2016).

Similarly, the precisely regulated system of judicial torture generated multiple abuses. Torture was used again and again when few or indeed any of the stated criteria were actually present (Clulow, 2019). All of this raises an obvious question. Why did a system with such clear safeguards fail in fact to protect? Here, again, there is a surprisingly clear parallel. For judicial torture, three basic factors contributed to its ongoing misuse in diverse European legal systems. First, there was often a basic misunderstanding about the content and meaning of the rules governing the use of judicial torture. This was a source of complaint by later writers like Bavius Voorda, who argued that the actual meaning of the original legal codes had been "mutilated" by inaccurate interpretations at odds with the original text (as cited in Brants, 2010; Van der Vrught, 1978). Second, these rules were frequently brushed aside in the moment as individual judges sought an expedited mechanism to secure a confession and, hence, a guilty verdict. In such instances, the "judge is not," one French jurist explained, "exempt from passion" (as cited in Langbein, 2006, p. 148). This was the case most famously with the witch-hunt trials that took place across large parts of Europe, but there are thousands of less well-known cases in which a divergence between theory and practice prompted a rush to torture (Langbein, 2006, p. 14). Third, there was no effective system of external policing. While occasional cases might generate a controversy that spilled beyond individual court systems or national boundaries, there was little capacity to monitor the enforcement of supposed safeguards and no possibility of an independent arbiter.

Similar issues are evident in the case of animal research. Despite the easy accessibility of Russell and Burch's (1959/1992) work, it is often striking how little contact there actually is with the foundational text (Tannenbaum & Bennett, 2015). The three R's have entered the policy and practice mainstream, but, in many cases, the original definitions have been lost on the way. Some practical interpretations of the three R's represent something close to a "mutilation" of the original text. Nowhere is this clearer than in statements related to replacement. For Russell and Burch, replacement relied on a basic distinction between two categories: conscious living vertebrates versus nonsentient tissue. This distinction is now essentially ignored both by policymakers and researchers, even as there has been no attempt to redefine the three R's. Similarly, whereas Russell and Burch indicated a clear hierarchy within the three R's, with replacement first and refinement last, policymakers and researchers often concentrate primarily on refinement, thereby inverting the original order (Lauwereyns, 2018).

At the same time, there has been an in-practice reality that animal ethics committees often work in inconsistent or inscrutable ways, sometimes under institutional pressure to process and approve applications (Lauwereyns, 2018; Tjärnström, Weber, Hultgren, & Röcklingsberg, 2018; Tsan et al., 2016; Varga, 2013). Despite the safeguards supposedly built into the system, such committees seldom turn down an application, limiting their decisions to requests for further efforts in refinement and more clarification with respect to the required numbers of animals or procedures (Röcklingsberg, Gamborg, & Gjerris, 2014; Silverman et al., 2015). Even if their individual members are motivated by the best of intentions, the fact remains that there is a basic dynamic built into the system that makes it very difficult for animal ethics committees to avoid the inevitable positive response. Moreover, there is effectively little or no external policing as individual universities or laboratories operate within an atomized environment in which the primary enforcement mechanism originates from within. The overall result for both animal testing and judicial torture is that the safeguards provide little actual safety.

IMPLICATIONS FOR THE CARE AND USE OF ANIMALS IN RESEARCH

For all the efforts of its interpreters and defenders, the system of judicial torture was ultimately abolished in the second half of the 18th century. Scholars dispute the nature of the key underlying dynamic, but most likely it was a combination of a series of factors, including the work of writers like Cesare Beccaria, who denounced the practice of judicial torture; changing standards of proof required to convict a subject; and the rise of Enlightenment ideals, which were championed by sympathetic monarchs (Wisnewski, 2010). By the early 19th century, the old regime of judicial torture had been largely eradicated from the continent.

Given this overall trajectory, what lessons does an examination of judicial torture hold for animal testing? Not surprisingly, there are different ways to interpret this. One way to read the comparison is that animal research will at some point be fully and completely abolished. This will likely come, as it did in the case of judicial torture, from a combination of changing dynamics. It may be that shifting standards of proof eventually require the use of human evidence whenever the ultimate target of the research is *Homo sapiens*. In such a scenario, the ideal subject would always be the human volunteer (Quigley, 2007). One can envisage a future in which moral reasoning rejects the basic brutality of subjecting animals to research for which no human volunteers can be engaged. The rule may thus become: "Do not do to an animal what you would not do to a human." This might be considered a variant of the so-called "Golden Rule" Bible verses (e.g., Matthew 7:12), including animals in the category of others. Alternatively, it may be that public sentiment against animal testing, perhaps driven by figures comparable to Cesare Beccaria, turns decisively against such practices.

Currently, however, such possibilities seem remote. Rather than pointing to a world of absolute abolition, we see two more valuable immediate lessons to be drawn from the comparison with judicial torture. First is a basic recognition that absolutes have a power that complex principles that are perpetually open to interpretation do not. For centuries, European legal scholars attempted to work around the edges of the system by providing elaborate manuals designed to improve the use of judicial torture. In the end, however, it became clear that only a clear absolute abolition would be effective. While this is not currently possible for animal research, the use of lesser or achievable absolutes may provide—and is already providing—one way forward. Based on public deliberation and collective decision-making, numerous countries have outlawed, and research agencies have discontinued funding for, biomedical research involving the use of great apes (Kaiser, 2015; Project R&R, 2017). Where the three R's provide a set of abstract principles that are all too easily lost in translation, an achievable absolute such as "no chimpanzees" sets a clear rule that can reduce abuses.

Such experiences suggest that rather than continuing focus on the three R's, the scientific community should shift its attention toward achievable absolutes, supported by a clear, evidence-based, and publicly deliberated rationale, in order to improve and facilitate research ethics. For instance, the abolition of research with great apes was based on scientific data (their similarity to humans) and moral reasoning (a concern for fairness, aiming to treat likes alike). The next achievable absolute along these lines may be to discontinue research with nonhuman primates. Based on scientific data with respect to the richness of sentient life, other achievable absolutes may be to discontinue the use of creatures such as whales, dolphins, and elephants. In such cases, public deliberation, informed by relevant data and moral reasoning, will serve to determine which absolutes are achievable, as incremental steps moving forward from current regulations.

From a different angle and with a focus on fairness, moral reasoning should lead us to consider likewise the use of animals in other domains of society including the food industry. An achievable absolute in this respect may be to require consistency across domains. For instance, it would be morally suspect to limit the use of certain animals in research if the same animals can be used for food. If pigs can be eaten, it would be strange to outlaw them for research (indeed, research is arguably a better usage than eating). Other achievable absolutes could target the way in which research is organized, setting rules on how to combat irreproducibility, or how to achieve scale enlargement by pooling data and sharing resources to optimize the benefit and reduce the harm from animal research. For instance, an achievable absolute with respect to combating irreproducibility would be to set standard practices for open science (McKiernan et al., 2016).

Second, the scientific community should make use of a unique opportunity available to enforce these achievable absolutes. In the case of judicial torture, the nature of domestic legal systems made it essentially impossible to imagine a situation of effective, international policing. Put another way, there was no possibility of an external arbiter sitting outside the confines of an individual system but with the ability to peer inside. In the case of animal research, the internationalized nature of the landscape means that there is a clear opportunity to move beyond a reliance on self-regulation and local regulation by research institutions and their animal ethics committees.

This stems from the existence of two key bottlenecks in the shape of grants and publications, which provide external mechanisms capable of effective monitoring. Although not all research is funded by grants, or published in refereed journals, it is fair to say that the direction of research trends is influenced by flagship journals and major funding organizations. Because of this, such bottlenecks offer a concrete opportunity for change. In order to obtain grants, researchers need to submit materials that are reviewed and evaluated in accordance with regulations set by funding agencies. Similarly, journals possess their own external mechanisms to review and reject manuscripts that do not meet certain tests. It could be comparatively straightforward to establish conditions and implement regulations that can effectively improve the care and use of animals in research. As soon as a major funding agency sets a new rule, it will immediately and directly impact any researcher who wishes to access this funding. Likewise, as soon as a leading journal implements a new requirement for the kind of research it will accept, it will inevitably influence the animal research that is submitted to it. As a proof of concept, modest initial steps are already being made in this direction. These include the ARRIVE guidelines (Kilkenny et al., 2010), which represent an effort toward improving the reporting of animal research, and counts as a submission requirement for journals such as *Nature*. The implementation of achievable absolutes in animal research can be realized via the use of these two bottlenecks. Journals and funding agencies can decide from one day to the next to refuse research with nonhuman primates or to disregard work that fails the standards of open science. In this way, research ethics will push beyond the fraught abstractness of the three R's toward a set of incremental improvements.

References

Bailey, J., & Taylor, K. (2016). Non-human primates in neuroscience research: The case against its scientific necessity. *Alternatives to Laboratory Animals, 44*, 43–69.

Balls, M. (2010). The principles of humane experimental technique: Timeless insights and unheeded warnings. *Alternatives to Animal Experimentation, 27*, 19–23.

Bayne, K., & Turner, P. V. (2019). Animal welfare standards and international collaborations. *Institute for Animal Laboratory Research, 60*(1). doi:10.1093/ilar/ily024

Brants, C. (2010). Legal culture and legal transplants. *Electronic Journal of Comparative Law, 14*(3).

Buchanan-Smith, H. M., Rennie, A. E., Vitale, A., Pollo, S., Prescott, M. J., & Morton, D. B. (2005). Harmonising the definition of refinement. *Animal Welfare, 14,* 379–384.

Clulow, A. (2019). *Amboina, 1623: Conspiracy and fear on the edge of empire.* New York, NY: Columbia University Press.

Directive 2010/63/EU of the European Parliament and of the Council of 22 September 2010 on the protection of animals used for scientific purposes. *Official Journal of the European Union L, 276,* 33–79.

Dougherty, M. R., Scheck, P., Nelson, T. O., & Narens, L. (2005). Using the past to predict the future. *Memory & Cognition, 33,* 1096–1115.

Franco, N. H. (2013). Animal experiments in biomedical research: A historical perspective. *Animals (Basel), 3,* 238–273.

Freshwater, M. F. (2015). Laboratory animal research published in plastic surgery journals in 2014 has extensive waste: A systematic review. *Journal of Plastic, Reconstructive, and Aesthetic Surgery, 68,* 1485–1490.

Glasziou, P., Altman, D. G., Bossuyt, P., Boutron, I., Clarke, M., Julious, S., . . . Wager, E. (2014). Reducing waste from incomplete or unusable reports of biomedical research. *Lancet, 383,* 267–276.

Godecharle, S., Fieuws, S., Nemery, B., & Dierickx, K. (2018). Scientists still behaving badly? A survey within industry and universities. *Science and Engineering Ethics, 6,* 1697–1717.

Goldberg, A. M. (2010). The principles of humane experimental technique: Is it relevant today? *Alternatives to Animal Experimentation, 27,* 25–27.

Henry, J. (1821). *Report on the criminal law at Demerera, and in the ceded Dutch colonies with an appendix on the nature of the office of fiscal.* London, England: Butterworth.

Holm, S. (2018). Precaution, threshold risk and public deliberation. *Bioethics, 33,* 254–260.

Huber, U. (1939). *The jurisprudence of my time (Heedensdaegse rechtsgeleertheyt)* (P. Gane, Ed.). Durban, South Africa: Butterworth & Co. (Africa) Ltd.

Hvistendahl, M. (2013). Corruption and research fraud send big chill through big pharma in China. *Science, 341,* 445–446.

Kaiser, J. (2015, November 18). NIH to end all support for chimpanzee research. *Science.* https://doi.org/10.1126/science.aad7458

Kilkenny, C., Browne, W. J., Cuthill, I. C., Emerson, M., & Altman, D. G. (2010). Improving bioscience research reporting: The ARRIVE guidelines for reporting animal research. *PLoS Biology, 8,* e1000412.

LaFollette, H., & Shanks, N. (1996). *Brute science: Dilemmas of animal experimentation.* New York, NY: Routledge.

Langbein, J. H. (2006). *Torture and the law of proof.* Chicago, IL: University of Chicago Press.

Lauwereyns, J. (2018). *Rethinking the three R's in animal research: Replacement, reduction, refinement.* Cham, Switzerland: Palgrave Pivot.

Li, G., Abbade, L. P. F., Nwosu, I., Jin, Y., Leenus, A., Maaz, M., . . . Thabane, L. (2018). A systematic review of comparisons between protocols or registrations and full reports in biomedical research. *BMC Medical Research Methodology, 18,* 9.

McKiernan, E. C., Bourne, P. E., Brown, C. T., Buck, S., Kenall, A., Lin, J., . . . Yarkoni, T. (2016). How open science helps researchers succeed. *eLife, 5,* e16800.

Olsson, I. A. S., Franco, N. H., Weary, D. M., & Sandøe, P. (2012). The 3Rs principle: Mind the ethical gap! *Alternatives to Animal Experimentation Proceedings, 1/12, Proceedings of WC8,* 333–336.

Peters, E. (1999). *Torture.* Philadelphia: University of Pennsylvania Press.

Phillips, K. A., Bales, K. L., Capitanio, J. P., Conley, A., Czoty, P. W., 't Hart, B. A., . . . Voytko, M. L. (2014). Why primate models matter. *American Journal of Primatology, 76,* 801–824.

Project R&R. (2017). *International bans: Countries banning or limiting chimpanzee research.* Retrieved from http://www.releasechimps.org/laws/ international-bans

Quigley, M. (2007). Non-human primates: The appropriate subjects of biomedical research? *Journal of Medical Ethics, 33,* 655–658.

Röcklingsberg, H., Gamborg, C., & Gjerris, M. (2014). A case for integrity: Gains from including more than animal welfare in animal ethics committee deliberations. *Laboratory Animals, 48,* 61–78.

Roelfsema, P. R., & Treue, S. (2014). Basic neuroscience research with nonhuman primates: A small but indispensable component of biomedical research. *Neuron, 82,* 1200–1204.

Rollin, B. E. (2017). The ethics of animal research: Theory and practice. In L. Kalof (Ed.), *The Oxford Handbook of Animal Studies* (pp. 345–363). New York, NY: Oxford University Press.

Russell, W. M. S., & Burch, R. L. (1992). *The principles of humane experimental technique.* Wheathampstead, England: Universities Federation for Animal Welfare. Retrieved from http://altweb.jhsph.edu/pubs/books/humane_exp/het-toc (Original work published 1959)

Schulz, J. B., Cookson, M. R., & Hausmann, L. (2016). The impact of fraudulent and irreproducible data to the translational research crisis—solutions and implementation. *Journal of Neurochemistry, 139*(Suppl. 2), 253–270.

Silverman, J., Lidz, C. W., Clayfield, J. C., Murray, A., Simon, L. J., & Rondeau, R. G. (2015). Decision making and the IACUC: Part-1 protocol information discussed at full-committee reviews. *Journal of the American Association for Laboratory Animal Science, 54,* 389–398.

Singh, V. P., Pratap, K., Sinha, J., Desiraju, K., Bahal, D., & Kukreti, R. (2016). Critical evaluation of challenges and future use of animals in experimentation for biomedical research. *International Journal of Immunopathology and Pharmacology, 29,* 551–561.

Smaldino, P. E., & McElreath, R. (2016). The natural selection of bad science. *Royal Society Open Science, 3,* 160384.

Stoop, B. C. (1996). *On Crimes: A Commentary on Books XLVII and XLVIII of the Digest* (Vol. 4): Cape Town, South Africa: Juta & Co.

Tannenbaum, J., & Bennett, B. J. (2015). Russell and Burch's 3Rs then and now: The need for clarity in definition and purpose. *Journal of the American Association for Laboratory Animals, 54,* 120–132.

Tjärnström, E., Weber, E. M., Hultgren, J., & Röcklingsberg, H. (2018). Emotions and ethical decision-making in animal ethics committees. *Animals (Basel), 8,* E181.

Tsan, M. F., Grabenbauer, M., & Nguyen, Y. (2016). Lapse in institutional animal care and use committee continuing reviews. *PLoS One, 11,* e0162141.

Van der Vrught, M. (1978). *De Criminele Ordonnantiën van 1570.* Zutphen, Netherlands: De Walburg Pers.

Varga, O. (2013). Critical analysis of assessment studies of the animal ethics review process. *Animals (Basel), 3,* 907–922.

Wisnewski, J. J. (2010). *Understanding torture.* Edinburgh: Edinburgh University Press.

About the Editors and Contributors

Andrew Linzey (editor) is director of the Oxford Centre for Animal Ethics and has been a member of the Faculty of Theology in the University of Oxford for twenty-eight years. He is a visiting professor of animal theology at the University of Winchester, professor of animal ethics at the Graduate Theological Foundation, and special professor at Saint Xavier University, Chicago. He is the author or editor of more than thirty books, including *Animal Theology* (SCM Press/University of Illinois Press, 1994), *Why Animal Suffering Matters* (Oxford University Press, 2009), *The Global Guide to Animal Protection* (University of Illinois Press, 2013), and *The Palgrave Handbook of Practical Animal Ethics* (Palgrave Macmillan, 2018).

Clair Linzey (editor) is a research fellow in animal ethics at Wycliffe Hall in the University of Oxford and deputy director of the Oxford Centre for Animal Ethics. She is also the Frances Power Cobbe Professor of Animal Theology at the Graduate Theological Foundation. In addition, she is director of the Annual Oxford Animal Ethics Summer School. She serves as coeditor of the *Journal of Animal Ethics* and coeditor of the Palgrave Macmillan Animal Ethics book series. She is the author of *Developing Animal Theology* (Routledge, 2021) and coauthor of *An Ethical Critique of Fur Factory Farming* (Palgrave Macmillan, 2022). Her coedited volumes include *Animal Ethics for Veterinarians* (University of Illinois Press, 2017), *The Palgrave Handbook of Practical Animal Ethics* (Palgrave Macmillan, 2018), *The Routledge Handbook of Religion and Animal Ethics* (Routledge, 2018), and *Animal Ethics and Animal Law* (Lexington, 2023).

Cheryl Abbate is assistant professor of philosophy at the University of Nevada, Las Vegas. She is the co-editor of *New Omnivorism and Strict Veganism: Critical Perspectives* (Routledge, 2023), and has published over 30 academic pieces on the ethical treatment of animals. Research interests include: theoretical and applied ethics, especially animal ethics, environmental ethics, and food ethics.

Alan W. H. Bates is medical director of Convit House Pathology Ltd, Essex, a fellow of the Royal College of Physicians, and a fellow of the Oxford Centre for Animal Ethics. He is the author of *Emblematic Monsters* (Rodopi, 2005), *The Anatomy of Robert Knox* (Sussex Academic Press, 2010) and *Antivivisection and the Profession of Medicine*

(Palgrave Macmillan, 2017). Research interests include: the history of medicine, and medical ethics.

Lauren Bestwick gained her undergraduate degree in History at Worcester College, University of Oxford in 2022. She is an alumnus of the Oxford University Animal Ethics Society. Research interests include: early modern history, and animal ethics.

Jacob Brandler is a DPhil (History) candidate at the University of Oxford; a postgraduate member of the Rothermere American Institute; and previous president of the Oxford University Animal Ethics Society. His master's thesis explored the issue of personhood in the caselaw of Missouri freedom suits and the *Dred Scott* decision (1857). His current project investigates the social construction of humanity by racial scientists and abolitionists in the antebellum United States. Research interests include: American history, legal history, human exceptionalism.

Adam Clulow is the Walter Prescott Webb Chair in History and Ideas at the University of Texas at Austin. He is the author of *The Company and the Shogun: The Dutch Encounter with Tokugawa Japan* (Columbia University Press, 2014), which won multiple awards including the Jerry Bentley Prize in World History from the American Historical Association, and *Amboina, 1623: Conspiracy and Fear on the Edge of Empire* (Columbia University Press, 2019). He is creator of The *Amboyna Conspiracy Trial*, an online interactive trial engine that received the New South Wales Premiers History Award in 2017, and *Virtual Angkor* with Tom Chandler, which received the American Historical Association's Roy Rosenzweig Prize for Innovation in Digital History and the 2021 Digital Humanities and Multimedia Studies Prize from the Medieval Academy of America.

Christene d'Anca teaches at the University of California, Santa Barbara. She is the co-editor of *Cultural, Social, Political, Religious and Economic Relations Between Serbs and Romanians from the Early 18th Century to the 20th Century* (Peter Lang, 2023) and has published the monograph *Medieval Mausoleums, Monuments, and Manuscripts: French Royal Women's Patronage from the 12th to the 14th Centuries* (Brepols, 2024). Research interests include: women and storytelling, alternate power structures, twelfth to fourteenth century European history, and female patronage of the funerary arts.

Carl Tobias Frayne is the director of the Institute of Devotional Arts. He holds a PhD in philosophy from St John's College, University of Cambridge, and an MA from the University of Chicago Divinity School. His articles include: "Animals in Christian and Muslim Thought: Creatures, Creation, and Killing for Food" (*The Routledge Handbook of Religion and Animal Ethics*, Routledge, 2018) and "Albert Schweitzer (1875–1965): The Life of Reverence" (*Animal Theologians*, Oxford University Press, 2023). Research interests include: applied ethics, aesthetics, comparative religion, and the history of food.

About the Editors and Contributors

Christina Hoenig is a former associate professor in Classics at the University of Pittsburgh. Her main areas of research are the Greek and Roman Platonic traditions. A central theme of interest was the translation of Greek philosophical vocabulary into Latin. Her monograph *Plato's Timaeus and the Latin Tradition* was published with Cambridge University Press in 2018.

Jan Lauwereyns is senior vice president of Kyushu University, and professor in the Faculty of Arts and Science, Kyushu University, Japan. Books include: *The Anatomy of Bias* (The MIT Press, 2010), *Brain and the Gaze* (The MIT Press, 2012), and *Rethinking the Three Rs in Animal Research: Replacement, Reduction, Refinement* (Palgrave Pivot, 2018). Research interests include: cognitive science and bioethics.

Marcello Newall gained his doctorate from the University of Leeds. He has published articles in academic journals on the intersection between Christian theology and veganism; Christian ethics, diet, and eschatology, as well as the book of Revelation. His PhD thesis was entitled "'Repairing the World': *Tikkun Olam* and Jürgen Moltmann's *Theology of Hope*". This work was an original discussion of the Jewish concept of *Tikkun Olam* (healing the world), and social and political action in the world, and its connection to Christian eschatology, and in particular Jürgen Moltmann's *Theology of Hope*. His research interests include: Christian eschatology, Jewish studies, political theology, Jürgen Moltmann, Christian ethics, and animal theology.

Violette Pouillard is assistant research professor at the French National Center for Scientific Research (IRHiS, UMR 8529 - CNRS-University of Lille) and a visiting professor at Ghent University. She is the author of *Histoire des Zoos par les Animaux (A History of Zoos via Animals)* (Champ Vallon, 2019). Research interests include: history of animals, zoo studies, history of (colonial) wildlife conservation policies, socio-environmental history, and more-than-human history.

Alison Stone is professor of philosophy at Lancaster University. Books include: *Frances Power Cobbe* (Cambridge University Press, 2022); *Women Philosophers in Nineteenth-Century Britain* (Oxford University Press, 2023). Research interests include: history of philosophy, environmental and animal philosophy, and feminist philosophy.

Felix Taylor is a library assistant at the Queen's College, University of Oxford. He has a DPhil in English and is currently writing a book about literature and the nineteenth-century occult revival, due to be published 2026. Research interests include: supernatural literature, occultism in literature, mythology, and fantasy.

www.ingramcontent.com/pod-product-compliance
Lightning Source LLC
Chambersburg PA
CBHW062128160426
43191CB00013B/2230